*Financial Systems and Economic
Policy in Developing Countries*

Financial Systems and Economic Policy in Developing Countries

EDITED BY

Stephan Haggard and

Chung H. Lee

CORNELL UNIVERSITY PRESS

ITHACA AND LONDON

First published 1995 by Cornell University Press.

Printed in the United States of America

♾ The paper in this book meets the minimum requirements of the American
National Standard for Information Sciences—Permanence of Paper
for Printed Library Materials, ANSI Z39.48–1984.

Library of Congress Cataloging-in-Publication Data

Financial systems and economic policy in developing countries / edited
  by Stephan Haggard and Chung H. Lee.
    p. cm.
  Includes bibliographical references and index.
  ISBN 0–8014–2892–0 (cloth: alk. paper).—ISBN 0–8014–8130–9
(paper: alk. paper)
    1. Finance—Developing countries—Case studies. 2. Credit control—Developing
countries—Case studies. 3. Asia—Economic policy—Case studies. 4. Latin
America—Economic policy—Case studies. I. Haggard, Stephan. II. Lee, Chung H.
HG195.F537 1995
332—dc20   95-18233

CONTENTS

PREFACE

The two editors of this volume joined forces to rectify shortcomings in the literature on finance and economic development. In the mid-1980s, Chung H. Lee began to question why countries such as Korea and Taiwan could achieve rapid economic growth with relatively underdeveloped and "repressed" financial systems. Specifically, he wanted to answer the question, Did the financial system really hinder the growth of the East Asian newly industrializing countries, or was there, in fact, some elective affinity between government intervention in financial markets and rapid economic growth? Though of obvious importance, this issue had been sidestepped in the economic literature owing to the relative neglect of the allocative function of financial systems. In other words, how different financial systems affect the flow of resources among different sectors and activities had not been adequately addressed. Drawing on Oliver Williamson's work on the properties of hierarchies, Lee published articles in *Economic Development and Cultural Change* (with Seiji Naya) and *World Development* suggesting how government intervention in the allocation of resources might be efficient. Though the observations put forth in those works were clearly of relevance to the debate about the role of the state in the development process, Lee realized that more work was needed in this important area.

During this same period, Stephan Haggard approached similar questions from a political economy perspective. Dissatisfied with dominant explanations of East Asian development, he sought to explore the politics of export-led growth in his book *Pathways from the Periphery* (Cornell University Press, 1990). That work, as well as collaborative work with Tun-jen Cheng and Chung-in Moon, focused largely on industrial and trade policy. But through a collective research project on the political economy of the debt crisis and the influence of two close colleagues and friends, Jeffry Frieden and Sylvia Maxfield, Haggard became increasingly interested in the political economy of finance. Central to his concerns were two questions: Why did countries pursue the financial policies they did? And, in particular, what political and institutional factors determined the effectiveness and efficiency of state intervention in financial markets?

In 1989, Lee invited Haggard to visit the East-West Center to work on a proposal on the political economy of financial markets in developing countries. An initial workshop was held at the East-West Center in April 1990 to discuss that proposal as well as the idea of a comparative project. Joining Lee and Haggard at that workshop were Shigeyuki Abe, Thomas Cargill, Luigi Ermini, Jeffry Frieden, Joseph Grunwald, Kazuhiro Igawa, Rolf Luders, Manuel F. Montes, Sang-Woo Nam, Seiji Naya, James Roumasset, and Phil Wellons.

Although the project was initially limited to East and Southeast Asia, it became clear to the participants that more could be gained by comparing East Asia's experience with that of some major Latin American countries. To make this possible, Rolf Luders helped in securing support from the International Center for Economic Growth for part of the Latin American studies.

Our approach in creating a research team was to bring together economists and political scientists to write complementary country monographs. Eight countries from Asia and Latin America were chosen for political analysis with particular attention to the use of preferential credit as a policy instrument and the politics of financial market liberalization. The papers by the political scientists were published in *The Politics of Finance in Developing Countries* (Cornell University Press, 1993), edited jointly by Stephan Haggard, Chung H. Lee, and Sylvia Maxfield.

The work done by the economists is presented in this book. Covering seven countries (Brazil, Chile, South Korea, Taiwan, the Philippines, Thailand, and Indonesia), the chapters focus on the economic determinants and effects of credit allocation policies, examining financial policy and its influence on economic performance, especially through its effect on credit allocation.

Generous support from the Korea Development Institute (KDI) and the Asian Development Bank (ADB) has made this project and these two volumes possible. We are particularly thankful to Bon-Ho Koo, president of KDI during the time this project was carried out, and to Sang-Woo Nam for coordinating relations between KDI and the East-West Center.

We are also grateful to Dr. Hakchung Choo, former chief economist at the ADB, for his support of the project. The East-West Center graciously and efficiently hosted two meetings to review the papers, the first in November 1990 and the second in October 1991. For their support, we thank Seiji Naya and Bruce Koppel, former director of the Resource Systems Institute and vice president for research and education at the East-West Center, respectively.

The economists contributing chapters for this volume benefited greatly from the chance to interact with the political scientists who wrote the parallel country studies: Laura A. Hastings (Chile), Leslie Elliott Armijo (Brazil), Paul D. Hutchcroft (the Philippines), Andrew J. MacIntyre (Indonesia), Byung-Sun Choi (Korea), Tun-jen Cheng (Taiwan), and Richard Doner and Daniel Unger (Thailand). We are also thankful for the useful comments we received from Yoon-Je Cho, Un-Chan Chung, David Cole, Betty Slade, Jeffry Frieden, Yun-Hwan Kim, Nathaniel Leff, Sylvia Maxfield, Walter Miklius, Yung Chul Park, Hugh Patrick, Joseph Ravalo, James Roumasset, Pearl Imada-Iboshi, and David Timberman.

We thank Roger Haydon of Cornell University Press for his interest in and support for publishing this work, an anonymous external referee for highly constructive comments, and Professor Hugh Patrick for his valuable comments on an earlier version of the manuscript. Our final thanks are to Ann Takayesu, whose efficient typing made this publication possible; to Mendl Djunaidy for her organization and management skills; and to Janis Togashi, senior editor at the East-West Center, who, with cheerfulness and good sense, helped us see the end of this project.

CHUNG H. LEE

Honolulu, Hawaii

STEPHAN HAGGARD

San Diego, California

CONTRIBUTORS

TEIN-CHEN CHOU is Professor of Economics and Director of the Institute of Economics, National Chung-Hsing University, Taipei, Taiwan

CARLOS DÍAZ is Assistant Professor at the Instituto de Economia, Pontificia Universidad Católica de Chile, Santiago, Chile

DANIEL L. GLEIZER is Economist at the International Monetary Fund, Washington, D.C.

STEPHAN HAGGARD is Professor in the Graduate School of International Relations and Pacific Studies, University of California at San Diego, La Jolla, California

FELIPE LAGOS is Associate Professor at the Instituto de Economia, Pontificia Universidad Católica de Chile, Santiago, Chile

CHUNG H. LEE is Professor of Economics, University of Hawaii at Manoa, and Director of the Center for Korean Studies, University of Hawaii at Manoa, Honolulu, Hawaii

MANUEL F. MONTES is Fellow at the East-West Center, Honolulu, Hawaii

ROBERT J. MUSCAT is Executive Director at the Institute for Policy Reform, Washington, D.C.

SANG-WOO NAM is Senior Fellow at the Korea Development Institute, Seoul, Korea

JOHNNY NOE E. RAVALO is Senior Economist and Director for Policy Research at the Bankers' Association of the Philippines, Manila, Philippines

WING THYE WOO is Professor of Economics, University of California at Davis, Davis, California

*Financial Systems and Economic Policy
in Developing Countries*

INTRODUCTION

ISSUES AND FINDINGS

Chung H. Lee and Stephan Haggard

Ever since the seminal contributions by McKinnon (1973) and Shaw (1973), the role of finance in economic development has been analyzed in terms of two ideal types: a free-market financial system and a "repressed" financial system. In a free-market system, savings are mobilized and credit is allocated on the basis of market-determined interest rates. As with markets for other goods and factors, the cost of money reflects its scarcity value. In a repressed financial system, by contrast, the government maintains artificially low interest rates and thus plays a direct or indirect role in rationing credit.

Because financial repression implies state intervention, the controversy over appropriate financial policy has been closely related to the broader debate about the suitable role of government in economic development. The neoclassical view is that state intervention, including financial repression, leads to a misallocation of resources. First, allocative decisions are in the hands of government bureaucrats who lack both the information and the incentives to allocate credit efficiently. Second, government actors are likely to be influenced by considerations other than rates of return, including distributive pressures from rent-seeking groups. Third, because subsidized credit lowers the cost of capital, it leads to the adoption of overly capital-intensive techniques. Preferential credit policies are thus likely to reinforce other biases in the system of incentives, such as the emphasis on import substitution in manufacturing over export-oriented manufacturing or agriculture. The Philippines and a number of Latin American and African countries are usually singled out as providing evidence supporting these arguments against financial repression.[1]

1. See, for example, Fry 1988, pp. 143–53 and 410–17, and Polak 1989, chap. 3.

There is, however, the puzzling phenomenon of East Asia's economic development. The economic success of postwar Japan and the rapid economic development of Korea and Taiwan since the early 1960s seem to contradict the conventional wisdom on financial repression. The financial systems in all three countries appear to be "repressed" by conventional standards, and these governments have been actively involved in managing the allocation of credit. Yet the allocation of resources appears to have been efficient, and growth has been undeniably rapid.

Furthermore, the recent experiences of the Southern Cone countries of Latin America—that is, Argentina, Chile, and Uruguay—have raised questions about the economic and policy conditions under which financial market liberalization is appropriate and, in particular, about the sequence in which reforms should be initiated. Many reasons have been offered for the disastrous results of the Southern Cone experiments with radical financial liberalization, including inconsistent policies, especially with reference to the real exchange rate; high spreads between domestic currency–denominated and dollar-denominated credit; and inadequate bank supervision among others (Corbo and de Melo 1985, 1987). A new consensus has emerged from the Southern Cone experiences, however: if financial liberalization is to bring about a more efficient allocation of credit, a government must provide not only macroeconomic stability but also prudential bank supervision. As remarked by some prominent analysts, a distinction must be made between wholesale liberalization of financial markets and properly monitored deregulation (Corbo and de Melo 1987; Dooley and Mathieson 1987).

But even under optimal conditions of macroeconomic stability and credible and efficient regulation, financial liberalization may not deliver what its advocates have promised. Because of the asymmetric and imperfect information that is characteristic of all financial markets, a liberal financial system operating under optimal regulatory conditions can still misallocate resources. It is thus possible that under certain conditions, government intervention in credit allocation can contribute to more efficient resource use and more rapid growth. Just as the existence of market failures does not necessarily warrant government intervention, so the existence of government failures does not necessarily mean that intervention is detrimental to economic growth.

In this chapter, we review the debate about financial market liberalization and offer an alternative theoretical framework that highlights the conditions under which the government can play a more active but positive role in resource allocation. Admittedly, these conditions are relatively scarce in the developing countries, and consequently, government intervention in financial markets frequently constitutes a drag on economic growth. But two sorts of important exceptions demand further exploration. First, we find countries, or, more accurate, periods and programs within countries, that combine government intervention and "financial repression" with efficiency and high growth. Second, we also find cases in which financial liberalization proves costly precisely because of the failure of governments to monitor and regulate financial markets adequately.

We first review recent work that has raised objections to the neoclassical perspective, particularly the theoretical work that emphasizes asymmetric and imperfect information. We then examine the literature on the firm as an internal capital market, drawing a parallel between internal capital markets and business-government relations in "repressed" financial systems. This analogy is further elaborated in a framework of a quasi-internal organization, after which we summarize the findings from the case studies of seven middle-income countries—Korea, Taiwan, Indonesia, Thailand, the Philippines, Chile, and Brazil—on the influence of the financial system on the allocation of resources. We conclude with discussion of some policy implications.

I. Asymmetric and Imperfect Information

Operation of a free competitive market, whether it is for financial instruments or commodities, is constrained by asymmetric and imperfect information and costly contract enforcement. These problems of market imperfection affect financial markets particularly strongly because every financial transaction involves an exchange of present certainty for a future promise. Thus, as Stiglitz (1989) has argued, the problems of adverse selection, moral hazard, and contract enforcement are inherent characteristics of financial markets. As a result, these markets do not operate in the manner of textbook models in developing or developed countries; credit and equity are rationed even in financial markets that are free of government intervention.

Credit rationing by banks—allocation of credit at interest rates below a market-clearing rate—may occur because of the asymmetry of information and because banks are risk averse (Stiglitz and Weiss 1981). In the absence of well-functioning equity markets, financial liberalization can then lead to inefficient allocation of credit (Cho 1986). But even if there is an equity market, equity rationing will also take place because of problems of adverse selection. In the absence of good information, equity markets may be unable to differentiate between good and bad issues and thus may discount the share prices of good issues (Stiglitz 1989). Unwilling to see their net worth decrease, "good" firms will be reluctant to issue new shares and will rely more on internal financing for capacity expansion, which can result in an inefficient allocation of resources.

Though these problems are inherent in all financial markets, they are especially serious for developing countries. Capital markets are generally less developed and the economy is subject to greater uncertainty, particularly where the political system is unstable. The small scale of business enterprises in most developing countries implies greater difficulty in collecting, evaluating, and disseminating information, which poses problems for financial intermediaries. Small firms also lack the scale to maintain their own internal capital markets capable of allocating funds efficiently among diverse subunits. Yet even where firms are large, the relative weakness of regulatory institutions impedes full disclosure and the adequate provision of information to the market.

The fact that rationing of credit and of equity exists does not necessarily call for government intervention. Private institutions, such as the horizontally diversified *grupo* structure that is common in a number of Latin American countries, emerged in part to cope with imperfect financial markets.[2] Moreover, government intervention to correct imperfect markets may result in less, not more, efficient allocation of capital. Deepak Lal (1985) has made the most forceful argument against "second-best" defenses of government intervention: "No general rule of second-best welfare economics permits the deduction that, in a necessarily imperfect market economy, particular *dirigiste* policies will increase welfare. They may not; and they may even be worse than *laissez-faire*" (p. 16).

Lal's defense of the market is, in fact, quite tepid. The critical issue centers on the *conditions* under which various policy regimes are likely to yield the predicted results. Just as the Southern Cone cases cast doubt on arguments for unfettered laissez-faire, so the East Asian newly industrial-

2. *Grupo* that exists in certain Latin American countries is a large multiunit enterprise and can thus be viewed as possessing an efficient internal capital market (Leff 1976). In Nicaragua, business groups are composed of several wealthy businessmen and families. Their principal function seems to be that of financial intermediation between the members with excess savings and those with investment opportunities but without sufficient savings. An advantage of this internal capital market is cheaper, more reliable credit (Strachan 1976).

izing countries have been at the center of a controversy about the costs and benefits of dirigisme. Interventionist policies have at least accompanied, if not contributed to, extremely rapid growth in Japan, Korea, Taiwan, and Singapore. It is too facile to dismiss this empirical observation with the argument that if these economies had pursued a more liberal policy course, they would have grown even faster.[3] As a recent World Bank study on the East Asian "miracle" admits (1993), the analytic task is to understand the conditions that contributed to efficient intervention.

The new theoretical literature on financial markets raises several issues that are germane to our discussion.[4] In addition to emphasizing the potential for important inefficiencies in *all* financial markets regardless of the policy regime, this work also draws greater attention to the institutional setting in which credit is allocated.

The "financial system" is usually taken to mean the collection of financial markets in a given economy, be they formal credit markets, stock markets, or curb markets. It also refers to financial institutions such as banks, credit unions, insurance companies, and so forth. But the mobilization and the allocation of financial resources, even in highly

---

3. There is now extensive literature on the role of government in the economic development of these countries. See, for example, Alam 1989; Amsden 1989; Bradford 1986, 1987; Cho and Kim 1991; Johnson 1985; and Lee 1992. In all these writings a common theme is that in these countries the governments did more than just "get prices right." The following quote from Bradford 1986 succinctly summarizes this theme: "Sectoral priorities and industrial policies have been essential ingredients in the East Asian success stories. In Korea, Taiwan, and Singapore, the evolution of the production structure and the composition of exports was not left to the market but was the result of deliberate government design. On balance, the exchange rate, the interest rate, the tax system, and public sector investment were not neutral factors subordinate to market forces in these cases; rather, they were leading indicators and important instruments of development strategy" (p. 123).
4. We should also note here the neostructuralist critique of "orthodox" stabilization policies such as those advocated by the International Monetary Fund (IMF) and the World Bank. The core of the neostructuralist argument is the need to take into account the existence of efficiently functioning curb markets in developing countries (e.g., Bruno 1979; Taylor 1979, 1983; van Wijnbergen 1982, 1983a, 1983b, 1985). Neostructuralists assume that time deposits in the formal segment of the market are a close substitute for curb deposits; in contrast to neoclassical analyses such as McKinnon's, the portfolio shift into time deposits, which occurs as a result of rising interest rates, comes out of curb market deposits and not out of "unproductive" assets such as cash, gold, and commodities. The crucial question that divides the neoclassical and structural views (Cho 1990), however, ultimately centers on the relative efficiency of formal and informal credit markets. For a variety of reasons, the McKinnon-Shaw school views the informal credit market as inefficient and the (liberalized) formal credit market as efficient; these include the limited scope and insufficient risk pooling in the informal markets (Cho 1990; Fischer 1989). The neostructuralists, though, tend to see the informal credit market as efficient and hold that it is typically the formal credit market that is characterized by distortions.

developed countries, are not limited to these market institutions. Nonfinancial institutions, be they households or manufacturing firms, also carry out the mobilization and the allocation of financial resources. These internal capital markets are not necessarily primitive institutions preceding the development of a market but rather institutional innovations that evolve in response to market imperfections. Because the mobilization and the allocation of financial resources clearly take place within organizations as well as in markets, the neoclassical picture of the financial system as a collection of financial markets is partial, even for a highly developed market economy. We therefore need a theoretical framework that encompasses the role of institutions, including the government, in credit allocation.

II. Markets and Organizations

The theoretical foundation for such a framework exists in the new institutional economics (Williamson 1975, 1985). The core insight of this literature is the pervasiveness of transactions costs and the role of organizations and organizational innovation in reducing them. In a capitalist market economy, organizations, including the firm, emerge because they are more efficient in carrying out certain economic transactions than are markets, given the existence of transactions costs. Because financial transactions are especially subject to moral hazard and costly contract enforcement, we would expect organizations to be particularly likely to develop internal capital markets for the purpose of allocating financial resources.

Clearly not every internal capital market is efficient because of limited size and scope. For such a market to be efficient, it would ideally be large enough to have diversified investment opportunities. Such an internal capital market does exist in the M-form (multidivisional) structure of a large modern enterprise, however. Economic transactions that take place within such an internal market are not wholly price-mediated but may nevertheless be less costly than price-mediated market transactions. With its strategic planning capacity, ability to allocate resources, and monitoring and control apparatus, the M-form structure can effectively reallocate cash flows among its subunits to high-yield uses.

The advantages of the hierarchical M-form structure are clearly spelled out by Williamson (1985) and are worth quoting at length:

> The M-form structure removes the general office executives from partisan involvement in the functional parts and assigns operating responsibilities to

the divisions. The general office, moreover, is supported by an elite staff that has the capacity to evaluate divisional performance. Not only, therefore, is the goal structure altered in favor of enterprise-wide considerations, but an improved information base permits rewards and penalties to be assigned to a division on a more discriminating basis, and resources can be reallocated within the firm from less to more productive uses. *A concept of the firm as an internal capital market thus emerges* [emphasis added].

Effective multidivisionalization thus involves the general office in the following set of activities: (1) the identification of separable economic activities within the firm; (2) according quasi-autonomous standing (usually of a profit center nature) to each; (3) monitoring the efficiency performance of each division; (4) awarding incentives; (5) allocating cash flows to high-yield uses; and (6) performing strategic planning (diversification, acquisition, divestiture, and related activities) in other respects. The M-form structure is thus one that *combines* the divisionalization concept with an internal control and strategic decision-making capability. (Pp. 283–84)

To analyze the efficiency or inefficiency of financial repression, we can compare a financial system in which the government has a role in credit allocation with the M-form corporate structure. The M-form structure is hierarchical, and its internal capital market is therefore hierarchical as well. What is commonly called "financial repression" can also be modeled as a hierarchical system, with the government performing the role of the general office and the enterprises that receive credit resembling divisional subunits. In carrying out such a comparison, we propose to replace the term *financial repression* with *hierarchical system of credit allocation*.

In discussing the efficiency of intraorganizational versus market transactions, Williamson (1975) focuses on certain advantages that organizations may enjoy in handling informational imperfections:

(1) Hierarchy extends the bounds on rationality by permitting the specialization of decision making and economizing on communication expense; direct channels of communication may be more efficient than reliance on parametric signaling that takes place in the market.

(2) Hierarchy reduces opportunism as it permits additional incentives and control techniques to be brought to bear in a more selective manner.

(3) Hierarchy reduces uncertainty by permitting interdependent units to adapt to unforeseen contingencies in a coordinated way.

(4) Hierarchy permits small-number bargaining indeterminacies to be resolved by fiat.

(5) Hierarchy improves information by extending the constitutional powers to perform audits, thereby narrowing the information gap that obtains between government and business under conditions of parametric signaling.

(6) As compared with parametric signaling, hierarchical relations may provide opportunities for a less calculating or mistrustful atmosphere and thus allow for the convergence of objectives between various units.

Private internal organizations that have evolved over time to economize transactions costs in a capitalist market economy would function differently from an institution created by the government or from the government itself for a number of reasons. A particularly critical issue in this regard concerns the possibility of rent-seeking behavior. Neoclassical political economy emphasizes that a major source of inefficiency is the ability of business and government to collude effectively through the provision of rents that advance the interests of politicians, bureaucrats, and their private sector clients at the expense of social welfare.

Yet it is important to underscore that opportunism is a characteristic of market transactions as well; indeed, the transactions cost literature assumes that private agents act not only to maximize self-interest but may use guile as well. Moreover, the literature on principal-agent relations shows that "rent seeking"—in the form of exploitation of monitoring and transactions costs and informational asymmetries—also occurs within firms. Though the existence of hierarchy does not eliminate problems of shirking and agency slack, it can mitigate them through effective monitoring and sanctioning (Tirole 1986).

The main point is that by regarding a financial system in which the government plays an active role as an internal organization, we admit the possibility that it can be more efficient than the market system of credit allocation; this alone is a significant departure from the conventional treatment of financial systems which takes nonprice-mediated transactions as ipso facto inefficient. The crucial question thus centers on the *conditions* under which a hierarchical system of credit allocation will, in fact, be more efficient.[5]

III. Quasi-internal Organization as an Internal Capital Market

Patrick (1990) has argued that for a highly competitive, market-based financial system to work efficiently, there must be an adequate institutional infrastructure. This infrastructure includes a system of laws, regu-

5. As pointed out by Wolf (1988), governments do suffer from nonmarket failures. The choice we are faced with is not, therefore, between an idealized model of the market and an idealized model of the government. Rather, it concerns the extent to which markets or governments should determine the allocation of resources in the economy.

lations, and courts; an effectual information system that minimizes uncertainties and costs of financial intermediation; prudential regulation ensuring the stability of the financial system and protecting depositors; and government supervision that minimizes moral hazard.[6] Patrick does not, however, discuss how this institutional infrastructure comes to be established or the choices governments confront between developing these institutions for the purpose of supporting market transactions and substituting for them through alternative organizational means.

For reasons we have outlined, it is possible for an internal organization such as an internal capital market to perform the tasks required of this institutional infrastructure more efficiently. Thus the question facing a developing country is whether it should invest in building the institutional infrastructure to support markets or devise an alternative system and hence bypass the imperfect financial market in whole or in part. Is investing in making the imperfect market less imperfect necessarily the best policy for a developing country?

Even in developed countries, the financial system consists of both market and nonmarket institutions, and as we have argued, private internal capital markets develop because of market imperfections and transactions costs. In developing countries, however, formal financial markets are likely to be characterized by both structural and policy-induced distortions, whereas private internal capital markets may not be efficient because of their limited size. In such settings, it may therefore be efficient for the government to create its own internal capital market in an attempt to improve the effectiveness of credit allocation. If a government-created "internal" capital market is to succeed as an effectual institution, however, it is likely to share features that are typical of those private institutions which have evolved and withstood the test of time in market economies.

The structure of a hierarchical system of credit allocation is made up of the government and a small number of enterprises that receive preferential credit allocated by the government. There may be financial institutions that function as intermediaries between government and enterprises, but in this hierarchical system their role is essentially that of distributing credit as directed by the government planners. As financial intermediaries and firms are not (necessarily) completely independent

6. One might even add here an observation made by Henry Bruton (1985) that "the market mechanism is importantly constrained by the larger environment within which it functions" (p. 1120). Its operation is thus affected by nonmarket institutions and the rules of a particular society.

institutions and as some transactions are clearly price-mediated, we may call the organization consisting of the government, financial intermediaries, and the recipient enterprises a *quasi-internal organization*. Because there are many other firms that do not belong to it, this quasi-internal organization constitutes only a subset of the entire market economy.

The similarities between the quasi-internal organization and the M-form structure of a modern corporation are worth specifying: decisions are made hierarchically; transactions between the government (general office) and select private enterprises that are the constituents of the quasi-internal organization (subunits) are internalized; and the activities of the subunits are monitored and coordinated by bureaucrats (salaried employees) instead of by the market mechanism. As the "bottom line" is a measure of performance of the subunits of the M-form structure, so the output and exports of constituent enterprises can be used as a measure of performance in the quasi-internal organization. Also, because of direct contact between the government and constituent enterprises, both sides are able to share information that would otherwise be conveyed only indirectly through prices. Decisions over the allocation of credit can thus be made before price changes signal the direction of credit allocation and private agents can respond to these signals.

But because the quasi-internal organization can function as an internal capital market does not necessarily mean that funds will be allocated efficiently; this will depend on the objective function of the political leadership and the internal structure of the quasi-internal organization. In a competitive market economy, the commitment of the firm's management to profitability is ultimately supplied by a combination of market pressures and institutional arrangements. Competition and the existence of equity markets ensure the survival only of those that, on average, choose the right products and production techniques. Yet even in such a setting, institutional arrangements matter. Through the monitoring of performance, shareholder organizations and boards are also capable of punishing and rewarding executives not committed to profitability.

Such checks may not operate to restrain governments, however. First, the quasi-internal organization does not face the competition that private firms face in the market. As it is the only such organization in the economy, it enjoys a monopoly position. Like a monopoly, the quasi-internal organization may prove "efficient" in achieving its own narrow objectives, but these may be predatory and come at the expense of the rest of the economy. Second, as in the model of the firm in which shareholders and board members monitor performance, imperfections typically exist in the capacity to monitor effectively: political leaders may be able to avoid punishment for bad performance. This is certainly true of some authoritarian governments, but it may also be true in democracies where powerful lobbies are capable of capturing policy for their own benefit.

Mechanisms do exist that can serve to constrain socially inefficient credit allocation. The first has to do with the broader policy setting in which the quasi-internal organization operates. If the government is committed to an outward-oriented strategy, the dependence of the economy on world markets acts as a check on government financial policy. For a small developing country committed to an outward-oriented development strategy, relative prices are parameters determined exogenously. Thus the government cannot arbitrarily change the prices of tradable goods to cover the consequences of an inefficient allocation of credit even though it can change the relative price of tradables to nontradables by varying the exchange rate. Because of this constraint, an inefficient internal allocation of credit which supports the wrong tradable goods industries will result in financial losses for the constituent enterprises. Although these enterprises may be able to survive with subsidies from the government, their losses become losses for the quasi-internal organization. Typically, governments of developing countries have financed such losses through money creation, with resultant inflationary pressures. For a small, open economy, this option is partly foreclosed. Put differently, the quasi-internal organization in an outward-oriented economy faces the equivalent of a hard budget constraint.

In contrast, a developing country that has adopted an inward-oriented development strategy can alter prices to cover the consequences of misguided internal credit allocations. Potential losses of the constituent enterprises can be made to disappear by changing prices with little noticeable effect on the treasury, at least in the short run. The quasi-internal organization can avoid losses that result from wrong credit allocations, and there is thus little or no incentive or compulsion to correct the existing pattern of allocation. Such a quasi-internal organization operates under a soft budget constraint.

As market competition is necessary to ensure the survival of efficient private internal organizations, so is competition necessary to ensure that the quasi-internal organization committed to economic growth makes efficient allocation of credit. For the quasi-internal organization, such competition exists only if it is forced to compete in world markets. Home markets may be protected for the benefit of certain constituent enterprises for a while, but their performance is ultimately judged by their export performance. For this reason, it is essential that the country be committed to an outward-oriented development strategy; we hold this as a central condition for the quasi-internal organizational model to be efficient.

Yet even if the policy environment is auspicious, that alone is not enough to guarantee the efficient operation of the quasi-internal organization. One problem that such an institutional arrangement faces is the existence of perverse incentives to the subunits, particularly the incentive to divert credit from its specified use to some other activity, such as real estate speculation or the curb market. In the extreme case of credit diversion, the receivers of rationed credit would get the rents accruing to their favored position, but the pattern of credit use would be no different from the one that would prevail under a free-market allocation of credit. The efficient functioning of the quasi-internal organization thus hinges critically on effective policy implementation.

Policy implementation within the quasi-internal organization differs from that in a market economy of the neoclassical mold. In the latter, government intervention is indirect through taxes and subsidies and rests on arm's-length regulations. Policy implementation works essentially by controlling market parameters that affect the behavior of economic agents; this is the market mode of policy implementation. In the "internal" mode of policy implementation, which is a characteristic of the quasi-internal organization, policy implementation does not rely on changes in market parameters but resides in negotiating and enforcing discrete contracts. The government provides credit, and the firm fulfills certain conditions.

This characterization suggests some of the organizational conditions that are likely to be important in making the quasi-internal organization effective. First and foremost, politics matters.[7] If the government in general, or the financial decision-making process in particular, is captured by the constituent firms, the conditional nature of credit provision naturally breaks down. Thus we would expect greater efficiency when decision makers are institutionally shielded from political pressures from firms, from the executive, and from other politicians who may seek to use credit policy for political ends. This process of insulation is necessarily imperfect; any government official is ultimately accountable to some constituency, whether it is the electorate as a whole, interest

7. This is the subject of the companion volume to this project. See Haggard, Lee, and Maxfield 1993.

groups, or the military. Nonetheless, central banks, regulatory institutions, and executive agencies in a number of countries have achieved some degree of autonomy from political pressures, which has influenced their capacity to allocate resources efficiently.

Second, the structure of business is likely to matter as well. On the one hand, a highly concentrated industrial structure poses certain political risks because large firms are more likely to influence or even blackmail government officials (Haggard, Lee, and Maxfield 1993). On the other hand, an implicit assumption of the foregoing analysis is that the number of constituent enterprises within the quasi-internal organization not be so large as to make monitoring costly. As the quasi-internal organization expands, it is more likely to confront organizational failures and may lose its relative advantage over markets. These organizational problems may help explain why various studies have shown that rural finance programs have failed to benefit the intended targets (Adams, Graham, and von Pischke 1984), as well as the current move toward liberalization of financial markets in a number of newly industrializing countries.

Finally, the nature of the contract between the government and the firms must be clear and measurable, and the government must have instruments of enforcement. For example, a large conglomerate like a Korean *chaebol* may internally reallocate government credit among its subunits. Nonetheless, its overall export record provides a clear measure of performance. The government must then possess control techniques not only for monitoring but also for "disciplining" agents who fail to live up to their contracts (Amsden 1989). In addition to the political factors noted above, the problem of managing the principal-agent relationship will demand a relatively well-developed bureaucratic apparatus.[8]

Economic development may itself affect the efficiency of the quasi-internal organization. As the economy becomes larger and more complex, graduating from producing simple goods to more technologically sophisticated products, organizational failures are likely to become more burdensome than market failures. This development also helps to explain why a number of both developing and developed countries have recently initiated efforts to liberalize their financial markets.[9]

8. It is important to note that the government in the quasi-internal organization is capable of rewarding desirable behavior and penalizing undesirable behavior on the part of constituent enterprises in a consistent manner as in a private internal organization. If the government is incapable of doing so for one reason or another, its relationship with the enterprises cannot be referred to as that in a quasi-internal organization. The importance of incentive-compatible mechanisms in designing the proper microeconomic role of government was discussed by Krueger (1990).

9. On failures of centralized hierarchy, see Sah 1991.

IV. Summary of Findings

The discussion of the quasi-internal organization in the preceding section suggests that under a certain set of conditions, a hierarchical system of credit allocation *can* be more efficient than a free-market allocation. The accompanying case studies seek to explore this proposition in more detail by examining the relationship between financial market structure, credit allocation, and economic growth in seven East Asian and Latin American countries. We begin our preview of the chapters that follow with Korea, because its experiences have been crucial to the debate over the merits and demerits of state intervention in support of rapid growth.

Korea

Until the mid-1980s, Korea's financial system was clearly "repressed." The entire banking system was under government ownership after 1961. Interest rates were maintained well below the market rate, and credit allocation was not left to the discretion of private bankers but largely dictated by the government in pursuit of its developmental objectives. Loans were extended at preferential rates, partly with government funds but mostly with bank funds and through control over foreign capital. Major areas of preference included the export sector, heavy and chemical industries, and the sectors commonly neglected by financial institutions, such as small and medium-sized firms, housing, agriculture, and fisheries.

During the 1960s, export financing received the most favorable treatment. Given the limited experience of the Korean private sector in foreign markets and the high uncertainty surrounding new investment, the government-directed credit allocation netted impressive results. Preferential finance to export-oriented manufacturing, administered by a politically and administratively strong state, contributed to the rapid growth of trade and set the country on a policy course that was conducive to relatively efficient government intervention.

Government control over the financial system was used in the 1970s to promote heavy and chemical industries. The result of the policy was mixed: industries such as electronics and passenger cars grew into leading export industries, whereas heavy machinery and shipping faltered. The policy also gave rise to a number of problems, including sectoral imbalances, concentration of power in the hands of large conglomerates, and rapid price and wage increases.

An evaluation of the policy promoting the heavy and chemical industries in terms of achieving its objectives must be made with care, however. First, the country's outward orientation contributed to the ability of the South Korean government to correct policy mistakes. Second, several sectors—including shipbuilding, shipping, and overseas construction—were extremely successful at first but then became burdened with surplus capacity following the second oil shock. No one, including private firms in the advanced industrial countries, could predict the oil crisis or the subsequent collapse of prices, which had a profound effect on these industries. Thus, some of the "failures" of the heavy industry period were the result of exogenous shocks, not the policy itself.

To restructure the ailing industries, the government forced mergers of failing firms, assisted by the infusion of new credit. These restructuring programs were not very effective, however, for the failing firms expected the government to bail them out in case of financial difficulties. Yet it is not clear that a laissez-faire adjustment process would have been more effective, given the concentrated nature of Korean business. Even in the advanced industrial countries, such a restructuring process involving large firms has not occurred through the market alone; the Chrysler bailout and the management of the savings and loan crises in the United States provide examples.

Since 1983, Korea's financial system has gone through a fair degree of liberalization. Commercial banks have been privatized and now have greater managerial autonomy, but they are still subject to heavy government intervention and oversight, in part to manage the lingering problem of nonperforming policy loans.

Taiwan

Taiwan has had a closely regulated and heavily protected formal financial sector. Unlike in Korea, however, financial policy was not used as a central industrial policy tool. Taiwan thus poses a puzzle as to why a repressed financial system could yield such spectacular growth. Tein-Chen Chou finds his answer in the presence of an active informal curb market that has functioned efficiently under a policy of benign government neglect.

Most of the commercial banks in Taiwan are state-owned. Although Taiwan began the process of financial liberalization in 1986 by lifting restrictions on interest rates, the personnel of the state-owned banks are still civil servants; consequently, the banks do not have managerial autonomy and are not free in making loan decisions.

The informal financial sector has played a much more important role. According to Chou's estimate, for every one hundred dollars that a corporation borrowed from formal financial institutions, it borrowed forty-seven dollars from the curb market, and for every one hundred dollars a household deposited at financial institutions, it lent fourteen dollars in the curb market. In other words, the curb market has been an important source of capital and a place for household savings.

Chou contends that this curb market has functioned efficiently because of the government's benign policy toward it. By not strictly forbidding curb market activities, the government effectively allowed the market to develop and evolve as a source of funding for projects that had not been funded in the formal financial sector. Chou's econometric study shows that credit allocation in the formal sector was based more on the size of collateral than on profitability, thus providing further evidence to the observation that the formal sector's credit allocation went mostly to large and state-owned enterprises (SOEs). The curb market was the chief source of funds for export-oriented small and medium-sized enterprises. Because these have played a key role in Taiwan's success as exporters of manufactured products, it is the curb market—and the export-oriented strategy more generally—that has played an important role in the success of the Taiwanese economy.

Chou's chapter still leaves unanswered the question of what role the government-controlled banking system has played in Taiwan's overall economic development. As in Korea, the government in Taiwan did assist firms in making the transition to an export-led growth strategy through financial subsidies. It is also true that while the state-owned enterprise sector in Taiwan may not be as efficient as the small-scale sector, neither has it been a source of the gross inefficiencies visible in other developing countries, in part because of the strong controls exercised by the government over SOE operations. Wade (1990), for example, offers a contrasting portrait to Chou's perceptions on the role of the state-owned sector: "In many sectors public enterprises have been used as the chosen instrument for a big push. This is true for the early years of fuels, chemicals, mining, metals, fertilizer, and food processing; but even in sectors where public enterprises did not dominate, such as textiles and plastics, the state aggressively led private producers in the early years" (p. 110). Unlike Chou, Wade also sees the large-scale sector (mostly public) as having an important influence on the small-scale sector:

While the government's direct role in the small-scale sector resembles the Hong Kong approach, the sector works rather differently from Hong Kong's. The large-scale sector provides an envelope for its activities through interdependence on both the demand and the supply sides. Large amounts of credit, technical assistance, and skilled labor come to small firms directly from large firms. By setting directions for the large-scale sector, the government influences the configuration of risks and profit opportunities for small-scale firms. Indirectly, through its effect on investment within the large-scale sector, the government influences broad trends within the small-scale sector as well. (p. 306)

Taiwan's small-scale sector was largely excluded from the formal credit market and was helped by the efficiency of the informal credit market operating under the policy of benign neglect. But to the extent that small-scale firms also depended on large firms for credit and technical assistance, they have been indirectly affected by government intervention in the formal credit market.

Indonesia

Indonesia's banking system has been dominated by state-owned banks (SOBs). This dominant position is the result of the nationalization of Dutch banks and increased state intervention in the 1974–1983 period. Given that every bank was assigned a specific credit quota, entry into banking was minimized to make it easier for the central bank to administer credit ceilings. SOBs, along with the Bank of Indonesia, were also used by the state as a vehicle for disbursing oil revenue, including through selective credit programs. Starting in 1983, many of the restrictive measures were eliminated, and by 1990 the proportion of banking credits accounted for by the central bank and SOBs had fallen.

The state-owned commercial banks were assigned specific sectors for their lending activities, and they handled most "liquidity credits," that is, credits that were received from the central bank for loans that the banks had made for government credit programs at a designated lending rate. In 1969, 75 percent of liquidity credits was channeled into financing agricultural production and international trade, but by 1979, manufacturing surpassed agriculture as the most favored activity for liquidity credits.

Wing Thye Woo argues that selective credit policies did not appear to have had a strong effect on sectoral performance. Moreover, this selective credit allocation had some troubling features, which are indicative

of the difficulties of insulating the process of discretionary credit allocation from political pressures, including those emanating from the executive itself. First, the range of activities eligible for liquidity credits tended
to expand. Second, the terms of a program were inclined to become
more concessionary over time. Furthermore, because of the implicit
government guarantee, SOEs received a preferred status in selective
credit allocation. Thus, in spite of the official desire to accelerate industrialization through selective credit allocation, the bulk of long-term
credits to manufacturing went to two SOEs—Krakatau Steel and Perumtel, a telecommunications company. In fact, selective credit allocation intended to promote industrialization in Indonesia had the effect of
supporting SOEs.

The policy of selective credit allocation in Indonesia had a fortuitous
but nonetheless favorable effect on the economy. During the 1970s, the
Indonesian monetary authorities had little control over the money supply in the short run. As a result, the oil boom had the predictable effect
of raising the prices of nontradables relative to those of tradables, that is,
the so-called Dutch disease. But the Indonesian economy did not suffer
as much from the Dutch disease as it might have in the absence of the
policy of selective credit allocation. That policy favored the manufacturing and trade sectors—the tradable and near-tradable sectors—precisely the sectors most affected by the Dutch disease during 1974–1978.
The selective credit policy thus neutralized the adverse effects on the
tradables sector and reduced the dynamic inefficiency resulting from
short-term fluctuations in relative prices.

Selective credit allocation did not achieve its intended result
of developing manufacturing, because Indonesia lacked the well-trained
bureaucracy and solid statistical reporting system that are necessary
for government-directed credit allocation to work. Moreover, the
country's political system was such that the credit allocation process was
not well insulated from pressures from SOEs and the executive. To
a greater extent than in many other developing countries, however,
preferential credit was channeled to activities that were in line with
Indonesia's comparative advantage, including export-oriented manufacturing and agriculture. As Woo argues, this outcome was mainly due
to Suharto's concern to reduce the risk of rural unrest. These supports, in turn, partly offset the disincentives associated with the Dutch
disease.

The financial deregulation measures enacted since March 1983 have
brought substantial changes, mostly beneficial. The financial system in

Indonesia is now much more competitive, more extensive in the range of services provided, and more creative in the development of new financial instruments. Greater supervision of the financial institutions, which is necessary for the overall health of the financial system, has been slow in following the deregulation, however, and thus Woo argues that the system remains vulnerable.

Thailand

Thailand's economic policies since 1960, including its financial policy, have been largely that of a nondirigiste approach, in spite of the fact that the market for long-term funds is very limited, with publicly issued equity forming a relatively small source of funds for Thai companies. The market for long-term debt securities is also very small, the instruments of which consist almost entirely of government bonds held mainly by commercial banks.

Most of the financial institutions in Thailand are privately owned, and the banking industry is highly concentrated, with the largest banks holding about two-thirds of all commercial bank assets. Thai financial authorities seldom interfered with their operation for explicitly allocative purposes. When the authorities have intervened, their objectives were for short-run price supports for commodities, especially sugar; to promote the agricultural sector and, later, rural activities in general; and to encourage exports by extending subsidized short-term credit. The primary focus of the financial authorities, however, has been on the solvency and stability of Thailand's financial system, not on sectoral allocation of investment funds.

The only large-scale credit allocation policy concerns agriculture, and it was initiated during a period of political liberalization. Beginning in 1975, commercial banks were required to extend credit to the agricultural sector and were given a specific quota that has increased over time. The coverage area has expanded to include small-scale rural industries and rural individuals as well as agriculture itself. In the industrial and commercial sectors, Thailand has been relatively free of project-level intervention through selective credit allocation. The government has taken a neutral stand and has not made the effort to create new comparative advantages for private enterprises. It is interesting to note, however, that this hands-off approach itself rested on unique organizational features of the Thai government which are akin to those required for an efficient quasi-internal organization to operate, including the strength of the central bank and financial authorities and the highly diversified nature of the larger Thai groups, which came to encompass financial, manufacturing, and agricultural activities.

The Philippines

The financial system in the Philippines clearly typifies a case where a small group of powerful players in the private sector has maximized its share of rents at the expense of the rest of the country. This small group and the weak authoritarian government have formed, according to Manuel Montes and Johnny Noe E. Ravalo, a "quasi-public network" whose objective is the protection of the economic position of its members. Thus it differs from the quasi-internal organization found in Korea, in which the state exerted greater influence over the private sector and the bureaucracy was more coherent.

Selective credit allocation has been used by the Philippine government to support the country's traditional (agriculture, timber, and mining) exports and import-substituting industries. Although there have been attempts to change, the Philippines has in practice maintained an inward-oriented trade regime, with bank credit going to heavily protected industries. This situation is not surprising given the control of these industries by powerful family groups and, in effect, their control of credit allocation, both through their influence over government banks and through their ownership of banking institutions. In such a situation, the type of financial system—repressed or liberal—arguably matters little to credit allocation; credit would have gone to the same enterprises, even were the system deregulated.

In 1985 financial liberalization was introduced in the Philippines, and control over interest rates was completely eliminated. But interest rates on bank deposits remained fixed at low rates, savings mobilization did not increase much, and long-term lending continued to be inadequate. The reason is that financial liberalization in the Philippines has had little effect on the structure of the financial market, which is dominated by a few large banks, and thus little effect on their competitive behavior. Furthermore, because of its administrative weakness and lack of insulation, the government was unable either to break the banks' control or to institute prudential regulation of and supervision over the banks.

The Philippines appears to provide a clear case against government intervention. A small number of large crony firms dominated credit allocation and the rents from corruption. Yet Montes and Ravalo's analysis shows that these problems would have existed even had the government liberalized the financial system. Thus the Philippines deviates from the model of the quasi-internal organization because of political and administrative weaknesses, that is, the corruption of the political leadership, the dominance of large rent-seeking groups, and the weakness of the bureaucracy itself.

Chile

Beginning in the 1930s the government of Chile began providing the manufacturing sector with direct subsidies, tax exemptions, and restrictive trade measures, including tariffs, quotas, import licenses, exchange controls, and multiple exchange rates. Subsidized credit was also one of the policy instruments employed by the government to achieve its goal of import substitution. In the 1950s, the government's stated emphasis shifted from promoting manufacturing to promoting "productive activities," but this change was reflective of only the generally indiscriminate use of the credit policy instrument. Even this practice of sending notices to the commercial banks to encourage credit allocation to specific activities was stopped in 1959 because of its ineffectiveness. In sum, the government lacked both the ability and willingness to process information related to the allocation of credit and consequently was unable to control its ultimate use. As a result, there was substantial credit diversion. During the period of financial repression, the banks made recurrent losses. They were able to survive because they channeled a part of bank credit to ownership-related firms; that is, while the banks were losing money, other related firms were getting the benefit of cheap credit.

If there was a pattern to credit allocation, it appears to have been an appendage to the import-substitution industrialization (ISI) policy thrust. The manufacturing sector received the lion's share of credit allocated by commercial banks, and within this sector, the most protected industries received a relatively large share of credit. Despite limitations on the available data, anecdotal evidence suggests that credit was routinely diverted from its intended destination to other activities, including speculative ones, where profits were higher.

Although quantitative control over credit expansion was used by the central bank to reduce the inflationary pressure of financing the fiscal deficit with new money creation, in fact it resulted in the allocation of credit in favor of the public sector, neutralizing to a certain extent credit allocation channeled to "productive activities."

The Chile study argues that financial repression had a strong negative effect on the country's economic growth. But given that financial resources would have gone to the protected import-substituting industries even in the absence of government intervention, the policy of financial repression should be regarded as only a contributing, albeit negative, factor to the economic growth of Chile.

Beginning in 1975 the new military government undertook various measures of financial liberalization, as well as a gradual reversal of the previous industrial policy emphasis on ISI. Financial liberalization caused substitution away from real assets, such as consumer durables and foreign currency, into financial assets, thus increasing the amount of savings allocated by the financial institutions.[10] But the well-documented failure to regulate the newly emerging financial markets, as well as macroeconomic policy failures, resulted in a massive crisis in 1982–1983, and it was only with the ascent of a more pragmatic team and the strengthening of prudential regulation that Chile's economic performance did improve. By the end of the 1980s, capital markets appeared to channel savings to more profitable projects, and financial liberalization could be deemed a success. But this success came only after the severe financial crises of the early 1980s.

Brazil

The political economy of Brazilian policy toward financial markets is exceedingly complex. The liberalization of the mid-1960s was accompanied by continued government intervention, with the result that a variety of contradictory policies coexisted at the same time. Moreover, the coherence of financial market policy has been complicated throughout Brazilian history by high inflation and the emergence of extensive indexing, including indexing of financial instruments. The result is a complicated system characterized by a lack of transparency and a variety of regulations, exceptions, taxes, and subsidies, many of which appear to have the effect of canceling one another out.

Even though the financial reforms of the 1960s brought about financial deepening, they had very little effect on private saving and failed to create a market for long-term credit. Increasingly, medium-sized and large private enterprises had to resort to debt financing contracted with government institutions such as the National Economic Development Bank and state development banks and to the use of foreign resources.

The selective credit policies of Brazil have had a mixed record. As in Korea and Taiwan, they contributed to Brazil's export success beginning in the late 1960s; during the 1970–1985 period, total Brazilian exports

10. Although external savings increased as a result of the reforms, the effect of liberalization on total savings remains ambiguous because of an offsetting decrease in internal savings.

grew at an average rate of 17.3 percent a year, while its manufactured exports grew at around 30 percent a year. And the policies promoting agriculture were successful in that the subsidized credit has contributed to the modernization of the Brazilian agricultural sector since the mid-1960s.

Once interest rates were fully freed from government control in 1976, demands for subsidized credit multiplied. The state began operating with a negative spread because its liabilities were indexed, whereas its assets were denominated in nominal terms, with rates of return that were lower in most cases than was the rate of inflation. Given the government's limited ability to extract fiscal resources and thus its reliance on credit from the central bank, it was inevitable that inflation would reemerge in the 1970s. Capital flight and investment in short-term financial assets at the expense of real investment became the defensive measures taken by the private sector.

Brazil shows clearly the crucial role of the macroeconomic setting. No effort at state-directed credit is likely to be successful under conditions of extreme macroeconomic instability. Rather, that instability itself created strong pressure for subsidies, which subsequently became so complex that the government was unable to gauge either their costs or benefits.

A basic premise of those advocating financial liberalization is that it will bring about a higher rate of economic growth both by increasing the availability of financial resources and by allocating them more efficiently. New theoretical insights and cumulative empirical evidence on financial markets have raised questions regarding this premise. Given the asymmetric and imperfect information that plagues all financial markets, there is no a priori reason why financial liberalization should bring about an efficient allocation of resources, even in developed countries. For many developing countries where financial markets are highly concentrated and where the capability for prudential supervision is lacking, the case for sweeping financial liberalization is much weaker.[11]

Given the inherently imperfect nature of financial markets, the regime of "financial repression" in certain countries can be understood as an effort on the part of the government to create its own internal capital market for mobilizing and allocating financial resources for its developmental objectives. Drawing on the analogy of the emergence of internal

11. In their survey of five developing countries in Asia which undertook financial reform, Cho and Khatkhate (1989) conclude that reform did not seem to have made any significant difference to the volume of saving and investment activities. What it seems to have done, however, is result in an increase in the financialization of savings.

capital markets as an institutional response to capital market imperfections, we have proffered several theoretical reasons for why this government-created internal capital market can be relatively efficient, as well as the empirical conditions under which it is likely to be so.

First, the quasi-internal organization is likely to be more efficient where the government is committed to an outward-oriented growth strategy that both restrains it and provides information on the soundness of its investment choices.[12] By exposing domestic firms to international competition abroad, the emphasis on exports constrains the policies and actions taken by the government and provides standards against which government policy can be checked.[13] Second, the contracts with the private sector must be clearly specified and measurable, and the government must be politically and organizationally "strong" enough to monitor and enforce those contracts through sanctions. Third, the quasi-internal organization is likely to be more effective where the number of private-sector actors is relatively small.

Finally, we have noted the role of politics and political institutions (Haggard, Lee, and Maxfield 1993). Credit policy is likely to be more efficient where the government in general and the relevant bureaucracies in particular have achieved some degree of institutional autonomy from interest groups and from the executive itself. The internal coherence of the policy bureaucracy and the implementing agencies also matters. Bureaucracies may achieve such a status if incentives, such as promotion patterns, are right. Yet ideology may also be a factor in understanding the coherence of bureaucratic organization. If, as pointed out by Simon (1991), organizational identification—"we" versus "they"—motivates employees of private enterprises, there is no reason to think that such motivations may not also work to enhance the efficiency of the quasi-internal organization.

These are formidable institutional requirements for many developing countries, as the country studies in this book attest. We find that many developing countries lack these conditions, but we also find that in

12. It should be noted that because of capital market imperfections, an outward-oriented growth strategy in itself is not sufficient for economic growth.

13. Chowdhury and Islam (1993) argue that the importance of outward orientation for the quasi-internal organization implies that it is export orientation that has played a primary role in East Asian economic development and that state activism has played only a supplementary role. It should be noted, however, that outward orientation is important for the quasi-internal organization because it constrains the policies that can be taken by the government, whereas in the neoclassical explanation of the East Asian success, outward orientation is important because it provides neutral incentives between exportables and importables. As noted in the text, this is inconsistent with the strong government intervention observed in East Asia.

certain cases, governments have intervened effectively in promoting economic development. Clearly, establishing these conditions—that is, insulating the financial decision-making process from the executive as well as external influence, developing monitoring capabilities, and maintaining performance-based allocation of credit—is going to be a difficult and costly process for many developing countries. But it should also be noted that correcting market failures and improving the workings of the market are not going to be an easy and costless process either. The choice faced by developing countries is not, therefore, between government and the market but between improving government and improving the market, given limited resources. The point of our book is that developing and improving institutions is as important as improving the market.

The approach we have outlined here implies a more differentiated approach to financial market reform and to liberalization more generally. Liberalization may be an appropriate strategy where distortions are particularly large and institutions for formulating a coherent interventionist strategy are weak. But these conditions do not hold across all developing countries, especially middle-income countries. As a result, there may be continuing room for government in influencing the allocation of financial resources as a component of a more comprehensive strategy for longer-term growth. Moreover, our approach shifts the focus of normative debate. The current emphasis given to macroeconomic policies must now be supplemented by a more thorough analysis of institutions.

References

Adams, Dale, Douglas H. Graham, and J. D. von Pischke. 1984. *Undermining Rural Development with Cheap Credit.* Boulder, Colo.: Westview Press.

Alam, S. M. 1989. *Governments and Markets in Economic Development Strategies: Lessons from Korea, Taiwan, and Japan.* New York: Praeger.

Amsden, Alice H. 1989. *Asia's Next Giant: South Korea and Late Industrialization.* New York: Oxford University Press.

Bradford, Jr., C. I. 1986. East Asian "Models": Myths and Lessons. In *Development Strategies Reconsidered,* ed. John P. Lewis and Valeriana Kallab. New Brunswick, N.J.: Transaction Books.

———. 1987. Trade and Structural Change: NICs and Next Tier NICs as Transitional Economies. *World Development* 15(3): 299–316.

Bruno, Michael. 1979. Stabilization and Stagflation in a Semi-industrialized Economy. In *International Economic Policy: Theory and Evidence,* ed. Rudiger Dornbusch and Jacob Frenkel. Baltimore: Johns Hopkins University Press.

Bruton, Henry J. 1985. The Search for a Development Economics. *World Development* 13(10/11): 1099–124.

Cho, Lee-Jay, and Yoon Hyung Kim, eds. 1991. *Economic Development in the Republic of Korea: A Policy Perspective.* Honolulu: East-West Center.

Cho, Yoon-Je. 1986. Inefficiencies from Financial Liberalization in the Absence of Well-Functioning Equities Markets. *Journal of Money, Credit, and Banking* 18(2): 191–99.

———. 1990. McKinnon-Shaw versus the Neostructuralists on Financial Liberalization: A Conceptual Note. *World Development* 18(3): 477–80.

Cho, Yoon-Je, and Deena Khatkhate. 1989. *Lessons of Financial Liberalization in Asia: A Comparative Study.* Washington, D.C.: World Bank.

Chowdhury, Anis, and Iyanatul Islam. 1993. *The Newly Industrialising Economies of East Asia.* London: Routledge.

Corbo, Vittorio, and Jaime de Melo. 1985. Liberalization with Stabilization in the Southern Cone of Latin America: Overview and Summary. *World Development* 13(8): 863–66.

———. 1987. Lessons from the Southern Cone Policy Reforms. *World Bank Research Observer* 2(2): 111–42.

Dooley, Michael, and Donald Mathieson. 1987. Financial Liberalization in Developing Countries. *Finance and Development* 24(3): 31–34.

Fischer, Bernhard. 1989. Savings Mobilization in Developing Countries: Bottlenecks and Reform Proposals. *Savings and Development* 13(2): 117–31.

Fry, Maxwell J. 1988. *Money, Interest, and Banking in Economic Development.* Baltimore: Johns Hopkins University Press.

Haggard, Stephan, Chung H. Lee, and Sylvia Maxfield. 1993. *The Politics of Finance in Developing Countries.* Ithaca: Cornell University Press.

Johnson, Chalmers. 1985. Political Institutions and Economic Performance: The Government-Business Relationship in Japan, South Korea, and Taiwan. In *Asian Economic Development—Present and Future,* ed. Robert A. Scalapino, Seizaburo Sato, and Jusuf Wanadi. Berkeley: Institute of East Asian Studies, University of California.

Krueger, Anne O. 1990. Economists' Changing Perceptions of Government. *Weltwirtschaftliches Archiv,* Band 126, Heft 3: 417–31.

Lal, Deepak. 1985. *The Poverty of Development Economics.* Cambridge: Harvard University Press.

Lee, Chung H. 1992. The Government, Financial System, and Large Private Enterprises in the Economic Development of South Korea. *World Development* 20(2): 187–97.

Leff, Nathaniel H. 1976. Capital Markets in the Less Developed Countries: The Group Principle. In *Money and Finance in Economic Growth and Development,* ed. Ronald I. McKinnon. New York: Dekker.

McKinnon, Ronald I. 1973. *Money and Capital in Economic Development.* Washington, D.C.: Brookings Institution.

Patrick, Hugh T. 1990. The Financial Development of Taiwan, Korea, and Japan: A Framework for Consideration of Issues. Paper presented at the Conference on Financial Development in Japan, Korea, and Taiwan, Institute of Economics, Academia Sinica, Taipei, August 27–28.

Polak, Jacques J. 1989. *Financial Policies and Development.* Paris: Development Center, Organization for Economic Cooperation and Development.

Sah, Raaj K. 1991. Fallibility in Human Organizations and Political Systems. *Journal of Economic Perspectives* 5(2): 67–88.

Shaw, Edward S. 1973. *Financial Deepening in Economic Development.* New York: Oxford University Press.

Simon, Herbert A. 1991. Organizations and Markets. *Journal of Economic Perspectives* 5(2): 25–44.

Stiglitz, Joseph E. 1989. Markets, Market Failures, and Development. *American Economic Review* 79(2): 197–203.

Stiglitz, Joseph E., and Andrew Weiss. 1981. Credit Rationing in Markets with Imperfect Information. *American Economic Review* 71(3): 393–410.

Strachan, Harry W. 1976. *Family and Other Business Groups in Economic Development: The Case of Nicaragua.* New York: Praeger.

Taylor, Lance. 1979. *Macro-models for Developing Countries.* New York: McGraw-Hill.

———. 1983. *Structuralist Macroeconomics: Applicable Models for the Third World.* New York: Basic Books.

Tirole, Jean. 1986. Hierarchies and Bureaucracies: On the Role of Coercion in Organizations. *Journal of Law, Economics, and Organization* 2: 181–214.

van Wijnbergen, Sweder. 1982. Stagflation Effects of Monetary Stabilization Policies: A Quantitative Analysis of South Korea. *Journal of Development Economics* 10(2): 133–69.

———. 1983a. Credit Policy, Inflation, and Growth in a Financially Repressed Economy. *Journal of Development Economics* 13(1): 45–65.

———. 1983b. Interest Rate Management in LDCs. *Journal of Monetary Economics* 12: 433–52.

———. 1985. Macroeconomic Effects of Changes in Bank Interest Rates: Simulation Results for South Korea. *Journal of Development Economics* 18: 541–54.

Wade, Robert. 1990. *Governing the Market: Economic Theory and the Role of Government in East Asian Industrialization.* Princeton: Princeton University Press.

Williamson, O. E. 1975. *Markets and Hierarchies: Analysis and Antitrust Implications.* New York: Free Press.

———. 1985. *The Economic Institutions of Capitalism.* New York: Free Press.

Wolf, Jr., Charles. 1988. *Markets or Governments.* Cambridge: MIT Press.

World Bank. 1993. *The East Asian Miracle: Economic Growth and Public Policy.* New York: Oxford University Press.

PART I

ASIA

CHAPTER ONE

KOREA

Sang-Woo Nam and Chung H. Lee

The financial system that existed in Korea until the middle of the 1980s was a "repressed" system. Interest rates were artificially fixed below the market-clearing level, and credit allocation was directed by the government in support of industrial development. Given the well-known proposition that such a financial system retards economic growth, how the Korean economy could have grown rapidly under this system is a puzzle that challenges those interested in the relationship between finance and economic development.

This chapter begins with a discussion of the evolution of the Korean financial market and the nature of the financial and industrial policies undertaken during the past thirty years. After reviewing the consequences of these policies, particularly those dealing with credit allocation, we argue that Korea is an exemplary case of the quasi-internal organization discussed in the introductory chapter. Led by a strong, developmental state and supported by an efficient bureaucracy, the quasi-internal organization has been instrumental in bringing about rapid structural changes and economic development in Korea. We conclude that with the recent introduction of numerous liberalization measures, the usefulness of the quasi-internal organization as a developmental institution has diminished in Korea.

I. The Evolution of the Korean Financial Market

Formation of the Formal Financial System

Until the mid-1960s, the intermediary role of commercial banks was of little significance because of the negligible savings of the nation.[1] The primary purpose of financial institutions was to channel aid funds to rehabilitation projects and farmers. Two special banks, the Korea Development Bank (KDB) and the Korea Agriculture Bank, accounted for over 70 percent of total bank lending.

The role of financial institutions as mobilizers of savings was recognized only after the adoption in September 1965 of a schedule of high interest rates. The effect of this interest rate reform on marshaling additional domestic resources was remarkable. As bank deposits increased rapidly, the ratio of M_2 to gross national product (M_2/GNP) jumped from 18.5 percent during 1965–1970 to 30.2 percent during 1971–1973. Also, the commercial banks' share of total bank loans rose from 27 percent in 1964 to 55 percent within five years. But the interest rate reform of 1965 was too short-lived to sustain the momentum that the reform had initially generated. After 1968, bank interest rates were lowered in several stages, reaching levels well below the prereform rates by 1972.

Another important role played by the Korean banking system was to facilitate the inflow of foreign loans by guaranteeing repayment. Since 1966, commercial banks have joined the KDB to become active participants in the massive foreign loan guarantee business. The 1960s also saw the establishment of new financial institutions engaged in specialized activities desired by the government. The Medium Industry Bank (MIB) and the Citizens National Bank (CNB) were both created shortly after the military government came into power in 1961; in addition, the Korea Exchange Bank (KEB) and the Korea Housing Bank (KHB) were established in 1967.

Throughout the 1970s, with the financial system under increasing repression and with accelerated inflation, financial development was rather slow. Efforts in the early 1970s to reduce the unorganized money market (UMM) by establishing new nonbank financial institutions and to promote the capital market contributed significantly to the diversification of Korea's financial market. In connection with the Presidential Emergency Decree of August 1972, which froze the curb market, short-term finance companies and mutual savings and finance companies were established, and credit unions were modernized. Although the growth of these institutions has been constrained by various operational restrictions, including interest rates, they seem to have succeeded in

---

1. For a detailed discussion of the development of Korea's financial system and government policies during 1945–1978, see Cole and Park 1979.

attracting funds that otherwise might have been supplied to the curb market.

Until 1972, the Korean capital market was little more than a secondary market for national bonds issued during and after the Korean War. Only a limited number of equity shares were traded in the market, and no corporate bonds were issued in the market before 1972. Since then, however, the capital market has grown very rapidly thanks to strong promotional measures undertaken by the government. Together with creating measures geared to increase demand for securities, the government has given favorable corporate tax treatment to publicly held firms and has ordered selected companies to go public.

The entire Korean banking system came under government ownership in 1961 when the new military regime nationalized commercial banks as a way of confiscating "illicit" wealth accumulated under the previous regime. Furthermore, legislation limited the voting power of any private shareholder to a maximum of 10 percent. Since then and until the early 1980s, the government was the major stockholder of nationwide city banks, generally holding more than 20 percent of their total shares. With the privatization of these banks in the early 1980s, however, the maximum ownership of any single shareholder has been limited to 8 percent of total shares.

Workings of the Informal Credit Market

The unorganized money market has been an important source of short-term financing for Korean firms and individuals. Unlike organized financial institutions, professional moneylenders, relatives, and friends usually do not insist on collateral. The professional moneylenders seem to be efficient in evaluating the credit standing of borrowers, loan collection, and pricing. Interest rates are sensitive to the risk differentials among borrowers, changing demand and supply conditions in the money market, and the rate of inflation. The UMM is very inefficient in other respects, however; it is an extremely fragmented market, and information is much more costly than in the formal credit market. Moneylenders do business without licenses and usually do not pay income tax. Because of this illegal nature of the UMM, the risk premium is rather high.

There have been several attempts, mainly in the 1970s, to estimate the size of the UMM based on corporate tax return data and household budget and other surveys. A rather reliable estimate, obtained by the Presidential Emergency Decree in August 1972, which required all

UMM loans outstanding to business firms to be reported to the National Tax Office, is the reported volume of credit of 354 billion won, which is equivalent to over one-quarter of total domestic credit to the private sector. One particular feature disclosed by the decree was that almost 30 percent of total UMM loans lent to business firms were so-called disguised UMM loans: that is, the loans were made by major equity holders or executives of the borrowing firms. This phenomenon arose from the repressed nature of the financial regime as well as inadequate information in the UMM market.

These disguised moneylenders not only had superior information about the firm but also had influence over corporate (financial) decisions; with this influence, they could have their loans repaid ahead of others when the borrowing firm was in danger of going bankrupt. Despite this privilege of virtually subordinating other loans, the insider fund suppliers, disguising their identity, charged fairly high (market) interest rates. The corporate insiders certainly capitalized on their positions for their own benefit, yet there was little evidence that the firms could have saved on the cost of borrowing by relying on insiders' funds.

The relative importance of the UMM, however, is known to have declined thereafter, as new nonbank financial institutions that offered interest rates more in line with the UMM rates were established. Investment and finance companies now accommodate the short-term working capital needs of business firms in a rather speedy and flexible manner. With growing markets for financial assets whose return is market-determined, the supply of funds in the UMM appears to be dwindling.

Some moneylenders have been observed to lend money through financial institutions by making deposits on the condition that the money will be lent to a borrower designated by the depositor. The interest rate differential between the organized and unorganized financial markets is directly settled between the lender and the borrower. Unlike in a pure UMM transaction, which is not reported to the tax office, the borrower gets a tax deduction on the interest payment to the financial institution.

Growth of Financial Markets

Financial development more or less stagnated during the 1970s because of the negative interest rates throughout most of the period as a result of the two oil shocks. The M_2/GNP ratio, which stood at 0.32 in

1970, remained virtually unchanged ten years later. During the 1980s, the ratio rose from 0.34 to 0.41 thanks to the deceleration of inflation and the resulting positive real interest rates on deposits since 1982 (Table 1.1). But the growth of M_2, the major monetary target, has been constrained by the restrictive monetary policy, particularly during the first half of the 1980s, and the introduction of new financial assets such as commercial papers, repurchases, variants of trust deposits, and certificates of deposit (which are not part of M_2).

The M_3/GNP ratio thus grew much faster, rising from 0.43 in 1979 to 1.15 in 1990. Such rapid growth of nonbank financial intermediaries can be explained by lower entry barriers to these markets, introduction of new financial instruments, and more attractive interest rates offered to depositors (often circumventing interest rate controls by the authorities). This favorable environment for the growth of nonbank financial intermediaries can be attributed to the desire of the government to

Table 1.1. Trend of financial deepening (by percentage)

	M_2/GNP[a]	M_3/GNP[b]	Domestic financial assets/GNP	National savings rate
1970	0.32	0.37[c]	2.12	18.0
1975	0.31	0.39	2.17	18.2
1976	0.30	0.38	2.05	24.3
1977	0.33	0.42	2.12	27.6
1978	0.33	0.43	2.14	29.7
1979	0.32	0.43	2.16	28.4
1980	0.34	0.49	2.40	23.1
1981	0.34	0.51	2.57	22.7
1982	0.38	0.59	2.90	24.2
1983	0.37	0.61	2.94	27.6
1984	0.35	0.65	3.09	29.4
1985	0.37	0.70	3.28	29.1
1986	0.37	0.78	3.31	32.8
1987	0.38	0.87	3.51	36.2
1988	0.39	0.94	3.59	38.1
1989	0.41	1.06	4.10	35.3
1990	0.41	1.15	4.22	35.3

Sources: Bank of Korea, various years b, various years c.
Note: Stock of financial assets is on a year-end basis.
[a] M_2 includes currency in circulation and deposits at monetary institutions.
[b] M_3 is composed of M_2, deposits at other financial institutions, debentures issued by financial institutions, certificates of deposit, bonds sold with repurchase agreement, and commercial bills sold.
[c] Figure is for 1971.

absorb curb market funds and thus maximize the mobilization of financial resources through organized markets. Rapid growth of nonbank financial intermediaries has been largely represented by short-term finance companies (corporate bills discounted and resold), securities investment trust companies (sales of beneficial certificates), money in trust offered by banks, life insurance companies (reserves), deposits in mutual savings and finance companies, and mutual credit of agricultural cooperatives.

The role of the securities market in Korea's total financial savings has increased steadily throughout the 1970s and 1980s. Securities issues as a share of total outstanding financial assets rose from 13.2 percent in 1972 to 21.3 percent in 1979 and to 31.1 percent in 1989. Although the role of the equity market declined in the early 1980s, it was more than compensated for by the increasing role of public and financial debentures and corporate bonds. As the stock market recovered strongly in the latter half of the 1980s, this market accounted for more than 13 percent of total outstanding financial assets during 1988–1990.

The ratio of total domestic financial assets to GNP, the broadest indicator of financial development, also stagnated during the 1970s but showed rapid growth during the 1980s, rising from 2.16 in 1979 to 4.22 in 1990. Significantly positive interest rates, new financial assets, a more extensive network of financial services, development of the securities market, and sustained economic growth during the 1980s all contributed to this rapid financial development. Net accumulation of financial assets, however, does not find an exact parallel in the national savings rate. As analyzed by Nam (1990), although positive real interest rates certainly help, the national savings rate is influenced primarily by the growth of income.[2] This is clearly shown by the substantial drop in the national savings rate in the early 1980s and the drastic rebound of the rate since 1986.

II. The Nature of Financial Policy

In Korea, the monetary authorities determine the whole spectrum of interest rates on financial assets and liabilities in the organized financial markets. The only exceptions to this are bond yields in the secondary market and some money market and trust instruments whose returns

2. According to the analysis of Nam (1990), a 1.00 percentage point sustained increase in bank interest rates results, with a one-year lag, in a 0.27 percentage point rise in the household savings ratio and a 0.17 percentage point rise in the national savings ratio.

depend largely on investment performance of securities. The interest rate structure was very complicated until June 1982 because the rates were differentiated depending on the sources (government, banking, or foreign), uses, and suppliers of the funds. Interest rates on preferential policy loans were particularly complex until rate differentials between general and policy loans were largely eliminated in June 1982.

Although the monetary authorities seem to have changed interest rates in consideration of the need to absorb liquidity, to boost investment activity, or to keep in line with changing inflation rates, the determination has, to a large extent, been arbitrary. In general, interest rates have been maintained well below the market rate and have not been adequately flexible (Table 1.2). With the excess demand for funds which exists in the organized financial markets, there has always been room for the curb loan market.

As a result of arbitrarily low interest rates in the organized markets, credit rationing has been inevitable. Before the 1980s, the government had ensured that adequate funds were available to the sectors of the economy deemed to be strategic by setting aside part of the available funds for preferential lending. As these preferential loans grew faster than the total loanable funds, access to funds by the less preferred sectors was seriously limited. Although preferential loans are extended partly with government funds, they are mostly made up of bank funds and foreign capital. Major areas of preference include the export sector, heavy and chemical industries, and other sectors that tend to be neglected by financial institutions, such as small and medium-sized firms, housing, agriculture, and fisheries.

Export financing has received the most favorable treatment since the launching of the First Five-Year Economic Development Plan in the early 1960s. Both short-term operating funds and foreign currency loans for imports of machinery and equipment have been supplied. A large proportion of export credit has been automatically rediscounted at the Bank of Korea (BOK), accounting for a large portion of its total loans outstanding.

The burden of providing medium- and long-term investment financing has mainly been borne by specialized financial institutions. The KDB has given support primarily to key manufacturing and electric power–generating industries with government funds and through borrowing from the National Investment Fund (NIF) and foreign sources. The Korea Long-Term Credit Bank provides development loans with funds obtained from long-term credit debentures and borrowings abroad. Another development institute, the Export-Import Bank of

Table 1.2. Regulated and market interest rates (year average, by percentage)

	Regulated rates		Market rates					
	Bank one-year time deposit	General bank loans	Corporate bond yield	Curb rate	Average borrowing cost (manufacturing)	Consumer inflation rate	Real GNP growth	M₂ growth rate
1970	22.8	24.0	na	49.8	14.7	15.4	7.6	na
1975	15.0	15.5	20.1	41.3	11.3	25.4	6.4	27.0
1976	15.5	16.5	20.4	40.5	11.9	15.3	13.1	29.2
1977	15.8	17.3	20.1	38.1	13.1	10.0	9.8	37.0
1978	16.7	17.7	21.1	41.2	12.4	14.5	9.8	39.3
1979	18.6	19.0	26.7	42.4	14.4	18.2	7.2	26.8
1980	22.7	23.4	30.1	44.9	18.7	28.7	−3.7	25.8
1981	19.3	19.8	24.4	35.3	18.4	21.6	5.9	27.4
1982	10.9	12.5	17.3	30.6	16.0	7.1	7.2	28.1
1983	8.0	10.0	14.2	25.8	13.6	3.4	12.6	19.5
1984	9.1	10.6	14.1	24.8	14.4	2.3	9.3	10.7
1985	10.0	11.5	14.2	24.0	13.4	2.5	7.0	11.8
1986	10.0	11.5	12.8	23.1	12.5	2.8	12.9	16.8
1987	10.0	11.5	12.8	23.0	12.5	3.0	13.0	18.8
1988	10.0	11.5	14.5	22.7	13.0	7.1	12.4	18.8
1989	10.0	11.5	15.2	19.1	13.6	5.7	6.8	18.4
1990	10.0	11.5	16.4	18.7	na	8.6	9.0	21.2
June 1991	10.0	11.5	18.6	na	na	10.1	na	18.4

Sources: Bank of Korea, various years a, various years b.
Note: na = not available.

Korea, finances medium- and long-term trade, overseas investments, and major overseas natural resource development projects with funds mobilized chiefly by borrowing from the NIF and foreign or domestic banks and by issuing its debentures.

In addition to these specialized institutions, deposit money banks also provide development loans. In 1971 they began to extend term loans repayable in installments, and since 1974 they have contributed to the NIF. The latter makes funds available to specific projects by pooling financial resources contributed by financial institutions and through deposits from public organizations and funds. NIF money has been supplied mainly to the heavy and chemical industries, the electricity-generating industry, and "New Village" (*Saemaul*) factories. Other preferential loans for small and medium-sized firms, housing, agriculture, and fisheries are supplied from both government and banking funds primarily through specialized banks. All commercial banks are required to maintain their credit outstanding to small and medium-sized firms above 35 percent of their total loans outstanding.

The Promotion of Heavy and Chemical Industries in the 1970s

In the early 1970s, the deterioration of the external environment had serious implications for the development of Korea's industrial policy. The Nixon administration reduced the number of U.S. troops in Korea by one-third in 1971, a move that was seen as the first step toward an eventual full withdrawal. Furthermore, industrialized nations, after the oil shock, strengthened protectionist barriers against light manufactured goods from developing countries. The emergence of China and other second-tier newly industrializing economies (NIEs) was also seen as a threat to Korea's continued export-led growth.

Given this situation, the promotion of heavy and chemical industries (HCIs) was seen as critical for developing indigenous defense industries as well as for restructuring the commodity composition of exports in favor of more sophisticated, high value-added industrial goods. The industries included iron and steel, nonferrous metal, shipbuilding, general machinery, chemicals, and electronics. Promotion of these industries was the overriding objective of tax policy, credit and interest rate policies, and trade policy.

Although tax incentives for exports were actually reduced in the early 1970s, the tax incentive policy began to receive increasing emphasis as a means of influencing resource allocation among industries. In 1974, diverse incentives to promote key industries were unified in the Tax Exemption and Reduction Control Law, which provided three optional incentives for qualified firms: a tax holiday for five years, an investment tax credit of 8 percent for machinery and equipment investment, and a 100 percent special depreciation.[3] Assuming that firms took full advantage of the major tax incentives, the effective marginal corporate tax rate from the mid-1970s to the early 1980s was estimated to be below 20 percent for the favored industries, while that for other industries was around 50 percent (Kwack 1985).

Trade policy was also geared to protect the favored industries by limiting imports of competing goods. For the manufacturing sector as a whole, the import liberalization ratio, which had declined slightly to 40 percent during the first half of the 1970s, rose to 57 percent by 1980.[4] This increase resulted mainly from higher import barriers for machinery and transportation equipment. The maintenance of a fixed exchange rate regime during the latter half of the 1970s was, in part, due to considerations given to the HCIs, whose imported facilities were financed primarily by foreign loans. Had the nominal exchange rate depreciated to make the real exchange rate stable, the effective cost of overseas borrowing would have been much higher.

Credit allocation by the government through the banking system was the most powerful means of supporting the favored industries. As the NIF proved to be insufficient in financing large-scale investment projects, banks, which were practically owned by the government, were directed to make loans to the "strategic" industries on a preferential basis. During the latter half of the 1970s, the share of policy loans in domestic credit rose steadily from 40 percent to over 50 percent.[5] A more significant aspect of the policy loans was the interest rate differentials. During the latter half of the 1970s, bank rates for export-related loans and equipment investment loans in key industries averaged 8 percent and 13 percent, respectively, while the rate for general bank loans and the inflation rate were 17 percent and 16 percent, respectively.

---

3. The supported key industries included petrochemicals, shipbuilding, machinery, electronics, iron and steel, mining and metal refinery, power generation, and chemical fertilizers.
4. The import liberalization ratio represents the proportion of items out of 7,915 at the eight-digit level of the Customs Cooperation Council Nomenclature (CCCN) for which import approval is automatic under the regular trade notice.
5. Policy loans include funds lent to earmarked sectors at preferential or nonpreferential rates and unearmarked loans extended at preferential rates with policy considerations.

III. Financial Liberalization and a New Industrial Incentive System in the 1980s

In the early 1980s, top priority in economic policy making was given to fighting inflation. Fears that restrictive demand management that relied on monetary and fiscal policies alone would be overly contractionary led the government to use incomes policies as well. Such policies included setting informal wage guidelines, stabilizing government purchase prices of major grains, and controlling interest rates and dividend payouts. Paying close attention to curbing inflation, the Korean government also placed great emphasis on institutional and structural reforms aimed at increasing the efficiency of resource allocation. These efforts led to important steps toward major reforms in at least three areas—financial liberalization, realignment of the industrial incentive system, and promotion of competition between domestic and foreign firms.

Financial Liberalization

Financial liberalization efforts began with the lifting of restrictions on bank management and the divestment of government equity shares in all five nationwide city banks. Furthermore, entry barriers into the financial market were lowered, and financial services provided by different intermediaries were diversified and streamlined. Significant progress was also made in interest rate and credit management. By June 1982, most policy loans were no longer extended at preferential interest rates, which made it easier to scale down policy loans. Actually, the relative share of policy loans has declined as both the NIF, a major source of policy loans, and, more recently, automatic short-term export credit have been reduced. Since early 1984, flexibility in interest rate management has been introduced to allow financial intermediaries to determine their own lending rates within a given range.

Further financial liberalization, however, has been hindered by the legacy of the government's heavy intervention in resource allocation during the 1970s. The government would not let troubled firms go bankrupt for fear of enormous financial losses to the banking sector and the ensuing social and economic repercussions. Government actions included helping the banking institutions by permitting attractive new services while tightening controls on nonbank interest rates, providing subsidized central bank credit, as well as exempting capital gains tax on collateral supplied by the troubled firms.

It was only in December 1988 that more extensive interest rate deregulation was undertaken against the background of a favorable macroeconomic environment. Bank and nonbank lending rates, some long-term deposit rates, and most capital and money market rates were deregulated. But the result of this interest rate deregulation has so far fallen short of expectations. Bank lending rates and most rates in the primary securities market are still very rigid and unresponsive to market conditions, which indicates that the Korean financial market is still far from being fully integrated and operating on a purely competitive basis. This phenomenon seems to be due in part to limited interest rate deregulation and in part to an inertia and mentality inherited from the time when most financial institutions were run like public enterprises.

The New Industrial Incentive System

In the early 1980s, direct government intervention was widely blamed for the overcapacity in HCIs and the decline in some industries. In response, promotion of strategic industries through preferential credit and tax treatment gave way to a more indirect and functional support of industries. The tax reform of 1981 substantially reduced the scope of special tax treatment for key industries. The 100 percent special depreciation became the only available option for most beneficiaries, because the tax holiday option was repealed and the scope and the degree of the investment tax credit option were narrowed.

After the second oil shock, several Korean industries, including shipbuilding, shipping, and overseas construction, suffered severely from declining orders, overcapacity, and financial distress. To prevent major bankruptcies that could have serious repercussions in the labor and financial markets, the government undertook several measures designed to help many of the troubled firms. The government was criticized, however, for being inconsistent across cases, that is, for being largely firm-specific rather than industry-specific; for excluding the involved financial intermediaries in designing rationalization programs; and for failing to define clearly the extent of government commitment.

To further streamline the industrial incentive system and deal with industrial rationalization more efficiently, the government enacted the Industrial Development Law (IDL) in July 1986. The IDL, which replaced seven individual industry promotion laws,[6] defines the role of the government as mainly that of a "troubleshooter." In two areas where

---

6. The seven industries include machinery, electronics, textiles, iron and steel, nonferrous metals, petrochemicals, and shipbuilding.

"market failure" occurs, the government is supposed to intervene for industrial rationalization. One such area consists of industrial sectors that are vital to the economy but not internationally competitive when left to the market. In this case, the government encourages specialization through indirect incentives designed to promote technological advancement. The other area includes declining industries for which the government may intervene in the phasing-out process.

In this selective intervention, minimizing government discretion and seeking wide consensus are considered critical. Thus, discussions of the Industrial Development Deliberative Council play an important role in formulating a rationalization program. Under the law, eight industries have been designated for rationalization for two or three years.[7] Rationalization packages prepared for these four declining industries and four emerging industries include subsidized credit for upgrading capital equipment, mergers, barring entries, and long-term supply contracts.

IV. Consequences of Financial and Industrial Policies

1965–1982: Rapid Industrialization

What effect government-directed credit allocation has had on Korea's economic development is still a controversial issue. Some of the promoted industries, such as electronics and passenger cars, grew into leading industries in the 1980s, whereas others, such as heavy machinery, overseas construction, and shipping, foundered. Because of these mixed results, many have argued that the policy of promoting the HCIs in the 1970s was a failure.

According to Yoo (1990), for instance, capital efficiency measured in terms of nonlabor value added per unit of capital was lower for the favored HCIs than for other manufacturing industries during 1971–1978. The converse was true for 1979–1985 (Table 1.3). Capital efficiency of the HCIs and other manufacturing industries was lower when monopolistic and the most oligopolistic industries (tobacco and petroleum refinery, respectively) were excluded. The average capital efficiency of the HCIs (excluding the petroleum refinery industry) remained at 22.9 percent throughout 1971–1978, while that of other manufacturing industries (excluding tobacco) declined from 28.2 percent to 20.8 per-

---

7. Declining industries include textiles, ferroalloys, dyeing, and fertilizers. Emerging industries include automobiles, diesel engines, heavy electrical equipment, and heavy construction equipment.

Table 1.3. Growth, factor mix, and capital efficiency of the manufacturing industry

	All manufacturing		Favored HCIs		Others	
	1971–1978	1979–1985	1971–1978	1979–1985	1971–1978	1979–1985
Growth rates (%)						
Value added	18.6	7.3	24.5	9.3	16.1	6.0
Capital stock	18.7	10.2	23.8	10.7	16.2	9.9
Employment	10.7	1.6	16.4	5.2	9.5	0.4
Capital/labor ratio	7.2	8.5	6.3	5.2	6.1	9.4
Capital/labor ratio[a] (million 1980 won per laborer)	6.0	11.6	10.9	17.7	4.8	9.5
Capital efficiency (%)[a,b]	31.4	24.9	30.5 (22.9)[c]	26.8 (22.8)[c]	32.0 (28.2)[d]	23.8 (20.8)[d]

Source: Adapted from Yoo 1990.
[a] Figures for 1971–1978 are averages for 1970, 1973, 1975, and 1978, and those for 1979–1985 are averages for 1980, 1983, and 1985.
[b] Value added (VA) created by a unit of capital employed = (total VA—VA generated by labor)/capital stock.
[c] Excluding petroleum refinery.
[d] Excluding tobacco.

cent between the two subperiods. These results, according to Yoo, suggest that cheap capital in the 1970s led to excessive investment in the HCIs.

Amsden and Euh (1990) argue, in contrast, that the HCI promotion policy was far from being a failure. They point out that the share of heavy and chemical products in total exports rose from 24 percent in 1977 to 54 percent over a ten-year period, and heavy industries developed as Korea's new leading sector. Their share of gross domestic product (GDP) also increased from 8.6 percent in 1970 to 16.5 percent in 1980 and to 18.1 percent in 1990 (Table 1.4). Meanwhile, the manufacturing sector was observed to account for only a small share of total nonperforming loans, with the share for heavy and chemical industries being far lower than their share of total outstanding credit.

Whether the same results, albeit mixed, could have been achieved at a lesser cost under a liberal financial regime is a difficult question to answer. But the fact is that during 1965–1982, when financial repression was in place, the Korean economy became highly industrialized and grew rapidly. The answer to this puzzle lies in the special relationship between the government and the large private enterprises that constitute the quasi-internal organization discussed in the introductory chapter of this book.

In Korea, large private enterprises have played a critical role in export expansion and economic growth. Because the government has influenced the decisions of these enterprises with various policy instruments but, most important, with credit allocation, an understanding of the relationship between the government, the financial system, and the large private enterprises is key to understanding Korea's economic development.

One of the salient characteristics of Korea's private sector is its dual nature, that is, there are a relatively small number of large enterprises, many of which belong to business groups called *chaebol*, and a relatively large number of small and medium-sized firms. For instance, in 1982 there were 35,971 firms in the manufacturing sector; but 271 manufacturing firms belonged to large business groups, accounting for more than one-third of the value of shipment, value added, and capital in the entire manufacturing sector.

The expansion of large private enterprises during the 1960s and 1970s paralleled that of the Korean economy, and given their importance in the economy, the success of the Korean economy is, in effect, the success of these enterprises. In fact, during the 1975–1978 period, sales of the largest fifty and one hundred firms listed in the stock market

Table 1.4. Share of bank loans, capital formation, and GDP by industry (by percentage)

Sector	Loans and discounts	Capital formation	GDP
1970			
Agriculture, forestry, fishing, mining, and quarrying	12.6[b]	10.8[c]	28.0
Manufacturing	46.1	24.9	21.3
Light industry	23.5	10.8	12.7
Heavy and chemical industry	22.6	14.1	8.6
Public utilities, construction	12.7	7.8	6.5
Services[a]	28.6	56.5	44.2
Total	100.0	100.0	100.0
1980			
Agriculture, forestry, fishing, mining, and quarrying	7.8[b]	8.9	16.2
Manufacturing	53.8	22.9	29.7
Light industry	21.7	6.9	13.2
Heavy and chemical industry	32.1	16.0	16.5
Public utilities, construction	14.6	9.6	10.4
Services[a]	23.8	58.6	43.7
Total	100.0	100.0	100.0
1990			
Agriculture, forestry, fishing, mining, and quarrying	6.6[d]	7.7[e]	9.6
Manufacturing	44.0	33.0	29.2
Light industry	13.8	9.6	11.1
Heavy and chemical industry	30.2	23.4	18.1
Public utilities, construction	9.3	6.1	15.4
Services[a]	40.1	53.2	45.8
Total	100.0	100.0	100.0

Sources: Bank of Korea, various years a, various years b, various years c.
[a] Services include government services, private nonprofit services, and import duties less imputed bank service charges.
[b] Loans and discounts of deposit money banks and the KDB.
[c] Figure is for 1975.
[d] Loans and discounts of deposit money banks and other financial institutions.
[e] Figure is for 1988.

averaged 52.9 percent and 73.9 percent, respectively, of the total sales of all listed firms (excluding financial and insurance companies) (Chong 1990).

Many of these firms are not independent entities but belong to business groups such as Daewoo, Hyundai, Samsung, and Lucky-Gold Star. At the end of 1977, there were forty such business groups in mining, manufacturing, and services (excluding financial, insurance, and trading industries). The top thirty business groups controlled 126 enterprises in 1970, 429 enterprises in 1979, and 402 enterprises in 1982. During the 1971–1979 period, these groups made a net addition of 303 enterprises by establishing 202 new enterprises and by adding 135 through acquisition. Even during the contractionary period of 1980–1982, when the groups as a whole shed 27 firms, 30 new units were established and 25 units were added through acquisition.

Given this dual structure of Korea's manufacturing sector, the government's relationship with large private enterprises needs to be distinguished from that with numerous small and medium-sized firms. Even in Korea, the relationship of the government with these firms has been at an arm's length, with its control over market parameters serving as a key instrument. Its relationship with large enterprises, however, has been quite different, being more direct and intimate as in an internal organization. In fact, this relationship has been described as a partnership in which the government is the senior partner and the private enterprises are the junior partners (Jones and Sakong 1980). Such a connection between the government and business was maintained through channels such as "deliberation councils" and "discussion groups," facilitating an exchange of information which was more direct than would have been possible through markets.

The relationship between the government and these larger enterprises has, however, involved more than meetings of deliberation councils and discussion groups with the government sometimes going so far as to audit the balance sheets of targeted enterprises. But the most important instrument employed by the government was its control of the financial system and the access to subsidized credit by these enterprises. By regulating the enterprises' access to credit, the government was able to direct their decisions over resource allocation and thus the pattern of industrial development.

What was perhaps unique to Korea was the Monthly Export Promotion Conference, which was established in December 1962 and which came to be one of the most important administrative support mechanisms for exports. The meeting was attended by President Park Chung Hee, the minister of the Economic Planning Board, the minister of trade and industry, the director of the Korea Trade Promotion Corporation, the chairman of the Korea Traders Association, and other public officials and private experts concerned with trade. The progress of exports and the performance of exporting firms were routinely reported at the meeting, and almost every month the president awarded medals and citations to successful business executives.

At the conference, businesspersons were asked to present their problems and opportunities, and government officials were informed in front of the president of the problems that executives had faced in dealing with government offices. The conference thus served not only as a forum in which the president could hector business representatives to increase exports but also as a place where they could frankly discuss with the president various problems, including bureaucratic red tape, that they had faced in attempting to achieve their export targets.

Another administrative measure used for export promotion was the export-targeting system adopted in early 1962. Although the system was initially used to establish an annual target for total exports, by the second half of the 1960s it had become more elaborate, with annual targets set for major commodity groups and destinations. Targets for major commodity groups were then assigned to related industrial associations, and targets for destinations were given for implementation to the Korean embassies in the respective countries or regions. A "situation room" was installed inside the Ministry of Commerce and Industry to monitor export performance with respect to the annual targets. The status of export performance was then reported at the Monthly Export Promotion Conference. An important aspect of the export promotion policy in the 1960s is that most of the promotion measures were basically nondiscriminatory. For instance, preferential credit was given to any exporter of whatever product as long as the exporter could present an export letter of credit at a foreign exchange bank.

The program establishing HCIs in Korea is a clear case of how the quasi-internal organization operated to prepare the economy for changing international conditions and comparative advantage. Six industries were chosen for promotion at investment totaling US $9.6 billion between 1973 and 1981. These were targeted to become future leading industries, with their share of total commodity exports expected to be more than 50 percent by 1980.

The selection of these industries came as a matter of course to the top policymakers because they were fully aware that Japan had earlier taken the same path of industrial development with great success. Furthermore, the experience gained in helping the light manufacturing industries to become internationally competitive gave these policymakers greater confidence in Korea's ability to establish the HCIs as the next group of leading export industries.

In the early 1970s, virtually no Korean firms possessed the technical as well as the financial resources necessary for undertaking any one of the

HCIs. Furthermore, given the large-scale economies and the high risks that are inherent in such industries, not many firms, including the large business groups, were willing to undertake the projects. Thus to implement its plan, the government had to handpick suitable firms and in fact coerced them into undertaking the projects with offers of various incentives.

By the late 1970s, the HCI policy was a success in that it had led to the establishment of HCIs in Korea. But the second oil shock of 1979 brought about a severe world recession, and Korea found itself with excess capacities in those industries. A tight monetary policy adopted in the early 1980s as an anti-inflationary measure made matters worse. It must be said, however, that the creation of HCIs laid the foundation for the export boom that began in 1983.

The double-digit economic growth in the middle of the 1980s was led by the exports of and further investments in the HCIs. Those now in place in Korea allowed the substitution of domestic supply for hitherto imported industrial intermediate inputs. For instance, the users of petrochemical products could now rely on domestic producers for a stable supply of intermediate inputs even in the midst of a worldwide shortage and thus could continue to expand their exports. Likewise, the steel industry played a key role in sustaining the competitiveness of Korea's manufactured exports by serving domestic industrial activities despite a worldwide shortage in steel.

The HCI program did not succeed without a cost. A high concentration of investment in the HCIs gave rise to serious sectoral imbalances and macroeconomic complications. The favored projects preempted financial resources, thus crowding out other industries from the credit market. And given the huge capital requirement and weak business position of small and medium-sized firms, it was the large business groups that received the HCI projects, which furthered the concentration of economic power among a small number of large conglomerates.

The money supply grew rapidly, particularly in the latter half of the 1970s, because of the credit allocated to the HCIs as well as the boom in construction service exports to the Middle East.[8] Accelerating inflation made financial savings unattractive because nominal interest rates remained low. With subsequent disintermediation and stagnation in the financial sector, credit became tighter, especially for small and

8. In 1979 net revenue from exports of construction services and related merchandise was US $1,536 million (Lee 1991).

medium-sized firms, which began relying more on the unorganized money market, which, in turn, grew in size.

1983–Present: Financial Liberalization

It is generally believed that Korea's financial system went through a fair degree of liberalization and integration in the 1980s without much real liberalization of banks, which was possible because of the relatively rapid growth of the more liberalized nonbank financial sector. Nonbank financial intermediaries (NBFIs) have been much less constrained than banks in terms of their expansion and sectoral allocation of credit. They were often allowed to circumvent interest rate ceilings, which were already set at levels that were higher than those on bank deposits and loans. Requiring a large portion of borrowing as a compensating deposit balance has been the most commonly used means of circumventing interest rate ceilings. This variance in the level of government control of banks and NBFIs seems to be due to the perception of different externalities associated with the failure of financial institutions as well as the desire to maximize the mobilization of financial resources through organized markets while retaining certain institutions, namely, commercial banks, that can be used to provide low-cost funds.

Despite privatization and greater managerial autonomy by commercial banks, the banking system is still subject to heavy government intervention. Several reasons exist for this slow pace of financial liberalization. First, the heavy burden of nonperforming loans, which was caused in part by the government intervention in bank lending in the 1970s, has made it difficult to do away completely with interest rate regulation. Drastic financial liberalization could threaten the soundness and safety of the banks as it would put them in a seriously disadvantaged position vis-à-vis nonbank financial intermediaries. It is questionable whether adopting a different approach, such as relieving banks of the burden of nonperforming loans and exposing them to vigorous competition, is a better solution. Furthermore, this solution is realistic only if it is politically feasible.

Second, credit ceilings and other direct controls have been used as a substitute instrument for indirect monetary control, which the Korean government lacked. The discount window has played only a limited role because many of the central bank loans are automatic rediscounts of policy loans by the banking sector. Since banks have suffered from a history of chronic reserve shortage, changing the required reserve ratio has generally been difficult and ineffective. Also, open market operations have been constrained by an underdeveloped money market, inadequacy of traded securities, and the absence of a secondary market, all of which are attributable largely to interest rate regulation.[9] An efficient money market will have to be developed by improving the call market, introducing interbank deposit and bills markets, and fostering specialized money market dealers and brokers before full financial liberalization can be adopted.

Third, policy loans by banks still account for almost half of all domestic credit. Such loans include credits to development institutions such as the KDB, credits to the housing and agricultural sectors, loans to small and medium-sized firms, and foreign currency loans mainly for capital goods imports. Until the commercial banks are freed from the obligation to extend policy loans, the extent of financial liberalization will remain limited.

Finally, a major thrust for the continued regulation of most of the interest rates in Korea is to prevent any major financial crisis that could result from bankruptcies of highly leveraged business firms. Furthermore, the government has been reluctant to raise interest rates because it believes low interest rates will encourage the strong corporate investments necessary for structural adjustment in Korean industries. Its desire to borrow cheaply must also have influenced the interest rate policy.

The share of nonperforming loans (NPLs) in the total credit of seven nationwide commercial banks showed a steep rise from 2.4 percent in 1976–1980 to 10.5 percent during 1984–1986. This rising share of NPLs reflects the aggravated industrial situation that resulted from the worldwide recession subsequent to the second oil shock. The situation was most serious in the shipping, overseas construction, shipbuilding, and other HCIs, where the shrinking overseas demand fell short of the supply capacity that had expanded drastically during the 1970s.

In 1980 the Korean government attempted structural adjustments in the areas where overcapacity was most severe. Mergers were worked out in the heavy power-generating equipment and heavy construction equipment industries through negotiations between participating firms and the government. In addition, supportive measures such as blanket orders related to the construction of nuclear power plants, conversion of KDB loans into equity investment, and additional bank credit were

9. The monetary stabilization bond issued by the central bank has recently been the major tool for sterilizing liquidity. But these bonds have been issued at below-market rates and sold mainly to financial institutions by coercion. The ever increasing issues of these bonds have seriously affected the liquidity position of financial intermediaries, resulting in a crowding out in the shallow market and often drastically depressing the corporate bond market.

provided. In the motor vehicles industry, participating firms agreed on the division of labor by product line. In vessel diesel engines, electronic exchangers, heavy electrical equipment, and copper smelting, the government implemented its own restructuring program when the seventeen firms involved in the restructuring failed to reach agreement through negotiations.

During 1984–1985, two major ailing industries—shipping and overseas construction—were rationalized. In the case of shipping, the government reduced shipping capacity and the number of firms from sixty-three to seventeen through mergers, also lowering their tax and financial burden. By the end of 1985, about 3 trillion won of loan principal and interest owed by the shipping companies was rescheduled to be repaid over twenty years after a ten-year grace period at a 3 percent interest rate per annum. Restructuring the overseas construction industry was not very successful in spite of substantial financial support. Only five firms were either merged with financially healthier ones at the behest of their main banks or entered into management consignment.

Nonperforming loans cannot, however, be attributed entirely to the unexpected contraction in demand. Because of government-directed credit allocation, lending banks had little incentive to undertake serious credit evaluation or ex post monitoring. At the same time, availability of cheap credit and tax benefits caused many firms not to give enough attention to appraising their investment projects. As a result of such factors, these overly leveraged firms were very vulnerable when the industry experienced a recession. One may argue that every industry has a natural product-life cycle, thus making it inevitable for the industry to decline. Nevertheless, it seems clear that government-directed credit allocation contributed to the rapid rise and equally rapid decline of such industries as shipping, overseas construction, and shipbuilding.

Because of the central role played by the government in initiating and shaping the restructuring programs, the government failed to impose market discipline. The government continued to be viewed as an implicit risk partner, because the creditor banks were largely excluded from the major restructuring decision making, even though they generally had the best information about the prospect of the loans. As bank losses were to be assumed partially by the government, the banks had no alternative but to accommodate whatever packages the government came up with. In addition, having been subject to government control for a long time, the banks did not have enough expertise to work out such a restructuring program on their own. The uncertainty surrounding the government's continuing role as a risk partner also failed to eliminate the moral hazard problem. The restructured firms were reluctant to reduce capacity and tended to pursue risky strategies in anticipation of another government rescue should these fail.

In the 1960s, the primary goal of Korea's economic policies was export expansion, regardless of its effects on industrial composition. In the 1970s, however, the Korean government actively promoted HCIs, using the financial sector in particular to channel resources to the preferred or strategic sectors. It achieved this mainly through preferential loans extended at low interest rates and other guidelines for the management of financial assets. Thus the government has played an important role in promoting strategic industries and in upgrading the industrial and trade structure, but not without a cost.

First, the provision of preferential policy loans resulted in rapid monetary expansion, which was mainly responsible for the chronic inflation in the 1970s. High inflation was eventually contained in the early 1980s, but only at the expense of economic growth and employment. Second, the role of government as an implicit risk partner contributed to poor performance by some industries and their large financial losses. The cost of subsequent industrial restructuring was shared mostly by creditor banks, the central bank (consumers), and the government (taxpayers). Finally, having been subject to government intervention for such a long period, the Korean banking system remains underdeveloped and burdened with many nonperforming loans, with management that is not very efficient.

Despite these factors, the Korean economy showed strong performance in the 1980s. It became a major exporter of heavy industrial products such as consumer electronics, semiconductors, telecommunications and computer-related equipment, and passenger cars. This strong economic performance is clearly a consequence of the industrial targeting policy of the 1970s, whatever its costs might have been.

Clearly, the strong performance of the Korean economy was helped by the expansionary U.S. fiscal policy of the Reagan administration, the weakness of the won since the mid-1980s, and diversion (because of import restrictions) of some U.S. imports from Japan to Korea. It must be pointed out, however, that with its supply capabilities, Korea was in a prime position to take advantage of the favorable external demand conditions. Therefore Korea's export growth and structural changes should be viewed as a consequence of both the deliberate change in its comparative advantage toward HCIs and the favorable external environment.

To understand how direct government intervention in the economy could have contributed to its growth, we must regard the government and large private enterprises as constituting a quasi-internal organization. Extensive government intervention in the financial system can then be viewed as internal credit allocation, and as such it *can* be more efficient in allocating credit than the free financial market, especially if the latter suffers from various market imperfections.

Through the 1970s, policy making in Korea was highly centralized; a few people made the important decisions, and policy formulation was speedy and flexible. Furthermore, it was not uncommon for the government to intervene and influence the management decisions of firms. This intervention was highly effective because the government had such powerful tools as subsidized bank credit, repayment guarantees on low-cost foreign loans, tax investigation, and issuance of licenses and permits.

As the country's structural complexity grows with economic development, the challenge of picking the right industries for promotion will become more difficult, and the usefulness of the quasi-internal organization as a development institution will diminish. Nevertheless Korea has already undertaken numerous liberalization measures, and it has thus made a change in the right direction.

References

Amsden, Alice H., and Yoon-Dae Euh. 1990. South Korea's Financial Reform: What are the Lessons? Paper prepared for the United Nations Conference on Trade and Development Secretariat, New York, March.

Bank of Korea (BOK). Various years a. *Financial Statements Analysis*, various issues. Seoul: BOK.

——. Various years b. *Monthly Bulletin*, various issues. Seoul: BOK.

——. Various years c. *National Accounts*, various issues. Seoul: BOK.

Chong, B. H. 1990. Economic Concentration and Anti-monopoly Policies. Honolulu: East-West Center. Mimeographed.

Cole, David C., and Yung Chung Park. 1979. Financial Development in Korea, 1945–1978. In *Studies in the Modernization of the Republic of Korea*. Cambridge: Council on East Asian Studies, Harvard University.

Jones, Leroy P., and Il Sakong. 1980. *Government, Business, and Entrepreneurship in Economic Development: The Korean Case*. Cambridge: Harvard University Press.

Kwack, Taewon. 1985. *Depreciation and Taxation of Income from Capital* (in Korean). Seoul: Korea Development Institute.

Lee, Chung H. 1991. Promotion Measures for Construction Service Exports to the Middle East (1975). In *Economic Development in the Republic of Korea: A Policy Perspective*, ed. Lee-Jay Cho and Y. H. Kim. Honolulu: East-West Center.

Nam, Sang-Woo. 1990. Industry Promotion, Restructuring, and Their Impact on the Financial Sector. Paper presented at the Senior Policy Seminar on Financial Sector Performance and Industrial Restructuring, Seoul, Korea, September 18–21.

Yoo, Jung-Ho. 1990. The Industrial Policy of the 1970s and the Evolution of the Manufacturing Sector in Korea. KDI Working Paper no. 9017, Korea Development Institute.

CHAPTER TWO

TAIWAN

Tein-Chen Chou

For more than four decades, Taiwan has maintained rapid economic growth with stable prices and full employment. Its real GNP has grown at an average annual rate of 8.9 percent (except for the two brief periods of oil crises), while its inflation rate has stayed at around 3 percent, and its unemployment rate, as low as 2 percent. The per capita income of Taiwan, which was as low as US $100 in the immediate postwar period, exceeded US $8,000 in 1990, and the nation's economic structure is no longer that of a developing country.

Taiwan achieved this remarkable economic success with an outward-oriented development strategy that provided, by and large, a stable and neutral incentive structure between exports and import substitutes. Yet Taiwan's formal financial system has been anything but liberal: it has been closely regulated and heavily protected. In fact, Taiwan's financial system shows all the characteristics of financial repression. What is puzzling, therefore, is how the Taiwanese economy has been able to develop so rapidly under the mixed regime of an outward-oriented trade policy and financial repression. Our answer to this puzzle is that Taiwan has had an active informal financial sector that, although illegal, functioned efficiently under a policy of benign neglect.

Taiwan's financial system consists of a repressed formal sector and a free informal sector. According to Tsiang (1956) and Shaw (1973), these two sectors complement each other, and the presence of an informal financial sector in the economy can increase the total amount of savings. Exactly how this dual financial system has contributed to the economic success of Taiwan has yet to be convincingly demonstrated, but the policy implications are obvious: allowing the informal financial sector to flourish can be a positive factor to economic growth.

Another function of the financial system is the allocation of credit among competing uses, the efficiency of which can, therefore, clearly affect the economic performance of a country. Consequently, it is a matter of great interest to find out how Taiwan's dual financial system has allocated credit and what effect it has had on economic growth. In particular, it is important to determine how efficient credit allocation has been in the formal as compared with the informal sector. Because of the unavailability of data, however, it is impossible to examine directly the efficiency of the informal sector.

This chapter therefore takes an indirect approach to this question. I assume that if the formal sector is inefficient in the sense that profitable projects are not funded there, the projects would go for financing to the informal sector, thereby increasing its contribution. Conversely, if the formal sector is efficient and funds profitable projects, then the contribution of the informal sector would be less. One way of discovering the contribution of Taiwan's dual financial system to economic growth is thus to examine empirically whether credit allocation in Taiwan's formal financial sector—more specific, the allocation by the state-owned banks—has been efficient in the sense that loan decisions were based on profitability.

I. Taiwan's Dual Financial System and Its Development

A Historical Review

After a half-century of Japanese colonial rule, Taiwan was returned to the Republic of China in 1945. Most of the properties formerly owned by the colonial Japanese were nationalized, and as a result, the Nationalist government, which relocated itself to Taiwan in 1949, became the owner of a large amount of public land, enterprises, and financial institutions. These banks and insurance companies, along with the banks relocated from mainland China, were then reorganized into state-owned and state-controlled banks (Cheng 1991). But the savings and loan companies and credit cooperatives that were managed by the Chinese during the colonial period continued to remain in private hands. Between 1976 and 1978, savings and loan companies were transformed into regional banks serving small and medium-sized enterprises (SMEs). One of eight regional banks, the Taiwan SME Bank, is owned by a provincial government, and the rest are privately owned.

Changes in the financial system have been gradual in Taiwan. Overseas Chinese and foreign governments as well as nationals have made frequent demands to open up the system. Some concessions were made by the Taiwanese government, but most were made for political reasons. For instance, farmers' and fishermen's associations, which played an important role in local elections, were given permission to form credit unions and branches in rural areas.

Many foreign banks and insurance companies were allowed to establish their presence in Taiwan, especially in the 1980s, largely as a result of pressure from the U.S. government. By the end of 1990, thirty-five branches of foreign banks were firmly in place, despite regulations and limitations imposed on the number of branches and business lines. Although this number exceeded that of domestic banks, these branches of foreign banks accounted for a very small share of the total loans and deposits of the banking sector. In the insurance industry, the entry of foreign firms is more restrictive, with only American insurance companies allowed to enter the domestic market. As of 1991, there were eight branch offices of American life insurance companies.

Formal capital markets for bonds and stocks were established in 1961 when the Taiwan Stock Exchange came into existence. With the creation of the Fu Hua Stock Financial Company in 1980, funds could be legally loaned for transactions in the stock market. As a result of the emergence of more security companies and the massive increases in money supply resulting from the huge current account surplus in the late 1980s, the Taiwan stock market expanded rapidly, growing more quickly at one point than all other stock markets in the world.[1] The money market, which came into being in 1976, has developed into an important market for treasury bills and other financial instruments.

In 1986 Taiwan began its process of financial liberalization. Nearly all restrictions on interest rates were eliminated, and the granting of new bank licenses, the establishment of new branches, and the approval of business operations can now be done in a less cumbersome way. The personnel of state-owned banks are still classified as civil servants, however, and consequently, personnel management, budgeting, and business management are under the government's elaborate oversight. The state-owned banks thus lack managerial autonomy. Other regulations still remain, but the most important ones that pertain to lending decisions are the ratio of nonperforming loans to total loans and the revenue that banks are to render to the government.

1. In 1990 the contraction in the stock market was also greater for Taiwan (by 80 percent or so) than for other countries.

Multilayered restrictions and regulations have led to inadequate competition among banks. Moreover, because of a similar ownership structure and the regulatory environment, there is a strong tendency for collusive pricing among the banks. As a result, a large interest rate spread exists despite the fact that the rates have largely been deregulated. Between 1983 and 1987, the interest rate spread was 3.14 percent on average, and in 1988, it was 3.36 percent. Although these spreads are less than that in any previous subperiods for Taiwan, they are high in comparison to those in the industrialized countries. Clearly, in the absence of competition the banks have had little incentive to attract savings by offering higher interest rates and to increase their loan portfolios by charging lower interest rates.

Recently (as of 1991), the Ministry of Finance ratified fifteen new bank applications and is reviewing a policy allowing trust and investment companies to transform themselves into banks. When fully implemented, these new measures will certainly increase the number of banks and thus the competitiveness of the banking industry. But until then, Taiwan will continue to have a dual financial system with its formal sector burdened with high entry barriers and regulations beyond prudential necessity.

The Structure of Taiwan's Financial System

Among the various financial institutions and markets that belong to the formal financial sector, the postal savings system is the most important in terms of the number of units in operation (Table 2.1). Postal savings branches are widespread across the island, accounting for one-third of financial institutions in 1980. Since then, this percentage has dropped, but the postal savings system still accounted for 30.0 percent of financial units in 1990. Banks—domestic banks, branches of foreign banks, and SME banks—are the second most important enterprises, accounting for 26.4 percent of the total number of units in 1990. Third in importance is the system of credit unions belonging to farmers' and fishermen's associations, followed by credit cooperatives.

Postal savings branches redeposit the funds they receive in the central bank; hence they perform only the function of savings mobilization and not that of credit allocation.[2] The banks, however, perform both functions and therefore make up the largest financial institutional group in terms of the number of units that mediate between savers and

---

2. Since 1982 the central bank has allocated these deposits to four specialized banks—Communication Bank, China Farmer Bank, Central Trust Bank, and Taiwan SME Bank. Hence the postal savings system has an indirect intermediate function.

Table 2.1. Number of units of financial institutions

	1961		1970		1980		1990	
	Units	%	Units	%	Units	%	Units	%
Domestic banks	260	19.1	394	21.6	536	18.9	741	18.4
Local branches of foreign banks	1	0.1	7	0.4	21	0.7	43	1.1
Small and medium-sized enterprise banks	84	6.2	118	6.5	165	5.8	279	6.9
Credit cooperative associations	153	11.3	222	12.2	274	9.7	473	11.8
Credit departments of farmers' and fishermen's associations	385	28.3	393	21.5	724	25.6	1,052	26.2
Investment and trust companies	1	0.1	6	0.3	26	0.9	53	1.3
Postal savings system	451	33.2	610	33.4	952	33.6	1,205	30.0
Insurance companies	24	1.8	77	4.2	132	4.7	174	4.3
Total	1,359	100.0	1,827	100.0	2,830	100.0	4,020	100.0

Sources: Adapted from Shea 1990, table 1; Ministry of Finance 1990.
Note: The Central Bank of China and the Central Reinsurance Corporation, which do not have financial business with the general public, are excluded from the financial institutions enumerated.

borrowers. Domestic banks are also the most important in terms of their share of total assets, loans and investments, and deposits, although their significance has decreased over time because of the freezing of bank licenses as well as the expansion of nonbank financial intermediaries such as postal savings and trust and investment companies. In 1990, banks accounted for 53.5 percent of total financial assets, 62.6 percent of total loans and investments, and 46.3 percent of deposits (Table 2.2). Among domestic banks, the state-owned banks far outweigh the private banks in importance. Thirteen state-owned or state-controlled banks (six commercial and seven specialized banks) have 725 branches, which is three times the number of branches of the eleven private banks (228 branches) (Yang 1990, p. 54).

In terms of the market share of loans, government financial institutions accounted for 79.9 percent of total lending in 1963 and 66.6 percent in 1988; but even the lower figure for 1988 is twice as much as that for private financial institutions (Table 2.3). As for deposits, the government financial institutions attracted 65.2 percent in 1988, although their share has been generally decreasing over time (Table 2.4). Of all government financial institutions, three provincial government-

Table 2.2. Shares of financial institutions at year-end (by percentage)

	Total assets				Loans and investments[a]				Total deposits[b]			
	1961	1970	1980	1990	1961	1970	1980	1990	1961	1970	1980	1990
Domestic banks	80.2	70.5	64.5	53.5	81.9	76.4	67.5	62.6	75.6	65.8	55.6	46.3
Local branches of foreign banks	0.9	2.9	5.5	2.9	0.4	3.1	7.6	3.4	0.0	1.5	0.3	1.1
Small and medium-sized business banks	3.1	4.4	3.7	7.4	3.8	4.9	4.8	9.2	4.9	5.2	4.5	7.4
Credit cooperative associations	7.5	8.0	6.8	9.2	7.1	7.1	7.0	8.5	10.1	10.5	10.6	11.5
Credit department of farmers' and fishermen's associations	5.2	5.1	5.0	6.9	4.7	4.4	4.7	5.8	5.9	5.4	7.0	8.3
Investment and trust companies	1.3	1.4	4.3	4.4	1.6	2.0	6.3	5.5	—	—	6.2	5.3
Postal savings system	0.8	5.8	8.3	11.7	0.3	0.5	0.2	0.2	3.4	9.7	13.7	14.9
Insurance companies	0.9	1.9	1.8	4.1	0.3	1.7	1.9	4.9	0.1	1.8	2.1	5.2
Total	100.0	100.0	100.0	100.0	100.0	100.0	100.0	100.0	100.0	100.0	100.0	100.0

Sources: Adapted from Shea 1990, table 2; Central Bank of China, various years.
Note: The Central Bank of China is excluded from the financial institutions.
[a] Loans and investments include loans, discounts, portfolio investments, and the holdings of real estate.
[b] Total deposits include deposits held by enterprises and individuals, government deposits, trust funds, and life insurance reserves.

Table 2.3. Percentage of loans held by government and private financial institutions

	Government financial institutions		Private financial institutions	
	All	Three major commercial banks		
Year	Share (%)	Share (%)	Share (%)	Combined total amount (NT $m)
1963	79.9	21.3	20.1	21,793
1964	78.0	20.0	22.0	27,153
1965	77.7	19.3	22.3	33,344
1966	76.8	20.2	23.2	38,789
1967	77.3	24.1	22.7	46,623
1968	78.8	26.7	21.2	57,898
1969	79.4	28.8	20.6	71,819
1970	80.4	28.4	19.6	85,543
1971	76.2	28.8	23.8	106,578
1972	74.2	29.0	25.8	133,829
1973	71.2	24.0	28.8	203,826
1974	72.7	22.0	27.3	279,462
1975	73.8	22.2	26.2	368,861
1976	73.5	24.7	26.5	456,547
1977	72.7	25.4	27.3	569,799
1978	68.7	26.5	31.3	771,636
1979	68.1	24.5	31.9	900,265
1980	66.4	22.3	33.6	1,076,756
1981	62.9	20.7	37.1	1,214,715
1982	64.8	19.1	35.2	1,421,207
1983	66.1	19.3	33.9	1,670,850
1984	66.4	19.0	33.6	1,881,928
1985	66.9	18.5	33.1	2,033,854
1986	67.4	20.7	32.6	2,238,012
1987	66.6	21.3	33.4	2,630,093
1988	66.6	23.0	33.4	3,583,277

Source: Adapted from Yang 1990, table 4.

owned commercial banks (the First, Hua-Nan, and Chang-Hwa) together accounted for 23.0 percent of total loans and 25.0 percent of total deposits in 1988.[3]

Both the money and the capital markets have expanded significantly in recent years. Discounted bills in the money market were NT $7.4 billion in 1976, or 1.1 percent of GNP and 1.7 percent of total loans and advances from financial institutions in that year. By 1989, these figures had reached NT $580.3 billion, or 14.7 percent and 13.3 percent,

3. For a measurement of the concentration in Taiwan's banking industry, see Chou, Hwang, and Wang 1990 and Chou 1991.

Table 2.4. Percentage of deposits held in government and private financial institutions

Year	Government financial institutions		Private financial institutions	Combined total amount (NT $m)
	All Share (%)	Three major commercial banks Share (%)	Share (%)	
1967	76.8	30.2	23.2	55,598
1968	77.3	30.8	22.7	64,876
1969	78.1	32.8	21.9	75,417
1970	78.3	32.4	21.7	87,887
1971	77.1	32.7	22.9	110,666
1972	76.3	31.7	23.7	152,366
1973	72.8	28.5	27.2	209,671
1974	73.4	26.9	26.6	257,154
1975	73.1	25.7	26.9	326,594
1976	77.5	25.1	22.5	556,089
1977	65.7	20.6	34.3	847,768
1978	73.9	24.6	26.1	983,071
1979	71.9	24.0	28.1	974,588
1980	66.8	23.5	33.2	929,341
1981	65.8	22.8	34.2	1,105,138
1982	64.9	21.7	35.1	1,356,539
1983	64.0	21.8	36.0	1,716,079
1984	63.0	21.3	36.9	2,088,374
1985	65.2	22.2	34.8	2,465,762
1986	66.6	23.3	33.4	2,935,687
1987	66.1	23.3	33.9	3,608,054
1988	65.2	25.0	34.8	4,476,435

Source: Adapted from Yang 1990, table 5.
Note: Postal agencies and insurance companies are excluded from financial institutions.

respectively (Shea 1990, Appendix 8). Bond trading in the capital market is still quite limited, its value being only NT $0.88 billion, or 1.26 percent of GNP and 4.59 percent of total loans and advances from financial institutions in 1961. Although trading increased to NT $254.1 billion in 1989, it still accounted for only 6.41 percent of GNP and 5.81 percent of total loans and advances (Shea 1990, Appendix 8). Corporate debentures have not exceeded 15 percent of total bonds and thus do not seem to be an instrument that is often used to raise capital. Therefore it is evident that the bond market is much smaller than the money market.

The stock market has experienced rapid expansion. Its trading value reached US $970 billion in 1989, and it played the most important role in terms of direct financing. In that year, a total of 307 security houses

Table 2.5. Composition of the business sector's financing from the financial system (as a percentage of total)

Year	Financial institutions	Money markets	Capital market	Curb market	Total
1964–1970	57.1	0.0	15.7	27.2	52,354
1971–1975	67.4	0.0	9.8	22.8	205,548
1976–1980	57.2	4.5	13.9	24.4	650,803
1981–1985	52.2	10.6	13.9	23.3	1,514,550
1986–1988	51.7	6.0	14.8	27.6	2,345,052
1964–1988	53.7	7.1	14.0	25.1	770,245

Source: Adapted from Shea 1990, table 8.

existed, with 4.2 million investors participating in stock market transactions. In 1990, nineteen new companies went public, adding shares valued at NT $20.5 billion (US $774 million) to the market, whereas existing public corporations issued new shares valued at NT $77.7 billion (US $2.91 billion).

The amount of capital raised in the stock market, however, equaled only 2.2 percent of total loans and advances from financial institutions and was less than the trading value in the bond and money markets. In fact, although the trading value of Taiwan's stock exchange closely trailed that of Tokyo and New York,[4] capital raised in the market was quite limited. Although the amount raised for individual public corporations was not small, the total amount raised in the stock market for the entire corporate sector was negligible, which indicates that Taiwan's stock market still has great potential for expansion.

The size of the informal financial sector is more difficult to estimate.[5] We can try to approximate the size from both the demand side and the supply side. On the demand side, 53.7 percent of financing for businesses came from financial institutions, 7.1 percent from the money market, 14.0 percent from the capital market, and 25.1 percent from the curb market during the 1964–1988 period (Table 2.5). Thus, if a corporation borrowed $100.00 from financial institutions, it borrowed $46.80 from the curb market. These figures indicate the importance of the curb market for corporate financing in Taiwan.

4. At the end of 1989, the trading value of Taiwan's stock market reached US $970 billion, while the Tokyo stock market was US $2,431 billion and the New York stock market was US $1,542 billion.
5. Although financial installment credit companies and financial leasing companies belong to the formal sector in terms of their legal definition, they are not yet authorized by the Ministry of Finance to carry out financial business. For this reason, they are included in the informal sector.

Table 2.6. Household savings through the financial system, 1965–1988

	As a percentage of saving	As a percentage of total sources of funds
Financial institutions	87.4	59.7
Money market	0.9	0.6
Bond market	1.7	1.2
Curb market	12.4	8.5
Total	102.5	70.0

Source: Adapted from Shea 1990, table 14.

For the supply side of funds, we can look at the average structure of household savings between 1965 and 1988 (Table 2.6). During this period, 87.4 percent of household savings went to financial institutions, and 12.4 percent went to the curb market.[6] In other words, if a household saved $100.00 at financial institutions, it lent $14.19 in the curb market. The share of household savings going to the curb market seems rather small relative to the share of financing done by businesses in the curb market, but this disparity may be due to the fact that many small businesses are lenders as well as borrowers in the curb market.

Thus within Taiwan's formal financial sector, it is indirect financing, especially financing from the state-owned banks, that has played the most important role. Direct financing and financing by nonbank financial institutions have played a secondary role. Within the informal financial sector, it is the curb market that has served as the primary source of capital for businesses and as a place for household savings.

II. The Efficiency of Credit Allocation under Financial Dualism

Taiwan's financial system consists of, among other things, a highly regulated and collusive banking sector and a highly competitive curb market. Potential borrowers who cannot obtain credit in the formal sector can go to the curb market, and savers can channel some savings to the curb market for a higher rate of return. Although these are two separate financial markets, they are functionally connected to each other. Thus how the curb market functions depends in a very important manner on the way that the regulated formal sector operates. Consequently, the contribution made to the economy by the curb market

6. These figures are from a survey carried out by the Directorate-General of Budget, Accounting, and Statistics, Executive Yuan.

depends on the way the formal financial sector operates and on how the government treats the curb market.

Figure 2.1 depicts the formal financial sector without any government regulation, where the equilibrium transaction volume is OQ_0 and the equilibrium interest rate is OR_0. When the government sets the interest rate at $\bar{R}$ ($<R_0$), the demand for loanable funds goes up from OQ_0 to OQ_2 but the supply decreases to OQ_1, and there is excess demand of Q_1Q_2. If the government completely forbids illegal financial activities, then the supply of loanable funds is limited to OQ_1, and the distribution of funds is limited to this formal sector. If the government takes a benign attitude toward curb market activities, then the excess demand in the formal sector will spill over into the curb market, and an additional supply of funds will be forthcoming in the curb market because the funds are attracted by its higher interest rates. That is, in addition to OQ_1 of loanable funds in the formal sector, a supply of funds will be available in the curb market. The supply curve in the curb market will look like $B'S'$ instead of BS because of higher risks in that market than in the formal sector.

The excess demand in the formal financial sector can now be satisfied in the curb market by an amount equal to Q_1Q_3, thus increasing total financing in the economy to OQ_3. This amount is still less than the level of financing that would result in a completely free financial market (OQ_0), but more than the level of financing that would result without the curb market OQ_1. It follows that if for some social or political reason

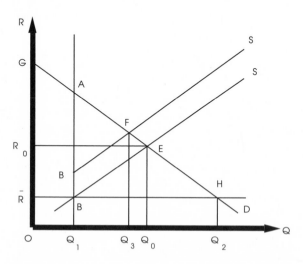

Figure 2.1. Formal financial sector without government regulation

the banking sector must be repressed, a second-best solution is to take a benign approach toward the curb market.

The case presented in Figure 2.1 is an extreme one. For the curb market to attain its equilibrium at point F, the formal sector must allocate credit to those projects for which the marginal efficiency or "profitability" is the area under GA of the demand curve. In other words, credit is allocated in the formal sector to the most profitable projects, and the curb market plays a residual role in financing those projects that are less profitable than ones financed in the formal sector. Obviously, there is no guarantee that the formal sector will necessarily finance only the most profitable projects.

An alternative scenario is the case where the formal sector finances the least-profitable projects, for instance, because of political interference. Such a case is demonstrated in Figure 2.2. Let point O' be such that $O'Q_2 = OQ_1$. The formal sector allocates funds to those projects that have profitability equal to the area under HH' of the demand curve, that is, the least-profitable projects. The projects not funded in the formal sector are more profitable than those funded, and the demand for the funds in the curb market is $G'H''$ $(=GH')$.

From the above, we may conclude that there is an inverse relationship between the efficiency of credit allocation in the formal sector and the economic contribution made by the curb market. If credit allocation in the formal sector is inefficient—that is, credit is allocated to projects with low profitability in the formal sector—then the contribution made by the

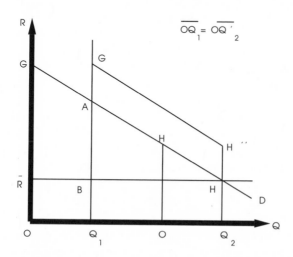

Figure 2.2. Formal financial sector funding of least profitable projects

curb market will be large because the projects funded there are likely to be of higher profitability. If credit allocation in the formal sector is efficient—that is, credit is allocated to projects of high profitability— then the contribution will be small because the projects funded there are probably of lower profitability. It is virtually impossible to observe directly whether the contribution made by the curb market is large or small. It is possible, however, to find out indirectly if the inverse relationship specified above holds. That is, if we can find out whether credit allocation is efficient in the formal financial sector, then we can make some inference about the economic contribution made by the curb market.

III. Credit Allocation in the Banking Sector

As noted above, the banking sector was under the strict control of the government until 1990 and consequently has been influenced in its allocation of credit by government objectives. For state-owned banks, two requirements have had a very important effect on the banks' decisions over credit allocation: the regulation on the bad-loan ratio; and the minimum profit requirement, which depends on, among other things, individual banks' past performance as well as the government's revenue situation. The ratio of bad or overdue loans to total loans is a criterion used not only for evaluating management performance but also for approving the request for opening new branches. In June 1984, for example, this ratio was set at less than 2 percent for those applying for permission to open a new branch. Since bank branches were very profitable because of the highly protected nature of the banking industry, the banks had a strong incentive to require large collateral for loans and thus keep the bad-loan ratio low.

The profits of the state-owned banks are an important source of government revenues, and the excess profits over the required amount is the only criterion for deciding bonuses for all bank employees. Again, this requirement led to conservative lending by the banks, which required substantial collateral for loans, as well as to their demand for large compensating deposit balances. This conservative tendency in the banking sector was further reinforced owing to lack of reliable credit information.

As pointed out by Patrick (1990), lack of reliable credit information has been the most severe problem for financial development in Taiwan. Collecting credit information is costly and subject to economies of scale.

ble 2.7. Structure of banks' loans

ar	Total loans (NT $m)	Long-term loans/total loans (%)	Total secured loans/total loans (%)	Short-term secured loans/short-term loans (%)	Long-term secured loans/long-term loans (%)
50	9,600	27.8	64.0	27.8	55.6
65	26,601	29.3	61.1	29.3	72.3
70	75,284	25.7	62.4	25.7	77.3
75	315,684	30.9	56.9	30.9	62.5
80	680,232	38.7	56.9	38.7	61.9
85	1,196,462	60.1	57.5	60.1	65.3
90	3,129,496	65.9	61.2	65.9	67.8

urce: Ministry of Finance 1990.

It is too costly to be done efficiently by many individual banks, although they could have in principle exploited economies of scale by focusing on a few companies and becoming monopoly suppliers of loans to them. This did not take place, however, probably because of a ceiling regulation on the amount that a bank might loan to a single customer. Furthermore, because of excess demand for credit, there has not been much pressure on banks to cooperate and construct a credit information system. But such a system would not have been very useful, for the financial statements provided by private enterprises bear little resemblance to the true financial status of the business. It is well known in Taiwan that, private enterprises prepare several editions of financial statements—one for the tax authority, another for the bank, and perhaps the true one for the owners themselves. Knowing this practice, the banks rely less on financial statements and more on the collateral offered in their decision making on loan applications.[7]

IV. Empirical Evidence on the Efficiency of Bank Credit Allocation

The Allocation of Bank Credit

Table 2.7 details the structure of bank loans by different terms of loan, namely, short-term (one year or less) versus long-term (longer than one year) and short-term secured versus long-term secured. The figures in

7. Foreign bank branches in Taiwan experienced a relatively high ratio of nonperforming loans when they made loan decisions on the basis of financial statements. After some bad experiences, they also began to require collateral as a condition for approving a loan. According to Yang (1990), the nonperforming loan ratio was, on average for 1977–1988, 8.81 percent for foreign bank branches, 4.41 percent for state-owned commercial banks, 4.65 percent for state-owned specialized banks, and 4.81 percent for private commercial banks.

the second column indicate that until 1985, long-term lending accounted for a small portion of bank loans (28–39 percent), which implies that most loans were short-term. But after that, long-term lending increased significantly as real estate mortgage loans increased pari passu with the boom in Taiwan's real estate market, where the average price of real estate doubled or even tripled between 1987 and 1990. It is also interesting to note that until 1985, many of the short-term loans were not secured, whereas the converse holds true for long-term loans. This reflects the banks' basic conservatism in their loan policy and is consistent with the measures they undertook to reduce the risk in long-term lending.

During the 1960–1990 period, private enterprises received between 41 and 66 percent of the total bank loans outstanding, whereas state-owned enterprises received from 8 to 38 percent. Over the same period, government agencies received less than 10 percent of all bank loans. State-owned enterprises, however, accounted for 18.4 percent of value added in the economy in 1960 and 14.3 percent in 1985 but received 40.8 percent and 28.6 percent of total bank loans for these respective years. It is clear that the SOEs' share of bank loans was larger than their relative contribution to the country's value added. Although this may result from the relatively high capital intensity of the SOEs, they must have received preferential treatment given that they were guaranteed against bankruptcy by the government.

In Taiwan, small and medium-sized enterprises have played a very important role in the economy, accounting for 60 percent of employment, 45 percent of production, and 60 percent of exports in manufacturing during the 1980s (Chou 1992). As shown in Table 2.8, however, the SMEs' share of bank loans was less than 30 percent before 1980, around 30–35 percent in 1981–1985, and slightly less than 36 percent in 1986–1989. Additionally, their share of short-term loans was over 90 percent, whereas the large firms' share of short-term loans was around

Table 2.8. Loans to small and medium-sized enterprises

Year	Loans to SMEs (NT $m)	Share of total loans (%)
1972	21,739	22.7
1975	60,797	21.6
1980	214,617	31.9
1985	488,822	35.7
1989	1,220,707	35.9

Sources: Small Business Integrated Assistance Center, various years.

70 percent in 1983 and 1986 (Chou 1988b, p. 34). Liu (1988) used the 1983 data of private firms to demonstrate the distribution of bank loans among firms of different sizes (p. 9). He found the ratio of bank loans to assets was only 5 percent for the group of smallest firms (that is, whose assets were less than NT $1 million) but 28.6 percent for the group of largest firms (namely, those whose assets were more than NT $1 billion). In contrast, the share of loans from the curb market was 42.6 percent for the former and 4.2 percent for the latter group.

Although exports have been an engine of economic growth for Taiwan, the share of bank loans targeted specifically for exports has been rather insignificant. In 1975, these export loans amounted to only 5 percent of total loans, and by 1990 the share had declined to less than 1 percent. It is likely that many of Taiwan's exporting firms have relied on the curb market for their working capital, although they, as manufacturing firms, must have received bank loans, as noted above. Subsidies forgone by not receiving export loans could not have been very much, however, because the difference between the subsidized interest rate on export loans and the curb market rate has been rather insignificant for some time.

In comparing the share of value added with the share of bank loans across industries, it is clear that manufacturing industries have a relatively high ratio of loans to value added. This is not surprising given that these industries are not only relatively capital intensive but have also been the priority sector for the government's development policy. Thus the loan policy of the banks has favored public and large private enterprises at the expense of SMEs and has been biased toward short-term loans. It may therefore be inferred that SMEs have received financing mostly through the curb market.

Testing the Efficiency of Bank Credit Allocation

The fact that banks have favored state-owned and large private enterprises does not necessarily mean that their credit allocation was inefficient. Such lending would be efficient if it followed a profit criterion. To determine the efficiency of bank credit allocation among industries, I ran the following regression:

$$BL = a_0 + a_1 SA + a_2 PS + a_3 GR + a_4 FA + a_5 FL + a_6 BL_{t-1}$$

where

BL = the ratio of bank loans to external funds,
SA = the ratio of sales to assets,
PS = the ratio of profits to sales,

GR   = industry growth rate,
FA   = the ratio of fixed assets to total assets,
FL   = the ratio of fixed assets to external funds, and
BL_{t-1} = a proxy for the relationship between the borrowing firm
         and the bank.

The ratio of bank loans to external funds (including bank loans and financing from both the money market and the curb market) indicates the loan decisions of the banks. Given that interest rates on bank loans were lower than the cost of money in both the money and the curb markets, potential borrowers would have an incentive to get as much bank credit as possible. Thus, a high value for this ratio for a given industry would mean that it was favored in credit allocation by the banks, whereas a low value would mean the opposite. The question is what determined the banks' decision to favor a particular industry.

If a_1, a_2, and a_3 are positive and significant, then loan decisions are based on the performance, profitability, and growth rate of the industry. In this case I would reject the null hypothesis that credit allocation among industries is inefficient. If a_4 and a_5 are positive and significant, however, then loan decisions are based on the size of the collateral, and I would not be able to reject the null hypothesis.

I used 1986 census data from *The Statistics of Revenue and Financial Structural Changes in Taiwan's Main Industries*, which is published by the Joint Credit Information Center of the Association of Banking Industry in Taipei. The cross-sectional data for 1986 covering seventy-nine industries were used to test the hypothesis. Using the ordinary least squares technique, we obtained the following results:

$$BL = 1.02 - 5.58SA - 0.18PS - 0.03GR + 0.26FA + 0.001FL + 0.74BL_{t-1}$$
$$(3.44) \quad (2.30) \quad (1.28) \quad (0.68) \quad (3.78) \quad (2.59) \quad (10.86)$$

$R^2 = 0.8963$; adjusted $R^2 = 0.8877$

The regression result shows that the first three variables have a negative sign and that two of the three are insignificant, whereas the remaining three variables have a positive sign and are all statistically highly significant.[8] In other words, on the basis of the regression result, we are unable to reject the null hypothesis that bank credit allocation is ineffi-

8. It is not easy to explain why the sign of SA is significantly negative, which is invalid from the theoretical point of view. But this negative sign again highlights that in making lending decisions, the banks did not place much emphasis on performance-oriented variables.

cient.[9] This regression result is consistent with the view that in their loan decisions, the banks tended to favor the enterprises with considerable assets, which could be used as collateral. These belong in many cases to relatively capital-intensive industries containing large-scale state as well as private enterprises. The banks' preference for them might, therefore, also reflect the relative capital intensity of these enterprises. It should be also noted that in Taiwan, the state-owned enterprises were not necessarily unprofitable, although loans to them might have been made for political reasons as well as for the purpose of building infrastructure.

In this chapter I have tried to explain how the Taiwanese economy could have developed so rapidly with a formal financial sector that was controlled and highly regulated by the government. Empirical evidence shows that the formal financial sector, especially the banks, allocated credit in a conservative manner, taking the size of collateral as a factor in loan decisions.

What perhaps distinguishes Taiwan's financial system from other repressed financial systems is that its curb market has been active in mobilizing and allocating savings under the policy of benign neglect by the government. The curb market could thus finance the profitable projects that were excluded from the formal financial sector. In fact, financial dualism in Taiwan parallels its dualistic industrial structure, which consists of domestic market–oriented industries and export-oriented industries.[10] The former consist mainly of small and medium-sized firms and have a highly competitive market structure with low barriers to entry. The latter are mainly large, capital-intensive enterprises and have a monopolistic or oligopolistic market structure with high barriers to entry. Most of the funds from the banking sector went to these industries, whereas the curb market was the chief source of funds for the export-oriented, small-scale industries. It is possible to argue, then, that even in a liberal financial system, the banks would have favored a large, capital-intensive monopoly or oligopolistic enterprises that would have a higher profit rate than highly competitive, small-scale enterprises.

Given the informal and illegal nature of the curb market, very little is known about its actual operation. But one can conjecture that under the

9. This result is consistent with that obtained by Shea (1990), who used 1965–1988 pooled data to test a similar hypothesis.
10. On the hypothesis of dichotomous market structure, see Chou 1986, 1988a. A study by Chen (1991), who examines the dynamic process of industrial concentration, also supports this hypothesis.

benign neglect of the government, the curb market has functioned as a highly competitive and efficient allocator of credit. It is quite possible that use of the curb market mitigated the unfavorable effect that financial repression in the formal financial sector might have had on the Taiwanese economy. Even then, a first-best policy would have been not to have a repressed financial system at all. But given that the government has kept the banks under control for political reasons, its policy of benign neglect toward the curb market can be regarded as a good second-best policy, for this policy made it possible for numerous small and medium-sized enterprises to finance their activities without a great cost disadvantage and thus for them to form a basis for Taiwan's export growth.

References

Central Bank of China (CBC). Various years. *Financial Statistics Monthly, Taiwan District, Republic of China,* various issues. Taipei: CBC.

Chen, G. L. 1991. Dynamic Adjustment of Market Concentration: The Impact of Industrial Policy. In *Conference on the Political Economics* (in Chinese). Taipei: Chinese Economic Association.

Cheng, T. J. 1991. Guarding the Commanding Heights: The State as Banker in Taiwan. Paper presented at the Conference on Government, Financial Systems, and Economic Development: A Comparative Study of Selected Asian and Latin American Countries, Honolulu, Hawaii.

Chou, Tein-Chen 1986. Concentration, Profitability, and Trade in a Simultaneous Equation Analysis: The Case of Taiwan. *Journal of Industrial Economics* 34(3): 429–41.

———. 1988a. Concentration and Profitability in a Dichotomous Economy: The Case of Taiwan. *International Journal of Industrial Organization* 6(4): 409–28.

———. 1988b. Loans to SMEs and Economic Development in Taiwan (in Chinese). *Taiwan Community Financial Journal* 17: 17–41.

———. 1991. A Measurement of the Concentration of the Banking Industry in Taiwan (in Chinese). *Bank of Taiwan Quarterly* 42(2): 40–56.

———. 1992. The Experience of SMEs' Development in Taiwan: High Export-Contribution and Export-Intensity. *Ritisita Internazionale di Scienze Economiche e Commerciali* 39(12): 1067–84.

Chou, Tein-Chen, P. I. Hwang, and C. L. Wang. 1990. Concentration Ratios of Taiwan's Banking Industry at Branch Level. *Taiwan Community Financial Journal* (in Chinese) 21: 61–73.

Liu, J. L. 1988. The Development and Prospect of Financial Institutions in Taiwan. In *Proceedings of Conference on the Modernization of Service Industries in R.O.C.* (in Chinese). Taipei: Chinese Economic Association.

Ministry of Finance (MOF). 1990. *Yearbook of Financial Statistics of the Republic of China.* Taipei: MOF.

Patrick, Hugh T. 1990. The Financial Development of Taiwan, Korea, and Japan: A Framework for Consideration of Issues. Paper presented at the Conference on the Financial Development of Japan, Korea, and Taiwan, Institute of Economics, Academia Sinica, Taipei, August 27–28.

Shaw, Edward S. 1973. *Financial Deepening in Economic Development.* New York: Oxford University Press.

Shea, E. S. 1990. Financial Development in Taiwan: A Macro Analysis. Paper presented at the Conference on the Financial Development of Japan, Korea, and Taiwan, Institute of Economics, Academia Sinica, Taipei, August 27–28.

Small Business Integrated Assistance Center. Various years. *Annual Report of Small Business Finance,* various issues. Taipei: Small Business Integrated Assistance Center.

Tsiang, S. C. 1956. Liquidity Preference and Loanable Fund Theories, Multipliers, and Velocity Analysis: A Synthesis. *American Economic Review* 46(4): 539–64.

Yang, Y. H. 1990. A Micro Analysis of the Financial System in Taiwan. Paper presented at the Conference on the Financial Development of Japan, Korea, and Taiwan, Institute of Economics, Academia Sinica, Taipei, August 27–28.

CHAPTER THREE

INDONESIA

Wing Thye Woo

When the Sukarno government invaded Dutch-held New Guinea in 1958, it also nationalized the Dutch-owned banks that dominated the Indonesian financial system. The second action rendered the banking industry, for all practical purposes, a state-owned industry. The ideological aversion of President Sukarno to capitalism in general, and to financial capitalism in particular, guaranteed an insignificant role for private banks through regulations on growth and entry. When the budget deficits began soaring in the 1960s as the result of disastrous economic policies, the government merged all state-owned banks into one institution, Bank Negara Indonesia (BNI), to facilitate the financing of the budget deficits.

The New Order government of President Suharto, which took formal power in March 1966, dismantled this monolithic structure through the enactment of Banking Act No. 14 of 1967 and Central Bank Act No. 13 of 1968.[1] The complex BNI structure was split into four components: a central bank (Bank Indonesia) with no commercial banking functions; five state-owned commercial banks (that is, deposit money banks); a state-owned savings bank; and a state development bank.[2]

Of the Rp 291 billion worth of gross assets held by the commercial banks in 1969, 75 percent was held by the five state commercial banks, 13 percent was held by foreign banks, and 10 percent was held by private commercial banks (Table 3.1). The dominance of the SOBs in 1969 was no doubt the legacy of Sukarno's policies, but its continued domination

---

1. For more details, see Nasution 1983.
2. A historical overview and analysis of the economic policies of the Sukarno years and the Suharto stabilization program in 1966 is given by Woo, Glassburner, and Nasution (1994).

Financial institution	Number				Gross assets (Rp billion)				Share of assets (by percentage)			
	1969	1972	1982	1989	1969	1972	1982	1989[a]	1969	1972	1982	1989
Bank Indonesia	1	1	1	1	417	675	13,706	38,880	58.9	40.7	42.7	29.3
Deposit money banks (DMB)					291	984	15,922	85,929	41.1	59.3	49.6	64.7
Nationl foreign exchange banks[b]	5	8	15	15	217	735	12,724	67,409	30.6	44.3	39.6	50.7
Foreign and joint venture banks	11	11	11	25	37	126	1,172	4,626	5.2	7.6	3.6	3.5
Development banks[c]	25	26	28	28	7	66	1,336	6,364	1.0	4.0	4.2	4.8
Other commercial banks[d]	122	126	61	73	30	57	690	7,510	4.2	3.4	2.1	5.7
Nonbank financial institutions	12	11	14	14	0	0	805	2,949			2.5	2.2
Savings banks			3	3	na	na	452	2,741			1.4	2.1
Insurance companies			83		0	0	587	na			1.8	
Leasing companies			34		na	na	114	na			0.4	
Pension funds[e]			78		na	na	277	na			0.9	
Other credit institutions[f]	8,619	9,366	5,861	7,740		na	56	120			0.2	0.1
Securities												
Listed bonds[g]	0	0	0	50	0	0	96	1,417			0.3	1.1
Listed equity shares[h]	0	0	14	85	0	0	100	794			0.3	0.6
Total financial assets					708	1,659	32,115	132,830	100	100	100	100
Memorandum												
Bank Indonesia claims on DMB					80	149	3,742	14,273				

Sources: Statistics from the Bank Indonesia, Ministry of Finance, Capital Market Executive Agency, and Central Bureau of Statistics.

Note: na = not available.

[a] Gross assets estimate is September 1989 figure.

[b] Consists of five state-owned banks, with the remainder being private banks.

[c] Consists of one state-owned national development bank and one private development bank, with the remainder being local development banks.

[d] Private national banks engaging in only domestic currency banks.

[e] Excludes pension funds not registered with the Ministry of Finance.

[f] Village, paddy, petty traders', and employees' banks as well as state pawn shops. Excludes assets of foundations and informal financial institutions for which data are unavailable. Number estimate for 1969 is from December 1968.

[g] Number of separate issues and values at initial offering.

[h] Number of listed companies and market values at end of period, including both Jakarta and Barasa Parelel.

in 1993, more than two decades later, is not. Until the 1988 financial reforms, entry into the banking sector was extremely difficult, and the establishment of branch offices was virtually impossible for private banks. The dominant position of the SOBs today is the result of two state actions taken in the 1974–1983 period: credit ceilings and selective credit allocation.

The first state action, the imposition of credit ceilings, was carried out in 1974 when oil revenue inflows created large balance-of-payments surpluses that caused the money supply to mushroom. Because every bank had to be assigned a specific credit quota, entry into the banking system was minimized to make it easier for the central bank to administer the credit ceilings. There were, in fact, forty-eight fewer deposit money banks in 1982 than in 1969. What is not often realized is that the credit ceilings created massive pressures on resource allocation because of their ineffectiveness as a macroeconomic instrument to fight inflation. As will be explained, the resulting inflation interacted with the fixed exchange rate to cause resources to move from the tradables sector to the nontradables sector.

The second state action, selective credit allocation, consolidated the dominance of the SOBs, for these banks were used by the state as a vehicle through which oil revenues were disbursed. Bank Indonesia not only gave direct credits to certain enterprises but also extended "liquidity credits" to the banking system (mainly to the SOBs) to promote targeted activities, which ranged from investment by indigenous entrepreneurs (as opposed to Indonesian entrepreneurs of Chinese descent) to acquisition of motorcycles by school teachers. The result was that Bank Indonesia and the SOBs supplied 86–90 percent of the banking credits during the 1974–1980 oil boom (Table 3.2).

With the steady fall in the price of oil since 1981, the resource transfer (fiscal) function of the SOBs declined in the 1980s. In 1983, Bank Indonesia and the SOBs extended only 79 percent of total banking credits, compared with 90 percent in 1975. Moreover, the new economic circumstances of the 1980s led to new financial policies—interest rate and credit controls were largely removed in 1983, entry barriers into the banking industry were lowered considerably in 1988, and the number of activities eligible for liquidity credits was drastically curbed in 1990—that served to erode further the financial power of the SOBs. By 1990, the proportion of banking credits accounted for by the central bank and the SOBs had fallen to 58 percent.

The important question is what this financial market liberalization implies for the future of economic growth in Indonesia. To answer this question, we have to examine how the credit ceilings, interest rate *e 3.2.* Banking system credits by source (Rp billion)

	1974	1975	1976	1977	1978	1979	1980	1981	1982	1983
k Indonesia direct credits)	231	894	1,212	1,229	1,935	2,163	2,454	2,649	2,771	2,356
e commercial anks	1,136	1,602	2,007	2,267	2,832	3,270	4,295	5,881	8,031	9,787
onal private anks	89	133	197	257	366	493	711	1,081	1,554	2,294
ign banks	117	122	150	184	262	342	414	548	666	862
al	1,573	2,751	3,566	3,937	5,395	6,268	7,874	10,159	13,002	15,299

ces: Bank Indonesia, various years.

controls, and selective credit allocation have affected macroeconomic management, resource allocation, income distribution, and economic growth. There should be no prior theoretical presumption that the financial policies of the 1974–1983 period were beneficial or detrimental to the Indonesian economy, as evidence from other countries is mixed.

On one hand, we have the voluminous literature associated with Fry (1988), McKinnon (1973), Shaw (1973), and the World Bank (1989) which argues that these types of "financial repression" reduce economic efficiency and retard growth. On the other hand, there is a growing literature, exemplified by Alam 1989, Diaz-Alejandro 1985, Lee 1992, and Stiglitz 1989, that argues the opposite case and documents how nonmarket credit allocation encouraged growth in a number of countries and how "financial liberalization" caused financial collapses in Latin America. Lee (1992) argues that because of the close ties between the Korean government and the conglomerates, "the extensive intervention by the government with Korea's financial system can be viewed as an internal capital market and, consequently, it could have led to a more efficient allocation of credit than possible in a free-market financial system" (p. 187).

I begin my analysis of how Indonesian financial market policies affected economic development in the 1974–1983 period[3] by evaluating the effectiveness of the credit ceilings in achieving the macroeconomic goal of inflation control and showing how this influenced resource allocation. I will show that the selective credit policy of the 1974–1983 period benefited the Indonesian economy in a way that was unanticipated by the protagonists in the financial repression debate. The

3. Other analyses of this topic include those by Nasution (1989), Cole and Slade (1990), and Layman (1990). I differ from these authors by focusing on resource allocation effects.

selective credit policy, by favoring the manufacturing and trade sectors, reduced the negative impacts of the overvalued exchange rate (which had been created by expansionary macroeconomic policies) on these sectors. The existence of a sizable tradables sector when the negative balance-of-payments shocks hit after 1981 enabled Indonesia to earn enough foreign exchange to service its external debts and thus avoid the type of prolonged economic crisis experienced by Latin America.[4] Because the selective credit policy was not undertaken with the expectation of negative balance-of-payments shocks, its beneficial effects on economic development were entirely fortuitous.

I. Using Credit Ceilings to Fight Inflation, 1974–1983

The Control of Monetary Aggregates

The chief instrument of monetary control before April 1974 was direct central bank credit to state and private enterprises. Because these credits were extended for a contractually fixed period of time, there was no way to reduce the money supply quickly. Thus when the oil boom began and the government financed its increased expenditures by converting the dollar earnings from oil exports into rupiah at the fixed exchange rate, the domestic money stock exploded.

In 1972, when oil revenues increased by Rp 90 billion over 1971 revenues (an increase of 64 percent), growth of reserve money was 46 percent compared with the 29 percent expansion of the previous two years. When the price of oil quadrupled at the end of 1973, reserve money grew 57 percent in 1974, while the inflation rate for that year was 41 percent. In April 1974 the central bank responded to this monetary anarchy by setting ceilings on lending rates in the banking system. But the credit ceilings were not able to cut the link between the reserve base, which was directly affected by oil export earnings, and the money supply. When reserve money grew by 33 percent in 1975, M_1 expanded by 35 percent. This conclusion is further evidenced by the upsurge in money growth in 1979 (32 percent) and 1980 (36 percent) when the OPEC-2 price increase occurred.[5]

The main reason why the credit ceilings did not control the money supply effectively was because they were extremely cumbersome to

4. It must be stressed that the selective credit policy constituted only one of the policy actions that preserved the economic viability of the tradables sector.
5. The reason why M_1 growth slowed down in 1977 and 1978 may be due more to the slowdown in oil revenue increases rather than to the credit ceilings.

change. Not only were quick ceiling changes difficult because there were separate ceilings for each kind of credit, but the ceiling for the same credit category also varied across banks, and the changes were made only after consultation with each bank. Such consultation was necessary because most bank loans were extended for a fixed period of time. Thus, any unilateral action by the central bank to lower the total amount of credit could potentially bankrupt some banks or automatically make criminals out of them (because the banks could not for contractual reasons reduce their outstanding loans). The standard operating procedure that emerged from this complicated situation was to change the credit ceilings at the beginning of each year.

An asymmetry in the management of bank credits also existed. Banks could request, and many times received, higher ceilings during the year; the central bank, however, was reluctant to lower credit ceilings in response to economic events that had occurred during the year. It is thus misleading to say that the central bank had three instruments of monetary control—that is, credit ceilings, reserve requirements, and central bank credit—because the first two instruments could not be used with any frequency to reduce credit on short notice.

During times of low credit demand, the credit ceilings were operative by default, that is, demand was lower than supply at the controlled interest rate. But whenever total domestic credit demand was higher than the aggregate credit ceiling, the excess demand would be partially relieved by some rise in the interest rates,[6] by some relaxation of the ceilings (occasionally), and by credits from abroad. The last mechanism is possible because there has been no control on capital account transactions since 1971.[7] The result was that large Indonesian firms could supplement their domestic credit with credit from international banks stationed in Singapore and Hong Kong whenever domestic bank lending was reduced. The conversion of private external credit through the balance of payments automatically increased the domestic money supply because the credit ceilings could not be constantly reset to offset the capital inflows. Furthermore, sterilization through open market operations was not possible because of the absence of developed financial

6. Although the deposit and lending rates of the state banks were controlled by the government, the rates of private and foreign banks were not. Nevertheless, the state banking system dwarfed its competitors in terms of both business volume and number of branches.
7. Indonesian policymakers are (rightly) convinced that the weakness of the administrative structure and the openness of the economy together make capital controls unenforceable. Any wavering on the open capital account policy would end the possibility of the return of any capital flight.

markets. It is crucial to note that private capital inflows increase the
money supply only by the amount of the increase in the monetary base
when the credit ceiling is binding. The money multiplier had a value of
one because the credit ceiling prevented the banks from expanding
credit in line with the rise in deposits.[8]

In summary, the Indonesian monetary authorities had little control
over the money supply in the short run during the 1970s. The open
capital account policy made this inevitable because of the difficulties (or
unwillingness) to change credit ceilings more than once a year and the
absence of organized domestic financial markets, which made open-
market operations impossible. From a medium-term perspective, the
government had two options for monetary control: continue to use
credit ceilings or develop the financial markets to enable open-market
operations. For reasons to be explained later in this chapter, the government chose to pursue the former option.

It is frequently claimed that even if Bank Indonesia has an open-
market capability, it cannot control the domestic interest rate (that is,
the money stock) under a fixed exchange rate regime because of the
proximity of Singapore's well-developed financial markets. But this
claim is not true for Indonesia in the 1974–1983 period, because the
credit ceilings prevented Indonesian banks from arbitrating away the
difference in interest rates. Since the bulk of Indonesian firms do not
have access to international credit, the persistence of an interest differential in a fixed exchange rate setting is possible.[9]

*The Consequences of Not Having Adequate Monetary Control on Resource
Allocation*

The credit ceilings might have slowed down the rate of price increase;
nevertheless, the inflation rates could have been even lower if Bank
Indonesia had developed the domestic financial markets and conducted
open market operations to neutralize the monetary consequences of the
balance-of-payments surplus. The resource allocation effects of the high
inflation rates, which came from the use of a flawed macroeconomic
instrument, may not be obvious, but they were widespread and serious.
For with a fixed nominal exchange rate, the prices in the tradables
sector could not rise faster than the world inflation rate, which was lower
than Indonesia's inflation rate. In short, the interaction between the

8. The Indonesian banks would often deposit these excess reserves with international
banks in Singapore and Hong Kong, which meant that the foreign debt incurred by
domestic private agents became the foreign exchange reserves of the commercial banks.
9. Woo, Glassburner, and Nasution (1994) present a formal model on this point.

high Indonesian inflation rate and the fixed exchange rate produced a strong incentive for producers of tradables to switch to producing nontradables.

Woo and Nasution (1989) constructed two proxies of the tradables/ nontradables price ratio, that is, the ratio of wholesale import prices to the cost of housing in Jakarta and the ratio of wholesale (nonpetroleum) export prices to the cost of housing in Jakarta. They found that both prices declined by about 30 percent in the 1974–1978 period. The movement of resources from the tradables sector to the nontradables sector during an oil boom is popularly known as the "Dutch disease." This resource movement is a disease because it is a dynamic inefficiency: the resources will have to move back after the oil reserves are depleted.[10]

Note that not all industries producing tradables suffered equally from the Dutch disease. Many manufacturing industries producing import substitutes lobbied for and received protection against the more intense import competition. The effective rate of protection (EPR) for imports in the manufacturing sector rose from 65 percent in 1971 to 98 percent in 1975. Less-comprehensive data suggest that the protectionist surge continued after 1975. For example, of the ten largest import-competing manufacturing industries, seven had an EPR that was higher in 1978 than in 1975, and the EPRs of the remaining three industries remained over 100 percent.[11] The final upshot of the higher inflation caused by the inadequate monetary control was that the export industries suffered the biggest disincentive to produce.

II. The Use of Nonmarket Credit Allocation for Economic Restructuring, 1974–1983

The System of Liquidity Credits and Direct Central Bank Credits

Use of lending ceilings as a short-run stopgap measure to control monetary growth is understandable, but Indonesia continued to rely on the ceilings until June 1983 despite their clumsiness as instruments of monetary control. The government did so because the credit ceilings gave it an additional instrument to implement its social, agricultural, and industrial policies, as well as to consolidate its political base through

10. Woo, Glassburner, and Nasution (1994) formalize the types of dynamic inefficiencies involved. An equally important dynamic inefficiency occurs in the intertemporal consumption pattern.

11. Woo, Glassburner, and Nasution (1994) provide details in table 7.5 of chap. 7.

preferential credit access. To better achieve these goals, the government subsequently instructed the central bank to introduce detailed ceilings by type of credit for each bank. For example, banks were told to reserve a proportion of their allocated credit for *pribumi* (non-Chinese Indonesian) entrepreneurs. In addition, high-priority items such as the financing of rural participation in the government's rice intensification program and the financing of the scheme to stabilize the price of rice were specified at the beginning of the New Order government. High priority was later extended to several manufacturing enterprises.

Each of the five state commercial banks was assigned a sector on which to focus its lending activities; Bank Rakyat Indonesia was to focus on rural development and small-holder agriculture; Bank Bumi Daya, on estate agriculture and forestry; Bank Negara Indonesia 1946, on industry; Bank Dagang Negara, on mining; and Bank Ekspor-Impor, on exports. State-owned and private domestic banks received "liquidity credits" from the central bank in the following manner: if the bank extended a loan under one of the government credit programs at the designated lending rate, it could rediscount a certain proportion of the loan with the central bank at a rate that was set lower than the lending rate. This process is almost equivalent to the domestic bank borrowing funds from the central bank at very low rates of interest and relending the funds at higher interest rates set by the central bank. Most of these liquidity credits were handled by the SOBs, as there were many government credit programs in which the domestic private banks could not participate. This policy of ceilings-cum-selective credit thus protected the state banks from competition with the private banks. Perhaps in compensation, the deposit and lending rates of the private banks (unlike those of the SOBs) were not controlled.

Data on the sectoral allocation of central bank credits show that in 1969, 75 percent of the liquidity credits was channeled to revive agricultural production, and 83 percent of direct central bank credits was directed to facilitate international trade, two activities that had been badly hurt by the economic policies of the Sukarno regime (Table 3.3).[12] With the development of the petroleum sector and the 1973 OPEC price increases, liquidity credits to the other sectors were greatly increased. Investment credits rose from Rp 73 billion in 1972 to Rp 183 billion in 1977, and credits to the manufacturing industry jumped from Rp 4 billion in 1974 to Rp 106 billion in 1975. By 1979, the amount of

12. Details are given in Woo, Glassburner, and Nasution (1994).

Table 3.3. Credits supplied by Bank Indonesia (Rp billion)

	Liquidity credits to bank to be disbursed to designated activities				Direct credits to sectors			Total credits
	Total	Agriculture and primary products sector[a]	Investment credits	Manufacturing industry	Total	Mining	Trade	
1969	80	60	6	3	87	0	72	167
1970	113	67	26	6	97	0	62	210
1971	143	67	56	3	104	0	60	247
1972	150	63	73	2	127	0	89	278
1973	195	108	73	3	155	0	118	349
1974	294	181	82	4	235	0	193	529
1975	565	321	88	106	894	726	143	1,459
1976	640	372	122	90	1,212	1,020	167	1,852
1977	682	322	183	123	1,229	1,042	176	1,911
1978	846	414	173	169	1,935	1,679	238	2,781
1979	1,129	419	277	278	2,163	1,875	248	3,292
1980	1,722	418	419	449	2,454	1,849	507	4,176
1981	2,548	535	829	625	2,649	1,644	809	5,197

Source: Adapted from Odano, Sabirin, and Diwandono 1988, table 4.
[a] Includes items such as sugar, estate, agriculture, export, cotton, and wheat.

liquidity credits extended to promote investment activities and expansion of manufacturing had exceeded the amount extended to the agri-cultural sector.

One troubling feature of nonmarket credit allocation in Indonesia is the tendency for the coverage to increase. This tendency is due to the political difficulties in Indonesia associated with insulating the process of discretionary credit allocation from interest group pressures. The sugar, estate, and contractor lobbies gained access to liquidity credits in 1980; the education lobby, in 1982; and the consultants who prepare feasibility reports for investment projects, in 1987.

Another disturbing feature of the operations of nonmarket credit allocation in Indonesia is the tendency for the terms of a program to become more generous over time. Beginning in January 1978, contractors of some government projects had their borrowing rate lowered from 21 percent to 13.5 percent, the proportion of their loans that could be rediscounted by the central bank rise from 20 percent to 70 percent, and their rediscount rate reduced from 10 percent to 6 percent. Even contractors not associated with these government projects saw a lowering of their costs. Although it is quite usual in the Asian-Pacific context to subsidize exports, Indonesia went one step further and extended credit subsidies to cover import activities. Importers saw their borrowing rate decline from 24 percent to 18 percent in 1978, and the banks that financed import activities were allowed to rediscount 40 percent of these loans with the central bank at a rate of 6 percent.

Investment Credit and Agricultural Credit Programs

To understand the performance of the investment and agricultural credit schemes, let us review the institutional setup of the three best-known credit schemes: Kredit Investasi Biasa (KIB; Ordinary Investment Credit); Kredit Investasi Kecil/Kredit Modal Kerja Permanen (KIK/KMKP; Small-Scale Investment Credit/Permanent Working Capital Credit); and Bimbingan Massal/Intensifikasi Massal (BIMAS/INMAS; Mass Guidance/Mass Intensification). The key objective of the KIB and KIK/KMKP schemes was to promote the industrialization of Indonesia, whereas the objective of the BIMAS/INMAS scheme was to increase production of rice and secondary crops.

The KIB program, which began in April 1969, provided investment credits that had a maximum ten-year maturity if issued through the SOBs or the national private banks and a maximum fifteen-year maturity if issued through the national development bank, BAPINDO. The borrower had to pledge collateral worth 150 percent of the amount of the

Table 3.4. Allocation of funds in the KIB, KIK, and KMKP programs (Rp billion)

	1975	1976	1977	1978	1979
Kredit Investasi Biasa (KIB)	177.8	246.2	278.2	295.8	391.0
Public sector	64.1	129.1	165.0	181.8	211.1
Agriculture	21.9	33.7	46.3	53.9	71.0
Mining	0.0	4.0	3.0	3.0	1.5
Manufacturing	23.0	41.9	53.8	61.5	76.5
Services	12.3	43.4	53.8	49.9	83.7
Other	6.9	6.1	8.1	13.4	8.3
Private sector	113.7	117.1	113.2	114.0	149.9
Agriculture	5.0	5.2	5.7	6.6	6.6
Mining	143.1	277.7	277.7	276.4	110.2
Manufacturing	55.3	52.2	52.0	51.7	59.7
Services	49.9	56.6	52.7	53.2	80.5
Other	3.4	2.8	2.4	2.2	2.9
Kredit Investasi Kecil (KIK)	21.6	36.1	50.5	64.7	94.3
Manufacturing	4.5	5.9	7.6	8.9	11.4
Other	17.2	30.2	42.9	55.8	82.9
Kredit Modal Kerja Permanen (KMKP)	19.2	41.4	61.8	83.8	143.8
Manufacturing	6.9	7.4	9.0	11.8	19.7
Other	12.3	34.0	52.8	72.0	124.0

Sources: World Bank 1981 and 1982.

loan and provide at least 35 percent of the project cost in equity contribution. If the loan was more than Rp 200 million, the borrower was also required to submit a feasibility report, which normally cost the borrower 5 to 10 percent of the amount of the loan.

Most of the increases in KIB loans since 1975 have gone to SOEs. From Rp 64 billion in 1975, KIB loans to the SOEs increased to Rp 211 billion in 1979; over the same period, KIB loans to the private sector rose from Rp 114 billion to Rp 150 billion (Table 3.4). In particular, KIB loans to private manufacturing industries actually declined in nominal terms every year from 1975 to 1978. This public-private gap occurred for three reasons.

(1) The banks did not have sufficient qualified personnel to assess the merits of all the proposed projects, and bank officials were wary of relying on the consultant report that was required for large projects, because the consultant was paid by the borrower. Furthermore, since loans to SOEs were riskless because of the implicit government guarantee, it was natural for banks to loan more to SOEs than to private sector businesses.

(2) The loans that had been extended to the private sector had an extremely high rate of arrears; thus, banks sought to avoid the past pattern of lending.

(3) Many short-term credit programs had lending rate/discount rate differentials at least as large as those for the KIB program, and the former involved less paperwork and had faster approval from Bank Indonesia. The processing of a KIB loan took a minimum of six months and could take as long as fifteen months. It was therefore more profitable for banks to allocate their resources to extending short-term credits.

Thus banks were not very interested in making KIB loans, despite the large differential between the lending rate and the discount rate. The fact that KIB loans were not accessible to Chinese-Indonesian entrepreneurs after 1974 may also have contributed to the low amount of KIB loans to the private sector.

Soon after the KIB program began in 1969, it became obvious that very few of the loans were going to small-scale pribumi entrepreneurs. On the supply side, banks found that this group of borrowers had a much higher default rate and that it was more costly to process many small loans than one big loan. On the demand side, most entrepreneurs within this group did not have the resources to meet the collateral and equity requirements and pay for the consultant report (if required). As a result, the KIK and KMKP programs were launched in December 1973 to increase investment by small-scale pribumi entrepreneurs. The programs differed from the KIB program in that the national private banks were not eligible to participate, the collateral requirement was the project itself and was a maximum of 50 percent, the maximum loan amount was Rp 10 million, the maximum maturity was ten years for KIK and three years for KMKP, and no minimum equity contribution was required.

Despite the more liberal terms, the growth of KIK/KMKP loans did not meet the expectations of policymakers. More specific, policymakers had hoped that KIK/KMKP would greatly increase the number of small-scale manufacturing enterprises and boost labor absorption in rural areas. But, in fact, the proportion of loans to manufacturing fell between 1975 and 1979 from 21 percent to 12 percent for KIK and from 36 percent to 14 percent for KMKP (Table 3.4).

The slow growth of KIK/KMKP loans was due to the same reasons given for the slow growth of KIB credits to the private sector, that is, the lack of organizational capacity to assess loan applications, the high default rate within the targeted group (pribumi), a high collateral requirement, and the existence of more profitable lending alternatives. The response of the government was not to modify the existing investment credit programs to enhance their attractiveness to lenders and borrowers but to launch a new investment credit program in September

1979, Kredit Kelayakan, which had even lower collateral and capital requirements.

Given the official desire to accelerate industrialization in Indonesia, the bulk of all long-term credits to the manufacturing sector went to two state firms, namely, the perennial money-loser Krakatau Steel, which absorbed 52 percent of the credits, and Perumtel, the telecommunications company, which absorbed 13 percent. The 56 percent of KIB credits to manufacturing that had gone to public sector enterprises meant that SOEs received 79 percent of total long-term credits extended to the manufacturing sector. Hence, in the Indonesian case selective credit allocation to promote industrialization translated into SOE-based industrialization.

The BIMAS program, which was launched in 1965–1966, was the first large-scale credit program of the New Order government. The credits in this program sought to increase rice production by allowing farmers to buy high-yielding seeds, fertilizers, and pesticides. Over time, the BIMAS program broadened its coverage to other crops. The INMAS program, which started in 1969–1970, was meant to provide only extension services and to subsidize inputs. INMAS expanded in 1977–1978 to include credits for fertilizer purchases.

Bank Rakyat Indonesia (BRI), which was in charge of dispensing these credits, would lend to farmers at 12 percent and could rediscount the entire loan with Bank Indonesia at 3 percent. This generous interest rate differential was necessary to compensate BRI for establishing branch offices in every village unit cooperative (a KUD, which may consist of two or more villages) and to induce BRI to be aggressive in extending loans to what the government considered to be the highest-priority sector for economic development and political stability.[13] This rural banking system came to be known as the BRI Desa Unit (village unit) system.[14]

The concessionary nature of the BIMAS and INMAS credits is clearly seen by the real interest rates that were charged. For the food production programs, the real interest rate averaged − 5.5 percent from mid-1972 to the end of 1978, while the real interest rate for nonpriority borrowing averaged 5.3 percent. In fact, the credits extended to the food production sector were more than simply subsidized loans but were, in effect, grants, given their high default rates (Nasution 1983, table 4.6;

---

13. See Woo 1988 for a statement of the case that agrarian radicalism is one of the most important determinants of economic policy in Indonesia.

14. The BRI Desa Unit expanded the range of its credit programs over time. Kredit Mini was introduced in 1974 to finance nonagricultural activities, and Kredit Midi was introduced in 1980 to make larger nonagricultural loans.

World Bank 1982, tables 4.3 and 4.5). As one example, the 1980–1981 default rate on BIMAS loans was 60 percent for the rice program and 82 percent for the secondary crops program.

The operation of the BIMAS and INMAS programs actually promoted default. As reported by the World Bank (1982):

> The [BIMAS] program provides no *incentive* to repay because the repayment record of an individual farmer does not affect either the amount or the terms under which he can borrow. The only reward for repayment is that he can borrow the same amount again and at the same terms. . . . The readiness of the government to reschedule repayments or write off debts . . . has succeeded in giving the justifiable impression to farmers that sooner or later unrepaid loans will be granted a moratorium. This has been the foremost reason for the high rate of defaults. The approach of being conciliatory towards defaulters and the willingness to reschedule loans or give moratoria several times . . . results in the borrower treating the loans under the BIMAS program as government grants rather than as bank loans. . . . Moratory measures of one form or another have been announced for almost every year between 1970 and 1977. (Pp. 54–55)

The loan criteria of the KIK/KMKP loans were still too high for most SMEs to meet. This demand for credit and the tolerance of the Suharto government (unlike the Sukarno government) toward informal credit institutions have caused many such institutions to appear throughout the archipelago. The degree to which these informal credit transactions are integrated across maturities and regions is difficult to determine.

Survey evidence from Jogjakarta in Java by McLeod (1984) suggests that the cost of such informal credit is high. He reported that the interest rate for working capital in the late 1970s was 7.5 percent per month, which equals an annual interest rate of 138 percent: that is, the cost of informal credit was more than 110 percentage points higher than the interest rates charged by urban commercial banks. Nevertheless, McLeod suggested that informal credit allocation was efficient in the sense that the interest rate accurately reflected the risk characteristics of the borrower; specifically, that small firms' financing options steadily widened over time as they built up their assets and their reputation.

The interest rate premiums charged by the informal credit institutions could have stemmed from four factors: higher default costs as SMEs were inherently more risky than large enterprises; higher intermediation costs, that is, the cost of servicing many small loans was proportionally much higher than the cost of servicing one large loan; higher operating costs because the informal credit institutions were operationally less efficient; and the informal institutions had local monopoly power. We may conclude that the informal financial markets are efficient in the standard sense if the high interest rate premium reflected only the first two factors.

McLeod (1991) suggests that the second reason—the higher intermediation costs—was responsible for the high premium. According to him, assuming a standard wage for handling informal loans of Rp 250,000 per month, twenty-five working days in a month, eighty customers a day, and a loan size of Rp 50,000, then the cost of extending each loan was "nearly 8 percent per month . . . before making any allowance for the moneylender's own cost of funds" (p. 201).

McLeod's ingenious argument certainly represents an advance in the technical analysis of the efficiency debate, but his conclusion is highly sensitive to his assumption of a monthly wage of Rp 250,000. In fact, even if we assume that no income (value added) went to the owners of capital, GDP per worker in 1980 was only Rp 77,000 per month, and the agricultural value added per agricultural worker was only Rp 35,000. Thus, McLeod's wage rate for a rural worker appears to be too high for 1980.[15] If we assume instead a monthly wage of Rp 50,000, then the cost of each loan was only 0.05 percent per day, or 1.5 percent per month. And if we assume that the monthly wage was Rp 77,000 and that the number of customers was forty rather than eighty persons a day, the operating cost is only 4.7 percent a month. Thus, the rural moneylender could have afforded to pay his depositors an annual interest rate of 39 percent.

The Impact on the Banking Sector

Throughout the 1970s, the five state commercial banks and BAPINDO accounted for approximately 80 percent of the total assets, total deposits, and total loans of deposit money banks. These six banks also dwarfed their competitors in every category of credit. In December 1982, they supplied 72 percent of the working capital lent by the entire banking system, 95 percent of the investment capital, and 57 percent of the consumption loans.

The main reason for the strong position of the state banks was that they were the primary financial institutions used by the central bank to disburse credit to targeted groups. In addition to the profit margin guaranteed to SOBs for being the disbursement agents of central bank credit, the SOBs were designated as the only financial institutions with which state enterprises could deposit their working balances. The domi-

---

15. The Rp 250,000 monthly wage assumed in McLeod 1991, however, is quite close to the GDP per capita in 1990, which was Rp 232,000 per month.

nant position of the state banks was further entrenched by the policy favoring state banks in applications for establishing new branches.

It must be pointed out that if not for the incentives given to the SOBs to extend long-term loans, the amount of investment credits to the economy would have been much lower. Private national banks, which received very few liquidity credits, and foreign banks, which received no liquidity credit, had only 5 and 0.3 percent of their loan portfolios as investment credits, respectively. In contrast, investment credits accounted for 33 percent of the loan portfolios of the SOBs. Although the volume of long-term credits available is important for economic growth, also important is whether the bulk of these credits go to the industries with the highest rates of return. Data on the second issue are rather disheartening, indicating that most of the long-term credit went to shoring up the state steel company and other public enterprises.

To ensure the rapid growth of targeted activities, the government always set the lending rates of the state commercial banks well below those of the domestic private banks. For example, 93 percent of the credit extended by state commercial banks was at or below interest rates of 13.5 percent; in contrast, only 9 percent of domestic private bank credit and 3 percent of foreign bank credit was at or below the 13.5 percent lending rate. Moreover, only 0.5 percent of state bank loans was contracted at interest rates above 21 percent, whereas loans in excess of a 21 percent interest rate made up 79 percent of private domestic bank loans and 66 percent of foreign bank loans.

Not only were state bank loans extended at lower rates, but they were also deliberately extended to borrowers who would be deemed as being credit risks by normal appraisal procedures. The rationale for this policy was that the state "banks should be agents of development. What was meant was that sometimes these State banks, because of the role assigned by the Government and the expectations of the business community, had to be more pioneering than a normal bank would be: that they had to take more risks than a normal bank would be willing to take" (Saleh 1978, p. 18).

The combination of the four factors—that is, a guaranteed income to the state banks for their disbursement function, the imposition of entry barriers to protect the dominant position of the state banks, the subsidized interest loans, and the directive that normal risk appraisal procedures be waived—produced a situation where the state banks were not interested in engaging in any of the traditional banking activities, namely, mobilizing savings, making loans (as exemplified by the KIB and KIK/KMKP programs), and collecting repayments (as shown by the

BIMAS/INMAS programs). Such a situation is not surprising given that the chief shareholder was not placing any pressure on the management of the state banks to maximize profits. In this lax atmosphere of oil-generated wealth, the state banks, unlike the private banks, seldom used up all their prescribed ceilings.

One can speculate that the loan demand was actually high but that bad bank practices of the state banks made them unable or reluctant to reach out to small customers because this involved cumbersome operations and low profit per customer. It could also be that their inability to meet their prescribed ceilings reflected an inability of the state banks' officers to select projects that were both economically and politically acceptable. A third explanation is that the officers of state banks may have demanded too high side payments from prospective borrowers (to "divide the implicit rents" from the negative, zero, or low real interest rate). It has been suggested that the graft could be as high as 15 percent of the volume of the loan granted,[16] which would result in the real cost of interest rates from state banks becoming too high for prospective borrowers or competitive with interest rates at private banks. If the interest rate at state and private banks (onshore and offshore) were about equal, borrowers would have preferred to borrow from the latter to avoid long delays and harassment from state banks. All these factors could explain why the state banks seldom reached their permissible loan ceiling.

Despite the dominant and favored position of the state banks, they were not profitable operations because of mismanagement and high default rates. The World Bank (1981) has estimated that state banks had a zero rate of return to capital in 1976 (p. 97). Bank Bumi Daya, the primary bank for large estates, had to be bailed out by the government in 1977 after having suffered big losses since 1975. Several of the managing directors were later tried for corruption. It was reported that "at Bank Negara Indonesia 1946 . . . officials actually recorded unearned interest on bad loans in their profit and loss account and paid tax on it to the Government, an effective—if rather short-sighted—way of putting a good front on things" (Jenkins 1978, pp. 42–43). In addition, it is estimated that 30 percent of the outstanding loans at some state banks in 1978 were either overdue or uncollectible (Jenkins 1978).

In an attempt to increase the profitability of state commercial banks, the central bank in 1977 decreased the reserve requirement ratio from 30 percent to 15 percent. Based on the experiences of developed

16. The 15 percent figure is from Nasution 1983, p. 106. Jenkins (1978) reports a figure of 10 percent (p. 42).

countries, this measure would have worked if not for the fact that the domestic banking system was subject to credit ceilings. As it stood, the state banking system was already in a situation of chronic excess reserves, and the only additional income that the state banks received from this measure came from the interest earned by depositing part of the incremental excess reserves in offshore banks (and later from the interest that the central bank started paying in January 1978 on excess reserves to deter capital outflows).

The Impact on the Securities Markets

The Jakarta stock market, which was established in 1952 but closed in 1958 because of political and economic instabilities, was reopened in August 1977. The volume of trading activities was low until the 1988 financial deregulation. In September 1986, for example, only twenty-four equity stocks and three bonds were listed in the Jakarta stock exchange. Sixteen of the listed companies issuing equity were foreign companies, and eight were private domestic firms. The three bonds were issued by public enterprises.

Most of the listed shares were issued in the 1981–1984 period when many foreign companies had to go public to comply with the "Indonesianization" process that is required after operating for a certain period of time inside Indonesia. Because these foreign companies had access to international markets through their overseas networks, they did not really need to raise money in the small Indonesian capital market. Thus, "going public" for a foreign company was similar to paying an entrance fee to the Indonesian market. Another reason for the burst of equity issues during 1981–1984 was that the government gave generous tax concessions to companies for going public, ones so generous that they actually exceeded the value of the shares issued. (These tax concessions were rescinded very shortly thereafter.)

On the supply side, the availability of marketable securities was limited for many reasons. The government had never floated bonds in the domestic market because since 1968 its budget deficits had been financed by foreign aid and loans. Only 4 of the 220 SOEs had floated bonds in the Jakarta stock exchange, and none had issued equities. The capital needs of these public enterprises had been financed by direct government investment, foreign loans, and subsidized bank credit.

For the large domestic private companies, debt financing had been less expensive relative to the costs of raising and servicing equity because credit from state banks at subsidized interest rates was plentiful and could be easily rolled over for these big firms. In addition, during the 1970s it was not hard to tap foreign financial centers such as Singapore and Hong Kong. Moreover, in a country such as Indonesia, where the database on taxpayers was poor, the tax administration was inefficient, and the legal and accounting systems were underdeveloped, tax evasion was an important source of internal financing. For all these reasons, the costs of going public (that is, disclosure, regulation, tax liability, dividend payout, and dilution of ownership and control) were typically too high for private corporations.

On the demand side, the public was unfamiliar with the functions of the stock exchange and the benefits to be derived from it. Heavy-handed financial market intervention by PT Danareksa, a public company charged with the responsibilities of underwriting new issues and reducing stock market volatility, may have made investment in stocks unattractive. For example, PT Danareksa stabilized share prices within a narrow band with a maximum daily variation of 4 percent.

Finally, the existence of liquidity credits rendered the stock and bond markets unnecessary as firms that were large enough to be eligible for listing on the stock exchange had no need to be.

The Impact on Resource Allocation

We will consider two dimensions of the impact of the financial policies on resource allocation in the 1974–1982 period. The first is how financial policies allocated resources between the public and the private sectors, and the second is how they influenced the sectoral composition of GDP.

Despite the fact that SOEs received 54 percent of KIB investment credits and 79 percent of the long-term credits that went to the manufacturing sector and that the proportion of KIB credits going to SOEs has been growing over time, the public-private division of long-term credits may overstate the bias of the Indonesian banking sector toward financing SOE investment over private investment to the extent that the bulk of supposedly self-liquidating, short-term credits were automatically rolled over by the banks. That is, private firms could have spent a large proportion of their short-term credits on physical capital formation. The breakdown of total short-term and long-term credit between SOEs and private firms should therefore be used to corroborate or qualify the conclusions reached from the information on allocation of credits to SOEs.

The data in Table 3.5 confirm that the banking system has been channeling a large amount of resources to SOEs, but the data contradict the hypothesis that the proportion of credits going to SOEs has been growing. The proportion has, in fact, been falling, even before the 1983 financial market liberalization. In 1978, SOEs received slightly more

Table 3.5. Credit allocation to public and private enterprises (Rp billion)

	1978	1979	1980	1981	1982
Credit allocation					
Public enterprises	2,796	3,167	3,655	4,247	4,979
Private sector	2,604	3,159	4,339	6,095	8,312
Total domestic credit	5,400	6,326	7,994	10,342	13,291
Source of credit					
BI direct credits	1,958	2,188	2,483	2,692	2,853
BI liquidity credits	846	1,129	1,722	2,547	3,742
Banks' own resources	2,596	3,009	3,789	5,103	6,696
Credit allocation by source					
Bank lending to private sector	2,572	3,115	4,270	5,987	8,127
Bank lending to public enterprises	870	1,023	1,241	1,663	2,311
BI direct lending to private sector	32	44	69	108	185
BI direct lending to public enterprises	1,926	2,144	2,414	2,584	2,668
Allocation of liquidity credits					
Liquidity credits to private sector	540	645	1,043	1,394	2,284
Liquidity credits to public enterprises	306	484	679	1,153	1,458
Total BI credits to public enterprises (direct + liquidity)	2,232	2,628	3,093	3,737	4,126
Proportion of public enterprise credit coming from BI direct + liquidity (%)	80	83	85	88	83
Proportion of total credit coming from BI direct + liquidity (%)	52	52	53	51	50
Proportion of total credit going to public enterprises (%)	52	50	46	41	37

Sources: World Bank 1981, 1982, and 1983.

banking credits than did private firms, but by 1982, the amount received by the former was only 60 percent of the latter. In 1978, 52 percent of total banking credits went to SOEs; in 1982, this ratio had fallen to only 37 percent.

The fifteen–percentage point decline in the public sector's share of total banking credits occurred primarily because of the change in the composition of central bank credits away from directed credits toward liquidity credits and secondarily from the banks lending proportionally more of their own resources to the private sector. The former accounted for eleven percentage points of the decline, and the latter, four percentage points. The shift in the composition of central bank credits away from direct credits caused an increase in the private sector's share of banking credits because the banks normally disbursed 60 percent of the liquidity credits to the private sector, whereas the central bank disbursed less than 4 percent of the direct credits to the private sector. Note that the proportion of banking credits coming from Bank Indonesia varied very little during this period, holding steady at around 51 percent.

Any attempt to identify how credit allocation affects resource allocation is fraught with difficulties. A positive correlation between sectoral credit allocation and sectoral growth would be consistent with the hypothesis that financial policies determine the nature of economic growth. But this positive correlation cannot be regarded as conclusive evidence unless we can explicitly reject other competing explanations. Similarly, the absence of any correlation (or a negative correlation) between sectoral credit allocation and sectoral growth does not necessarily imply that financial policies do not have powerful effects on the sectoral composition of GNP. Besides the truly zero-effect possibility, the zero (or negative) correlation could have been produced by any one or a combination of the following:

(1) The invalidity of the ceteris paribus assumption. The effects of financial policies were offset (or more than offset) by policies implemented to achieve other goals. For example, large fertilizer subsidies and irrigation investments would greatly increase agricultural production even if there were no special agricultural credits.

(2) The fungibility of funds. The funds allocated to one sector were actually diverted by the borrower to finance its own activities in other sectors. It would not be irrational for an indigenous entrepreneur who has limited business experience to obtain a KIB loan at the subsidized rate and then redeposit the funds in a private bank to receive the market interest rate. Stories of such credit diversion were common in the 1974–1983 period.

(3) The dictates of technology. Some activities are more capital intensive than others. A sector with a low ratio of output to capital could receive many more investment credits than a sector with a high ratio, but its incremental output may still be smaller.

(4) The inflow of foreign capital. Because Indonesia has kept an open capital account since 1971, large enterprises could borrow from abroad without going through the foreign banks stationed in Indonesia and could invest in any sector that they perceived to be profitable. The fact that the domestic banking system allocated a small amount of credits to a particular sector does not indicate that massive capital investments were not occurring in that sector. The resulting output growth in that sector would thus appear "mysterious."

It is with the above considerations in mind that we attempt simple correlations between different measures of credit allocation and resource allocation.

Table 3.6 shows the sectoral allocation of banking credit and real GDP. The manufacturing, trade, and mining sectors received the bulk of

Table 3.6. Sectoral credit and output

	1973	1974	1975	1976	1977	1978	1979	1980	1981	1982	1983	Average
	Banking system credits by economic sector											
Rp billion												
Agriculture	87	116	220	266	270	345	438	526	813	1,025	1,226	
Mining	8	11	741	1,036	1,062	1,699	1,893	1,866	1,693	1,472	807	
Manufacturing	278	359	719	990	1,156	1,624	1,933	2,563	3,324	4,717	6,005	
Trade	428	627	766	858	911	1,114	1,338	1,977	3,062	4,129	5,132	
Services	79	122	172	260	319	389	422	573	675	1,046	1,425	
Other	180	338	132	156	218	223	244	375	592	633	704	
Total	1,060	1,573	2,750	3,566	3,937	5,394	6,269	7,880	10,159	13,022	15,299	
As percentage of total												
Agriculture	8.2	7.4	8.0	7.4	6.9	6.4	7.0	6.7	8.0	7.9	8.0	7.44
Mining	0.8	0.7	27.0	29.0	27.0	31.5	30.2	23.7	16.7	11.3	5.3	18.46
Manufacturing	26.2	22.8	26.1	27.8	29.4	30.1	30.8	32.5	32.7	36.2	39.3	30.36
Trade	40.4	39.9	27.9	24.1	23.1	20.6	21.3	25.1	30.1	31.7	33.5	28.89
Services	7.4	7.7	6.2	7.3	8.1	7.2	6.7	7.3	6.6	8.0	9.3	7.46
Other	16.9	21.5	4.8	4.4	5.5	4.1	3.9	4.8	5.8	4.9	4.6	7.39
Total	99.9	100.0	100.0	100.0	100.0	100.0	100.0	100.0	100.0	100.0	100.0	

Sectoral composition of real gross domestic product in 1973 prices

Rp billion												
Agriculture	2,710	2,811	2,811	2,944	2,981	3,135	3,256	3,425	3,594	3,670	3,846	
Mining	831	859	828	952	1,070	1,049	1,047	1,035	1,069	940	957	
Manufacturing	912	1,075	1,213	1,315	1,522	1,765	1,958	1,705	1,878	1,901	1,943	
Trade	1,118	1,224	1,294	1,351	1,438	1,530	1,681	1,852	2,043	2,159	2,240	
Services	634	683	723	791	929	1,033	1,112	1,900	2,037	2,164	2,281	
Other	548	617	763	805	942	1,056	1,111	1,308	1,435	1,492	1,577	
Gross domestic product	6,753	7,269	7,631	8,156	8,822	9,567	10,165	11,169	12,055	12,325	12,842	
Growth rate (%)												
Agriculture	9.3	3.7	0.0	4.7	1.3	5.1	3.9	5.2	4.9	2.1	4.8	4.10
Mining	23.3	3.4	−3.6	15.0	12.4	−2.0	−0.2	−1.2	3.3	−12.1	1.8	3.65
Manufacturing	16.0	17.9	12.8	8.4	15.7	16.0	11.0	na	10.2	1.2	2.2	11.13
Trade	8.8	9.5	5.7	4.4	6.5	6.4	9.9	10.2	10.3	5.7	3.8	7.36
Services	8.2	7.7	5.8	9.4	17.5	11.2	7.7	na	7.2	6.2	5.4	8.63
Other	6.6	12.6	23.6	5.5	17.1	12.0	5.3	17.7	9.7	4.0	5.7	10.89
Gross domestic product	11.3	7.6	5.0	6.9	8.9	7.7	6.3	9.9	7.9	2.2	4.2	7.08

Sources: World Bank 1983 and 1989.

Note: To be consistent with credit allocation categories, the following adjustments were made: pre-1980 construction data were put in manufacturing, and data for 1980 and beyond were put in services; and electricity, transport, and banking were combined with services. na = not available. See note 11.

Table 3.7. Impact of credit allocation on resource allocation

	1973	1974	1975	1976	1977	1978	1979	1980	1981	1982	1983	Average
Part A: Flow of real resources from bank credits, Rp billion in 1973 prices (change in nominal credit normalized by implicit sectoral deflator)												
Agriculture		23.6	72.9	27.7	2.3	34.6	32.3	25.7	75.3	51.7	43.7	39.0
Mining		0.9	243.5	95.7	7.7	156.9	29.5	(2.5)	(14.0)	(17.1)	(45.5)	45.5
Manufacturing		67.4	254.7	157.6	88.8	197.3	101.8	168.9	202.2	353.9	304.7	189.7
Trade		137.0	85.8	48.6	25.8	87.9	67.2	161.6	252.4	231.6	187.1	128.5
Services		29.6	29.7	46.4	30.4	23.7	9.4	52.1	31.6	97.7	83.5	43.4
Other		125.7	(140.0)	13.8	30.3	2.1	7.5	38.5	54.6	9.5	14.6	15.7
Total credit		348.4	710.9	430.3	172.7	575.1	255.1	388.1	499.2	595.1	418.3	439.3
Part B: Proportion of sector (% of GDP in current prices)												
Agriculture	40.1	32.7	31.7	31.1	31.0	28.0	26.9	25.2	24.9	25.4	25.3	29.3
Mining	12.3	22.2	19.7	18.9	18.9	17.6	19.7	24.1	24.0	20.5	20.0	19.8
Manufacturing	13.5	12.1	13.6	14.7	14.9	17.3	17.1	13.6	12.8	12.6	11.7	14.0
Trade	16.6	16.6	16.6	16.5	15.5	14.6	16.1	15.7	16.0	16.8	17.2	16.2
Services	9.4	9.2	9.6	9.8	9.4	12.4	11.4	11.8	11.9	13.9	14.8	11.2
Other	8.1	7.3	8.9	9.0	10.2	10.2	8.8	9.6	10.4	10.9	11.0	9.5
Gross domestic product	100.0	100.0	100.0	100.0	100.0	100.0	100.0	100.0	100.0	100.0	100.0	100.0

Part C: Proportion of sector (% of GDP in constant prices)

Agriculture	40.1	38.7	36.8	36.1	33.6	32.8	32.0	30.5	29.8	29.8	29.9	33.6
Mining	12.3	11.8	10.9	11.7	12.0	11.0	10.3	9.2	8.9	7.6	7.4	10.3
Manufacturing	13.5	14.8	15.9	16.1	17.1	18.4	19.3	15.2	15.6	15.4	15.1	16.0
Trade	16.6	16.8	17.0	16.6	16.2	16.0	16.5	16.5	16.9	17.5	17.4	16.7
Services	9.4	9.4	9.5	9.7	10.5	10.8	10.9	16.9	16.9	17.6	17.8	12.7
Other	8.1	8.5	10.0	9.9	10.6	11.0	10.9	11.6	11.9	12.1	12.3	10.6
Gross domestic product	100.0	100.0	100.0	100.0	100.0	100.0	100.0	100.0	100.0	100.0	100.0	100.0

Part D: Output-input ratios

	Change in real output between 1973 and 1983	Cumulated resource inflows from credit allocation, 1974–1983	Output-input ratio
Agriculture	1,135.6	389.8	2.9
Mining	125.5	455.2	0.3
Manufacturing[a]	1,292.5	1,897.3	0.7
Trade	1,122.2	1,284.9	0.9
Services[a]	832.2	434.2	1.9
Others	1,028.8	156.6	6.6
Total[b]	6,088.8	4,393.3	1.4

Sources: World Bank 1983 and 1989.

[a] Construction is excluded completely, so computed ratio understates true ratio because of inclusion of construction credits in the denominator.

[b] Total change in output includes change in construction output, which is 543.

credits, but only the growth rate of manufacturing was impressive.[17] Among the agriculture, services, and "other" sectors which each received about 7.5 percent of banking credits on average, the "other" sector grew the fastest. Seeking a correlation between sectoral credit allocation and sectoral growth rates may be an inappropriate way to test the hypothesis because the high growth rates of the services and "other" sectors may be due to the fact that they started from low bases.

Table 3.7 constructs different measures of both variables. In Part A the flow of real resources to each sector enabled by the flow of bank credits is calculated, and Parts B and C show how the sectoral composition changed over time. Part A shows that the manufacturing sector received most of the real resources. On an annual average basis, manufacturing received Rp 190 billion out of a total of Rp 439 billion, which is 50 percent higher than the next highest sector, four and a half times the amount allocated to the services sector, and twelve times the amount allocated to the "other" sector. But as shown in Part B, manufacturing's share of GDP in current prices actually fell slightly between 1974 and 1983 and in constant prices showed only a very modest increase. The next most favored sector, the trade sector, received Rp 129 billion of credits annually, and its share of GDP increased by only about one-half of a percentage point. Again, there is a zero correlation between credit allocation and resource allocation.

Part D of Table 3.7 shows the change in the output of each sector between 1973 and 1983, and the cumulated resource flow from the banking system to each sector in the 1974–1983 period. Note that the computed output-input ratios are not accurate indicators of either relative production efficiency or relative technological constraints because the influence of other variables on output are not controlled for. Thus, it may be incorrect to conclude from the low output-input ratios of manufacturing and trade that total output growth would have been greater if a greater proportion of banking credits had been allocated to the agricultural sector. At the end of this chapter I will argue that the zero correlation between credit allocation and output was caused by offsetting macroeconomic forces. That is, if the manufacturing sector had not been favored by credit allocation and trade protection, its output-input ratio would have been even lower.

17. Note that a "glitch" exists in the data. In the official sectoral credit data, credits to finance construction activities were included in the manufacturing sector figure until 1979; from 1980 on, they were included in the services sector figure. The result is that the 1980 growth rate was −12.9 percent for manufacturing and 70.8 percent for services. As these two strange 1980 growth rates are artificial, they were excluded from the table and from the calculations of the period average.

III. Financial Market Deregulation in the 1980s

The 1983 Financial Market Reforms

When oil prices began to fall in 1982, thus threatening a major balance-of-payments problem, the central bank sought in August 1982 to reduce domestic absorption by reducing the flow of liquidity credits to SOBs. This action decreased the profits of the state banks in two ways. First, because disbursement of targeted credit was guaranteed a profit margin and because liquidity credits accounted for 30 to 47 percent of SOB loans in the 1978–1982 period,[18] the reduction in liquidity credits resulted in a large income loss. Second, although deposit and lending rates of state banks were controlled, those of private banks were not. The liquidity squeeze that resulted from the reduced flow of liquidity credits led private banks to raise their deposit rates, which caused a big switch from state bank deposits to private bank deposits.

In March 1983, the government responded to the plight of the state banks by decontrolling the interest rates paid by state banks on deposits with less than a six-month maturity. But the financial problems of the state banking system were too great, and the government was faced with two options—either it could greatly subsidize the state banks or it could restructure the industry to make the state banks self-supporting, the latter of which was the only option the government could afford to pursue. Furthermore, the threat of a balance-of-payments crisis strongly suggested the need for a greater effort to mobilize savings, an activity that the SOBs had neglected.

The result was a sweeping financial reform package that was implemented in June 1983. Credit ceilings were abolished, deposit and lending rates were deregulated, and the number of programs eligible for direct central bank credits was cut. With the downsizing of the liquidity credit system and the reforms in the financial market, total excess reserves as a percentage of current rupiah liabilities declined from an average 18 percent in 1978–1982 to 10 percent in 1983–1986. At the same time, nominal interest rates increased significantly to raise the level of real interest rates substantially, a development that may have encouraged saving.[19]

The reduction in subsidized credit from Bank Indonesia necessitated

---

18. I do not find plausible the claim by the World Bank (1983) that "prior to the August 1982 regulation, less than 1 percent of state bank credit was not refinanced by liquidity credits" (p. 81).

19. The evidence on the response of savings to interest rate changes is mixed. See the review in Fry 1988.

that the BRI Desa Unit system transform itself from being a disbursement agent to a financial intermediary with a hard budget constraint. The subsidized credit programs were replaced by the KUPEDES (Kredit Unum Pedesaan; General Rural Credit) program, which carried interests that covered operating costs and default risks. The BRI Desa Unit system also sought to attract deposits by offering new services such as SIMPEDES (Simpanan Desa; village savings), which offered unlimited access to funds;[20] Deposito Berjangka (time deposits); and Giro (demand deposits).[21]

The macroeconomic financial reforms that were necessary for the central bank to exercise better control over the money supply came in February 1984. The central bank began weekly auctions of its own debt certificate, Sertifikat Bank Indonesia (SBI), and started a discount window to allow borrowing by financial institutions to tide over temporary reserve shortfalls. Access to the discount window was limited to 5 percent of deposits. The central bank subsequently ended interest payments on excess reserves to encourage the banks to use their excess reserves to buy SBIs.

These macroeconomic financial reforms, however, proved inadequate in allowing the central bank to control bank reserves. In September and October 1984, there were massive withdrawals of rupiah deposits from commercial banks on the expectation that there would be a devaluation to cope with the deteriorating balance-of-payments situation. The capital outflow was so large that the loss of reserves from the commercial banks exceeded the amount of credit that could be liquidated immediately. Because the amount of reserves required by the banks to meet the legal reserve requirement was greater than the legal limit on discount-window borrowing, the interbank interest rate soared.

When the interbank interest rate reached 80 percent (on an annual basis) on September 7, the central bank, fearing that too many firms would not be able to cope with the temporary high cost of working capital and hence be forced into bankruptcy, opened a special credit facility to pump reserves into the financial system. The interbank interest rate immediately stabilized and then fell to its prespeculation level.

The fact that a special credit facility had to be established in 1984 to increase the amount of reserves in the banking system was a clear indica-

20. Up to that point, the sole savings instrument offered by BRI Desa Unit was TABANAS (Tabungan Nasional; national savings), which allowed depositors only two withdrawals a month.
21. For a detailed history of the BRI Desa Unit system, see Patten and Rosengard 1990.

tion that the central bank did not have an institutionalized procedure to control the money supply quickly. The amount of SBIs outstanding was too small for reserves to increase significantly when the central bank redeemed the SBIs from the commercial banking sector. The October 1984 experience convinced the central bank that it should establish a money market facility whereby it could buy and sell commercial bills held by the commercial banks and thus directly control the amount of reserves. Hence a new money market instrument called SBPU (Surat Berharga Pasar Uang) was created in February 1985.

The SBPU is essentially a bankers' acceptance, that is, a liability of the financial institution that first endorsed them. Three types exist: promissory notes by eligible financial institutions, promissory notes issued by customers of eligible financial institutions when borrowing from them, and bills of exchange issued by third parties and endorsed by eligible financial institutions. The maturity of SBPUs was initially set to between one and three months but was later lengthened to six months. In reality, 98 percent of the SBPUs are in the form of promissory notes with maturity dates ranging from one to fourteen days.

The 1988–1990 Financial Reform Packages

Further financial reform packages were presented in October and December 1988 and in March 1989.[22] The common thread in these reform packages was the hope that increased competition would lead to greater efficiency. Entry of new private banks was permitted, the establishment of branches in other cities by domestic private and foreign banks was no longer subject to indefinite administrative delays, state enterprises could now put up to 50 percent of their deposits in private financial institutions, and nonbank financial institutions were allowed to issue certificates of deposit.

The task of savings mobilization and investment promotion was enhanced by making it easier for firms to be listed on the Jakarta Stock Exchange; stopping the heavy-handed interventions by PT Danareksa to stabilize share prices; establishing an over-the-counter equity market for small firms; simplifying entry requirements into insurance, brokerage, venture capital, and consumer finance activities; and granting the private sector the right to operate stock exchanges. The government also deepened the market for monetary instruments by increasing the maturities on these instruments and developing a secondary market for

---

22. For details of how the 1983–1989 financial reforms affected the banking system and the conduct of monetary policy, see Binhadi 1990 and Nasution 1990.

them. These last measures are necessary if market-oriented forms of monetary control are to be effective.

In January 1990, coverage of the liquidity credit system was decreased sharply, and the lending and rediscount rates were brought closer to market rates. Liquidity credits were made available only to farmers for working capital; cooperatives for food purchases; the national rice agency for stabilizing food prices; and development banks, nonbank financial institutions, and estates for investment credits. To ease the reduction of liquidity credits to small-scale enterprises, banks were commanded to direct 20 percent of their loan portfolio to small-scale enterprises.

The two most visible fruits of the deregulation packages are the expansion of the private banking sector and the heightened level of activity in the Jakarta stock market after 1987. The value of stocks traded in the last two months of 1988 was more than six times greater than that in 1981. The number of companies listed on the stock exchange jumped from 24 in 1987 to 132 in 1990, the value of shares listed increased from Rp 133 billion to Rp 8,034 billion, and the share price index soared from 83 to 418.[23]

The ineffectiveness of credit ceilings in containing inflation in a fixed exchange rate setting meant that prices of nontradables rose relative to the prices of tradables (where the latter is determined by the foreign prices of tradables, the exchange rate, and tariffs). Of the six sectors, services and "other" most closely fit the nontradables category, and agriculture and trade most closely fit the tradable category. Because of import bans on a significant number of manufactured goods, the manufacturing sector is considered to be only a "near-tradables" sector.[24]

The expectation from the macroeconomic side is that the services and "other" sectors would have expanded relatively quickly in the 1974–1978 period of high inflation and fixed exchange rates and relatively slowly in the 1979–1981 period following the 50 percent devaluation in November 1978, which reversed the decline in the tradables versus nontradables terms of trade.[25] The growth rate of the agricultural and

23. For details of the stock market growth, see Sjahrir and Naiborhu 1990 and Usman 1990.
24. In analytical terms, a tradable is converted into a nontradable once it is freed from international price competition, for example, after the imposition of an import quota.
25. I stop at 1981 because the 1982 global recession subjected Indonesia to large external shocks.

trade sectors would display the opposite pattern. On the basis of the sectoral allocation of credit, the microeconomic expectation is that the manufacturing and trade sectors would have registered the highest growth, and services and "other," the lowest. I found, however, that the ceteris paribus microeconomic expectation held only for the manufacturing sector. The overall correlation between sectoral credit allocation and sectoral output performance was zero.

I believe that the inability to find strong cross-sector (as opposed to within-sector) evidence of the selective credit policy is the result of resources in many sectors being pushed harder in the opposite direction by the credit ceiling policy. Proof that the resource allocation impact of the selective credit policy is smaller than that of the credit ceiling policy comes from the empirical studies of Pangestu (1988) and Woo (1992), which showed, through simulations of two independently estimated macroeconometric models, that Indonesia suffered a substantial bout of the Dutch disease in the 1974–1978 period.[26] The Pangestu and Woo findings are consistent with the emerging view that macroeconomic imbalances exert much more influence on resource allocation across sectors than do sector-specific policies.[27] The match between the actual time profiles of the growth rate of the services, "other," and trade sectors and the expected time profiles from macroeconomic considerations leaves no doubt that macroeconomic forces exerted strong pressures on resource allocation.

But there is a neglected beneficial outcome from the use of selective credit policy. Indonesia, by funneling most of the credits to the tradables and near-tradables sectors, softened the blow of the Dutch disease. The selective credit policy reduced the dynamic inefficiency by shrinking the amount of resources that had to move back and forth. More important, by helping to prevent many tradable industries from being bankrupted by the overvalued exchange rate in the 1974–1982 period, Indonesia was able to increase nonoil exports to earn additional foreign exchange to service its external debts when the price of oil plummeted in 1982.[28] The Latin American experience suggests that an external debt crisis would have resulted in protracted economic stagnation in Indonesia. The most important contribution of the selective credit policy to

26. Neither Pangestu (1988) nor Woo, Glassburner, and Nasution (1994), however, deny that the selective credit policy did affect the within-sector allocation of resources.
27. See, for example, Valdés 1986 and Krueger, Schiff, and Valdes 1988.
28. For a detailed analysis of why Indonesia did not experience an external debt crisis in the 1980s, see Woo and Nasution 1989 and Woo 1992.

Indonesia's economic development was (unfortunately) totally fortuitous. And there may be a second beneficial outcome. The selective
credit policy, by ameliorating the economic conditions in the tradables
sector, might have attenuated the sector's demand for tariff protection.
Under some circumstances, the protection of an industry by subsidizing
capital input is more efficient than protection by tariff.

On the issue of how the Indonesian experience relates to the traditional "financial repression" debate, we note that the spectacular success
produced by the special government-conglomerate relationship in Japan
and Korea has as its basis a well-trained bureaucracy and an excellent
statistical reporting system. Given the precipitous drop in the quality of
the civil service below the middle-ranking level and the paucity of economic data, Indonesia's selective credit policy did not (because it could
not) approximate the kind of "internal capital market" discussed by Lee
(1992). Another reason for why the selective credit policy did not mimic
an internal capital market is that the credit allocation process was not
sufficiently insulated from interest group pressures, as evidenced by the
broadening of the range of activities eligible for liquidity credits and by
the deepening of concessions associated with each credit program.

The financial instruments, SBIs and SBPUs, still do not provide sufficient control over the monetary aggregates, as their markets are still too
shallow, which is made clear by the way in which the money supply had
to be contracted in response to the speculative runs on the rupiah in
1987 and 1991. In the first case, capital flight began in earnest in the
second quarter of 1987 when a current account deficit that was higher
than had been expected was reported. In June 1987, the minister of
planning ordered the SOEs to withdraw Rp 1.3 trillion from SOBs and
place the funds in central bank securities. This action, together with the
sale of Rp 800 billion of open-market instruments to banks during the
month, sharply reduced bank liquidity and caused the interbank rate to
rise to 46 percent in early July. The liquidity shortage forced the banking
system to sell its foreign assets to meet its rupiah reserve requirements.
Other domestic corporations soon began repatriating capital to meet
their current operating needs. This severe credit squeeze succeeded in
convincing private agents that the government was prepared to adjust
other policies to ensure the viability of the existing exchange rate, and
the speculation against the rupiah came to an end.[29]

29. For an excellent discussion of the 1991 speculative attack on the exchange rate, see
Parker 1991. Note that the methods of ending the capital flights of September 1984 and
June 1987 could not have been more different. The former involved increasing the supply
of credit, whereas the latter involved decreasing the supply of credit. In Woo, Glassburner,

There is no doubt that open-market operations capability is sorely needed for better economic management. The market-based method of withdrawing funds is superior because it allows the government to have greater control over the final level of the interest rate. Bank Indonesia, for example, may not want the interest rate to exceed a particular value and as a result to threaten the stability of the banking system. With market-based, open-market operations, Bank Indonesia could ensure that the interest rate will be below the critical rate by trading SBIs. In contrast, the nonmarket method of ordering each state enterprise to withdraw a specific amount from the commercial banking system could lead to an interest rate either above or below the target level. The market-based method can guarantee that the interest rate will not over-shoot and inadvertently crash the stock market.

The cutback of liquidity credits has made the development of an efficient capital market a necessity. Private banks have never been impor-tant sources of long-term credit and are unlikely to become so in the near future. In fact, the immediate impact of the financial deregulation has been to reduce the amount of long-term credit. Banks are still unsure of how to deal with the resulting volatility of sources and costs of funds, and they have reacted by increasing the share of short-term assets in their portfolios.

Although serious imperfections in the Indonesian financial system still exist, it is important to acknowledge that the financial deregulation measures enacted since March 1983 have brought great and beneficial changes. The financial system is now much more competitive, more extensive in the range of services provided, and more creative in the development of new financial instruments. The large amount of financial deepening since 1983 is well captured by the behavior of the ratio of quasi money to GDP (an indicator of financial market sophisti-cation), which was 1.8 in 1969, 4.9 in 1972, 6.3 in 1982, and 23.2 in 1989. The seventeen–percentage point leap in the ratio of quasi money to GDP from 1982 to 1989 is unprecedented and indicative of the range and amount of new financial instruments that have been developed with the financial deregulation.

---

and Nasution (1994), I argued that both methods succeeded in ending the capital flight because the overall policy posture and market developments had convinced agents that the existing value of the exchange rate in each case was compatible with the balance-of-payments equilibrium. The current account deficit dropped from US $6.4 billion in 1983 to US $2.0 billion in 1984, US $4.1 billion in 1986, and US $2.3 billion in 1987. The inflation rate dropped from 12 percent in 1983 to 9.1 percent in 1984, 9.2 percent in 1986 and 1987, and 5.6 percent in 1988.

Table 3.8. BRI desa unit losses over time (Rp million)

Year	Income	Expenses	Profit (loss)	Total yearly administrative subsidy
1970	5	77	(72)	0
1975	4,720	6,717	(1,997)	1,126
1980	13,303	20,140	(6,837)	8,096
1981	22,822	33,114	(10,292)	7,068
1982	22,255	30,394	(8,139)	13,595
1983	21,069	33,719	(12,650)	21,980
1984	25,853	50,976	(25,123)	21,444
1985	72,565	73,501	(936)	1,243
1986	126,932	117,086	9,846	0
1987	177,873	155,394	22,479	0
1988	229,613	198,973	30,640	0
1989	330,629	293,715	36,914	0

Source: Adapted from Patten and Rosengard 1990.

The best example of the positive effects of the financial deregulation is the turnaround in the performance of the BRI Desa Unit system (Table 3.8). Unlike in the past when it required subsidies every year to cover its losses, the BRI Desa Unit has been a profitable enterprise since 1986.

It must be stressed that the removal of government regulations alone is not enough to bring vibrant financial markets into existence. In Indonesia, greater supervision of the activities of the financial institutions has been slow to follow the deregulation, thus rendering the financial system more susceptible to collapses. The foreign exchange market loss of US $420 million at Bank Duta in 1989 and 1990 through off-balance-sheet transactions[30] and the more recent collapses of Bank Umum Majapahit Jaya, Bank Sampurna, and Bank Summa[31] (because of excessive bad loans to companies affiliated with the bank owners) are warnings of what could go wrong during a period of transition when optimism prevails over caution.

30. For details of Bank Duta's loss, see *Asian Wall Street Journal Weekly,* October 8, 1990, and *Far Eastern Economic Review,* September 20, 1990.
31. The liquidation of Bank Summa in December 1992 is especially noteworthy because it resulted in the Suryadjaya family losing control of its flagship company, Astra International, which it founded thirty years ago and which is the largest listed company on the Jakarta Stock Exchange. See *Asian Wall Street Journal,* January 18, 1993.

References

Alam, S. M. 1989. *Governments and Markets in Economic Development Strategies: Lessons from Korea, Taiwan, and Japan.* New York: Praeger.

Bank Indonesia. Various years. *Indonesian Financial Statistics,* various issues. Jakarta: Bank Indonesia.

Binhadi. 1990. Banking and Monetary Policy in Indonesia. Mimeographed.

Cole, David C., and Betty Slade. 1990. Indonesia Financial Development. Harvard Institute for International Development Working Paper no. 336 (April).

Diaz-Alejandro, Carlos. 1985. Good-bye Financial Repression, Hello Financial Crash. *Journal of Development Economics* 19(1/2): 1–24.

Fry, Maxwell J. 1988. *Money, Interest, and Banking in Economic Development.* Baltimore: Johns Hopkins University Press.

Jenkins, David. 1978. Indonesia Adds Up after 10 Years of Bad Debts. *Far Eastern Economic Review,* August 18, pp. 42–43.

Krueger, Anne O., Maurice Schiff, and Alberto Valdes. 1988. Agricultural Incentives in Developing Countries: Measuring the Effect of Sectoral and Economywide Policies. *World Bank Economic Review* 2(3): 255–71.

Layman, Thomas. 1990. The Development of Indonesia's Financial Sector: Past, Present, and Future. Paper presented at the International Conference on the Economic Policy-Making Process in Indonesia, Bali, Indonesia, September 6–9.

Lee, Chung H. 1992. The Government, Financial System, and Large Private Enterprises in the Economic Development of South Korea. *World Development* 20(2): 187–97.

McKinnon, Ronald I. 1973. *Money and Capital in Economic Development.* Washington, D.C.: Brookings Institution.

McLeod, Ross. 1984. In Defense of the Capital Market: A Study of the Financing of Small Business in Indonesia. Working Paper no. 101, Working Papers in Economics and Econometrics, Australian National University (May).

——. 1991. Informal and Formal Sector Finance in Indonesia: The Financial Evolution of Small Business. *Savings and Development* 15(2): 187–209.

Nasution, Anwar. 1983. *Financial Institutions and Policies in Indonesia.* Singapore: Institute of Southeast Asian Studies.

——. 1989. The Role of the Financial Sector in Indonesia's Economic Development. Mimeographed.

——. 1990. Reform of the Banking Sector in Indonesia, 1983–1990. Paper presented at the International Conference on the Economic Policy-Making Process in Indonesia, Bali, Indonesia, September 6–9.

Odano, Sumimaru, Syahiril Sabirin, and Soedradjad Diwandono. 1988. Indonesian Financial Development: From Government Intervention to Liberalization. *Southeast Asian Studies* 25(4): 625–52.

Pangestu, Mari Elka. 1988. Adjustment Problems of a Small Oil-Exporting Country: Did Indonesia Suffer from the Dutch Disease? Paper presented at the East Asian Economic Association meeting, Kyoto, Japan, December.

Parker, Stephen. 1991. Survey of Recent Developments. *Bulletin of Indonesian Economic Studies* 27(1): 3–38.

Patten, Richard, and Jay Rosengard. 1990. Progress with Profits: The Development of Rural Banking in Indonesia. Paper written for Harvard Institute for International Development (April).

Saleh, Rachmat. 1978. Statement made in the *Far Eastern Economic Review*, August 18, p. 18.

Shaw, Edward S. 1973. *Financial Deepening in Economic Development.* New York: Oxford University Press.

Sjahrir, and Justarina Naiborhu. 1990. The Indonesian Capital Market from a Recent Phenomenon to a Permanent Future. Paper presented at the International Conference on the Economic Policy-Making Process in Indonesia, Bali, Indonesia, September 6–9.

Stiglitz, Joseph E. 1989. Markets, Market Failures, and Development. *American Economic Review* 79(2): 197–203.

Usman, Marzuki. 1990. Indonesian Capital Market: Lesson in How to Change a Dormant Market into an Active One. Paper presented at the International Conference on the Economic Policy-Making Process in Indonesia, Bali, Indonesia, September 6–9.

Valdés, Alberto. 1986. Impact of Trade and Macroeconomic Policies on Agricultural Growth: The South American Experience. In *Economic and Social Progress in Latin America, 1986 Report.* Washington, D.C.: Inter-American Development Bank.

Woo, Wing Thye. 1988. Devaluation and Domestic Politics in Developing Countries: Indonesia in 1978. *Journal of Public Policy* 8(3/4): 335–52.

———. 1992. The External Debt Situation in Indonesia: Performance and Prospects. *Asian Economic Journal* 6(2): 191–212.

Woo, Wing Thye, Bruce Glassburner, and Anwar Nasution. 1994. *Macroeconomic Crisis and Long-term Growth: The Case of Indonesia, 1965–1990.* Washington, D.C.: World Bank Press.

Woo, Wing Thye, and Anwar Nasution. 1989. Indonesian Economic Policies and Their Relation to External Debt Management. In *Developing Country Debt and Economic Performance*, bk. 1, vol. 3, ed. Jeffrey Sachs and Susan Collins. Chicago: University of Chicago Press.

World Bank (WB). 1981. Selected Issues of Industrial Development and Trade Strategy. In *Financial Policies for Industrial Development*, annex 4. Washington, D.C.: WB.

———. 1982. *Indonesia: Rural Credit Study.* Washington, D.C.: WB.

———. 1983. *Indonesia: Policies for Growth with Lower Oil Prices.* Washington, D.C.: WB.

———. 1989. *World Development Report, 1989.* New York: Oxford University Press.

CHAPTER FOUR

THAILAND

Robert J. Muscat

Thailand's financial policies and the role of Thai financial institutions in the country's economic development are interesting on at least two counts. First, although it did not match the growth performance of the economies of Asian newly industrializing countries (NICs), the Thai economy has grown faster and more consistently over the past three decades than most developing countries. Over the four-year period from 1987 through 1990 in particular, Thailand was among the fastest growing economies in the world and is regularly hailed in the financial press as the next "Asian Tiger." The Thai financial sector has grown faster than domestic output, with assets growing at a compound annual rate of nearly 20 percent over the period 1970–1988. The ratio of broad money to GDP rose from 23.0 percent in 1960 to 38.5 percent in 1981 and then shot up during the 1980s to reach 65.0 percent by 1989. At that time, only seven out of 68 low- and middle-income countries had broad money ratios that were higher than Thailand's (World Bank 1991). While the Thai financial system still lacks many of the instruments available in more mature economies, it has become relatively deep by the standards of the developing countries.

Second, the Thai government has been much less interventionist in the financial sector than has commonly been the case among the developing countries; this relatively noninterventionist orientation matches the broadly nondirigiste approach of Thai economic policy generally since about 1960. Thus, Thailand's experience is worth examining, in light of the country's strong growth record, as a case of financial policy where less is more.

I. The Structure of the Thai Financial System

Of the total assets of all formal financial institutions in Thailand at the end of 1988, about 59 percent was held by commercial banks; 6 percent, by the Government Savings Bank; and 10 percent, by finance companies. All other financial institutions (excluding the central bank) accounted for only 9 percent of total assets. The majority of these organizations were privately owned, holding about two-thirds of the system's total assets. Only 4.8 percent of the assets were earmarked, by the nature of the institution, for allocation to specified sectors of economic activity. The Industrial Finance Corporation of Thailand (IFCT), with 1.2 percent of the assets in the system, lends to the (broadly defined) industrial sector; with a 1.7 percent share, the Bank for Agriculture and Agricultural Cooperatives (BAAC) lends to farmers, as do the agricultural co-ops (0.7 percent); and the Government Housing Bank (1.0 percent) lends out funds for housing.

The financial system shows a high degree of concentration. Although the twenty-nine (fifteen Thai and fourteen foreign) private commercial banks held 48 percent of the total assets of the system, a share that has been rising over the years, the four largest banks alone held about two-thirds of all commercial bank assets and about the same share of the market (as measured by loans and advances). At the end of 1988, the fifteen Thai banks had 2,046 domestic branches throughout the country, whereas the fourteen foreign banks were limited to sixteen branches in Bangkok. The largest of the commercial banks, the Bangkok Bank, commands a 30 percent market share; the remaining three together command about 36 percent. The second-largest bank of the system, the Krung Thai Bank, is government-owned. The fourth-largest bank, the Siam Commercial Bank, is unusual in that the major shareholder is the Crown Property Bureau, a significant financial and real estate holding institution that in effect stands apart from both the public and the private sectors as an independent, technocratically managed investment fund (the bureau director formally reports to the minister of finance) that pursues developmental objectives while generating income allocated to the support of the royal establishment. The Thai Military Bank, the sixth largest in terms of assets, is normally classified as a private commercial bank; ownership is held by the Thai military, not the ministry of finance, and for most purposes, it is managed and operated as are other privately held commercial banks.

The finance and securities sector has developed only since the mid-1970s. Finance companies obtain funds through issuance of promissory notes and engage in a range of lending, mostly short-term and consumer-oriented lending. The *crédit foncier* (mortgage loan society) companies finance immovable property.

Only one institution, the Small Industries Finance Office, is dedicated to lending to small-scale, nonagricultural enterprises. The Government Savings Bank, which was established in 1946 and inherited postal savings set up in an earlier form in 1913, places most of its funds in government securities and is allowed by the Ministry of Finance to lend only a small fraction to state enterprises and private nonbank enterprises.[1]

The Securities Exchange of Thailand (SET) dates from 1974. Although the number of listed companies grew rapidly beginning in the late 1980s, as has the volume of trading (based to a considerable extent on foreign portfolio investment, both individual and in the form of mutual funds listed in New York, London, and other foreign markets), publicly issued equity still forms a relatively small source of financing for Thai companies. Thus, large companies tend to be highly leveraged, relying on internally generated funds and commercial bank credit. Medium-sized and small companies rely heavily on the informal credit market.

No money market exists in which commercial banks can obtain funds by issuing debt instruments. As a result, the banks depend primarily on depositors and their capital base as sources of loanable funds. The market for long-term debt securities in Thailand is very small, and the instruments consist almost entirely of government bonds, the holders of which are largely commercial banks.

The Informal Credit Market

Although the informal credit market is important in Thailand, it has not been the subject of much study and is inherently difficult to document and quantify. Traditional, rotating mini–credit clubs remain widespread. Seasonal credit extended within families and by merchants remains especially important in the small-scale and low-income farm sector that is not reached by BAAC credit. Evidence exists that small-scale enterprises also depend significantly on informal credit, but conventional wisdom about the informal credit market is not reliable. For example, it is commonly thought that high interest rates in the informal market (50 percent a year is often cited as the top rate) reflect a high risk

---

1. In 1989 the Government Savings Bank was forced to hold large amounts of cash; the government budget was in surplus, and the expanded revenues were used to retire government debt. Yet the Ministry of Finance denied authority for the bank to expand its nongovernmental lending.

of default and the difficulty of securing legal redress. On the other hand, it is known that much of the informal rural credit goes to better-off farmers, who are presumably lower-risk borrowers, and there is some evidence that default rates are, in fact, very low. Under these circumstances, there would appear to be substantial scope for intermediation between borrowers who are creditworthy for commercial banks and low-risk farm borrowers who are not creditworthy for the commercial banks but whose credit needs are also not met by the BAAC.

It is also commonly thought that the lending practices of commercial banks discriminate against small and medium-sized enterprises. This discrimination arises from the fact that commercial banks have not generally used the loan interest rate as an allocation device. Loan decisions are based on a judgment of the borrower's reliability and the amount and type of collateral offered. Variation in the degree of risk is reflected in the amount that the bank is willing to offer in relation to the value of the collateral. In provincial towns, the discrimination against SMEs is probably less than in Bangkok; bank branch managers in these relatively small communities are in a better position to develop personal knowledge about local entrepreneurs. Forced to rely heavily on the informal credit market, the SMEs are assumed to be facing interest rate costs that choke off some range of investment potential which would otherwise be feasible and economic, measured by both private and social returns, if such projects could have been financed at formal market rates. There are several problems with this hypothesis and no empirical evidence that such a range of frustrated investment actually exists. In any case, it can also be argued that the solution to this problem lies in reforms of financial policies to make them neutral with respect to the size of the enterprise, rather than with directed and institutionalized SME allocation programs. Now that the Bank of Thailand (BOT) is decontrolling loan rates, it should become evident whether its long-standing policy of maintaining a ceiling on loan rates has, in fact, been inhibiting the commercial banks from using interest rate variation as a means of extending more lending to Bangkok-based SMEs.

The Ownership and Control Relationship between Financial and Nonfinancial Institutions

Within the financial sector are interrelationships that cross between categories. Some of the leading nonbank finance companies are owned and controlled by commercial banks, which thereby enables the banks to have a financial interest in types of lending which are permitted to finance companies but denied to commercial banks under BOT regulations. In 1990, the BOT launched a broad liberalization program that is aimed at reducing the restrictions that have limited the activities of financial institutions to specified functions for each respective category. The commercial banks are in effect required to place substantial funds on deposit with the BAAC at below-market interest rates, but this involves no other legal or operational relationship. Krung Thai and three of the private commercial banks are minority shareholders in IFCT.

In Thailand the domestic banks are not owned by nonbank trading or industrial groups. In fact the reverse is true; most of the banks began as family-held financial institutions designed to mobilize funds for the nonbanking operations of these families. They have evolved, however, into financial flagships through which the controlling interests—now mainly in the banking business (or more accurate, the senior figures of these families are essentially bankers, whereas other members closely tied to the respective bank may be identified as essentially executives of nonbanking enterprises related to the flagship)—extend relationships of varying degrees of interest into the nonbank sector.

The number of major family-initiated banks is small. Although some generalizations can be made, the key cases must be understood as individual examples with unique business-family-corporate histories and evolution. In general, the family banks evolved as a business "culture" that operated with minimal public disclosure and occasional, even frequent, masking of financial and operating information from BOT inspection. In earlier years, especially through the 1950s, they were required to cope with anti-Sinic economic policies by forming "protective" relationships with leading military/political figures. Most of the banking families represent "new" money, that is, the banks have not emerged from families that were prominent or wealthy before World War II. The banks were formed during an era when the industrial sector in Thailand was still only nascent. Rice trading and alcoholic drinks were among the products in which the founding families dealt; in other words, no inherent industrial allocation pattern existed among these founders which had any lingering stamp on the development of Thai industry through the intermediation of the family banks. And in recent years, especially since the financial crisis in the mid-1980s, the Thai banks have become increasingly professional in their management, with declining family ownership shares and/or operational control, and have come under stricter BOT supervision and stronger legislation aimed at eliminating fraudulent practice, reducing family use of owned banks for insider financing, and putting the troubled banks back into sound financial condition. The Krung Thai Bank has also gone through a financial crisis, for different reasons, and has had to be guided back to financial strength under close BOT scrutiny.

The finance companies went into an even deeper crisis in the early 1980s, with a large number threatened by outright collapse. Lacking a deposit insurance system, the BOT had to take special measures to keep the finance companies in operation and to shore up the weaker banks. Many of the finance companies remain in difficulty.

II. The Nature of Financial Policy

The Thai financial authorities—the Ministry of Finance and the Bank of Thailand—have intervened in financial markets at various times for the following objectives:

(1) To sustain viability and restore financial health to individual or groups of financial institutions that have fallen into difficulties that thereby threaten the interests of depositors or may impose wider damage to the general confidence in the country's financial system

(2) To counter inflationary pressures using standard instruments of central bank intervention and to stimulate activity in periods of economic recession

(3) Occasionally, to require the extension of commercial bank credit to support specific, short-term commodity price-support schemes (the outstanding case involved sugar, the one agricultural commodity where producers (growers and millers) are well organized into pressure groups)

(4) To encourage or channel more credit to the agricultural sector or, in alternative formulations of this policy, to farmers, to small-scale rural industries, or to areas outside the Bangkok metropolis

(5) To reduce the extent of ownership concentration in the leading commercial banks

(6) To encourage exports through extension of concessionary interest rates on short-term trade financing

The BOT also manages the Exchange Equalization Fund to maintain orderly operation of the foreign exchange market and has occasionally employed other instruments to intervene against destabilizing capital movements.

It is important to recognize the strong element of continuity which exists between recent financial policy in Thailand and the financial policy tradition of the century preceding World War II. Following the reopening of the country in 1855 to trade with the West, pursuit of a conservative financial policy was viewed by the Siamese monarchs as an integral part of their overall strategy for sustaining national independence in the face of colonial encroachment. To avoid creating any justification for foreign intervention, the government emphasized financial stability and creditworthiness over investment and economic expansion as policy objectives. In effect, the country operated no independent monetary or demand management. A major implication of this policy was a complete absence of any attempt to use the financial system as a deliberate instrument for industrial promotion. These policies contributed to Siam's success as one of the few Third World countries to avoid being colonized.[2]

Technocratic influence over economic policy has been strong in the postwar period. Continuity with the conservative traditions of the past was reinforced by (1) the neoclassical, nonideological orientation these technocrats absorbed in their foreign university training mainly in the United Kingdom and the United States; (2) the realization by the technocrats that the post-1932, postmonarchical political system had not (by the 1950s and 1960s) developed to the point where military/political leadership could be relied on to pursue policies characterized by probity and economic restraint and rationality if the tight legal and technical reins of financial policy were released; (3) the experience of the war years and the economic dislocation of the immediate postwar period, in which inflation had introduced widespread corruption into the traditionally sober bureaucracy as well as extensive smuggling and other trade-related violations of the law; and (4) a traumatic financial experience in the mid-1950s in which an unsound venture into quasi-private industrial development involving government guarantees of foreign supplier credits to a poorly planned and managed conglomerate threatened Thailand's creditworthiness and mortgaged the development budget for several years.

Finally, in 1959, at the very beginning of the modern period of systematic planning and orientation of government toward economic development, the financial authorities were confronted with a manage-

2. Some historians have argued that the financial conservatism of the nineteenth and early twentieth centuries was motivated by monarchical self-interest. Most historical scholars agree that the reluctance to push economic development faster through more-aggressive external borrowing to finance infrastructure projects was a central aspect of Thai foreign policy, designed to ensure that foreign financial interests did not become too large and that the country would not be exposed to the risk of defaulting on external debt service and to the gunboat diplomacy that such exposure might entail. The history of Thai financial conservatism is explored by Brown (1988).

ment and solvency crisis of the private Agriculture Bank which focused their attention at once on institutional soundness as the key problem of the financial sector. The Ministry of Finance was forced to take over this bank, which subsequently became the Krung Thai Bank. Interventions by the BOT in three additional cases were necessary to pull the institutions out of insolvency crises through one solution or another (Asia Trust in 1984, First Bangkok City Bank in 1986, and Siam City Bank in 1987). Several other commercial banks suffered mild to severe deterioration in their financial condition and were helped (or are still being helped) to restoration through expansion of their capital base, subventions from BOT in the form of low-interest loans, and measures to strengthen management.

For many years, a substantial fraction of commercial bank credits has been extended in the form of overdrafts. The importance of overdrafts is that they introduce considerable uncertainty into the mere recording of sectoral allocation of commercial bank loans. They would therefore make it difficult for the financial authorities to monitor credit allocation at the sectoral level even if the authorities attempted to use credit allocation as a device for controlling the allocation of real resources. Besides the fact that many enterprises are units of conglomerates, it is generally believed that borrowers often deliberately misstate to their banks the intended use of loans. These difficulties in the way of an interventionist credit allocation policy are compounded by the relative disinterest and inexperience of the banking system in project-based loan analysis. For arm's-length lending, that is, outside the family management's own interests, most banks rely on collateral or personal guarantees of trusted individuals rather than on close analysis of intended uses. Practices appear to vary with respect to loans for family- and management-owned nonfinancial enterprise interests. In some banks, such loans have been subject to less scrutiny and lower collateral requirements than is normally applied to arm's-length borrowers. In other cases, management is said to select the best project opportunities, as revealed by professional loan analysts, for placing both loans and management's own participating interests.

Although the above describes the essential character of commercial bank lending in the past, as a result of the lessons learned during the banking crises of the 1980s and the resultant pressures from the BOT, bank management practices are undergoing a transition toward separation of ownership from management, dilution of family ownership through issuance of equity on the stock exchange, increasingly professional management, and changes in lending practice toward more attention to risk analysis. Nevertheless, as rapid economic development and change presented new perspectives and new policy challenges, the financial authorities (especially the more proactive among the personalities who at different times have occupied the positions of minister of finance and governor of the BOT) have introduced policies to influence credit allocation in the pursuit of specific economic and social objectives. These policies have not, in practice, represented substantial departures from the conservative, noninterventionist traditions of the past.

Interest Rate Policy and Credit Allocation

The only large-scale sectoral credit allocation policy in Thailand concerns agriculture. Beginning in 1975, commercial banks were required to extend credit to the agricultural sector in an amount equal to 5 percent of the previous year's lending. In 1976 the base for calculating the amount each bank had to lend to agriculture was changed to the total deposit liabilities outstanding at the end of the previous year, and the required percentage was raised to 7 percent. The allocation rate was gradually increased to 20 percent, which is the current level. From the very start of this system, the commercial banks found themselves unable to reach their targets, and the resulting shortfalls had to be deposited with the BAAC, where the commercial banks earned a lower return than they would have under alternative uses of their funds. In 1978 the mandated amount was divided into two categories: the larger one continuing as "agriculture" in general with individual farmers as the target, and the smaller one being a new category of agribusiness and agro-industries. The general agriculture category was further broadened in 1987 to encompass the "rural sector," including small-scale rural industries and individuals from rural areas who needed financing to cover the up-front costs of obtaining employment in the Middle East. Although the banks have been able to meet the agribusiness/agroindustry lending targets, they have continued to fall short even on the liberalized rural sector definition of the larger proportion target.

Whereas the BAAC is required to lend at (moderately) below-market interest rates, commercial banks are under no mandated interest rate policy with respect to loans to the agricultural or any other sector. Commercial bank lending rates have been constrained from time to time by ceiling rates set by the BOT, but within these ceilings, the banks set loan rates based on the individual borrower and the collateral, irrespective of sector. In a recent estimation of the interest subsidy created by the requirement that commercial banks deposit their shortfalls with

BAAC, the World Bank concluded that there has been a "relatively minor" interest rate distortion on mandated lending and that in terms of subsidy per agricultural borrower from BAAC, the amounts have been "small" (World Bank 1990, p. 130). In short, the interest subsidy, as a second instrument for promoting credit to the agricultural sector, has been a minor intervention.

To channel an increasing fraction of bank loans to the provinces, the BOT has linked permission to open new branches in the urban areas (mainly Bangkok) to the opening of new provincial branches—a policy that in effect discriminates against the smaller banks that have very few branches outside Bangkok. In addition, rural branches are required to lend 60 percent of the volume of locally derived deposits to borrowers in the same local area; a third of this 60 percent must be allocated to agriculture.

Insofar as agribusiness/agroindustries are concerned, it appears unlikely that this system has resulted in any additional credit allocation, because the targets have always been exceeded. But one may ask whether the impact of the mandated lending for general agriculture, especially the shortfall deposits with BAAC, has involved a significant market distortion through some denial of credit availability to competing nonagricultural investment demand. Several considerations would have to be taken into account. First, there have been recurrent periods of high commercial bank liquidity, with the inflow of funds into the banking system exceeding the ability of banks to place these funds in loans. Second, for a number of years prime industrial borrowers have had ready access to offshore loan sources when offshore terms were more favorable than those being offered by the domestic banks. It has been a common observation that, except for brief periods when the BOT has restrained credit expansion for short-run countercyclical reasons, Thai businesses have had easy access to funds if one takes into account equity, supplier credit, and other sources in addition to commercial bank loans. The large share of offshore funds available to Thai businesses also reflects the ability of Sino-Thai business families to tap funds from overseas Chinese communities in Southeast Asia, an ability not limited to prime-rate enterprises. Third, although the commercial banks have asserted that their agricultural lending is of low profitability,[3] the large-scale financial pressures on the banks in the mid-1980s were derived from nonperforming, not merely low-profit, loans in the commercial

3. For example, the president of Bangkok Bank has stated, "We have a very strong social commitment to Thailand . . . for example, our agricultural credit business represents 13 percent of total assets and yet brings in little or no return" (*Nation* 1986, p. 39).

and industrial sectors and foreign exchange losses resulting from devaluation. Thus, it is unlikely that the funds allocated to agricultural loans had a high opportunity cost.

Finally, there have been occasional ad hoc interventions, initiated within the Thai cabinet (quite apart from the BOT), in which suasion or political pressure has been applied on the commercial banks or selected larger banks to accommodate the financial needs of a specific policy or project. Participation in the short-term financing of the operations of the sugar price-support scheme was a major example in the agricultural sector.

In the industrial and commercial sectors, Thailand has been relatively free of project-level intervention through the financial system. Intervention has taken the common forms of import duties and controls and tax and other fiscal incentives for foreign or domestic projects in specified product or service lines. But intervention has not extended into matching potential investment projects in these "promoted" lines with credit allocation. There have been a few exceptions to this general policy orientation. In one of the most celebrated cases (in 1986–1987) involving a large fertilizer production proposal intended as one of the major industrial enterprises to be sited at the Eastern Seaboard complex, certain major banks refused to provide financing needed to float the project despite heavy pressure from some senior cabinet members. The fertilizer case was a salient example of the 1980s whereby, in the absence of legally mandated instruments, the increasing power of the private sector to resist pressure of an "informal" character was demonstrated.

As far as interest rates are concerned, it was only in the 1980s that the BOT liberalized and dismantled its long-standing policy of setting general ceilings on loan and deposit rates. Until then these ceilings imposed relatively moderate degrees of general financial repression in most years. Thanks to relatively low inflation rates, real deposit rates were, however, positive in the 1960s and early 1970s (between 0 and 5 percent) and substantially positive in the 1980s (between 2 and 13 percent). Moderate to substantial negative real deposit rates were experienced in the aftermath of the first oil shock (1973–1974) and in the inflationary late 1970s.

Bank of Thailand: Credit Allocation through Accommodation

In addition to its regulations requiring the commercial banks to allocate portions of their credits to specified sectors or classes of borrowers, the BOT has operated its own rediscount facility that, through criteria of selected eligibility, has served as a direct and fine-tuned instrument for channeling credit to specified classes of borrowers. Although the eligibility categories have overlapped,[4] the rediscount facility has been the only significant source of credit directed toward industry by the monetary authorities (apart from the specialized Industrial Development Finance Corporation of Thailand). The facility was set up in the late 1950s and for several years financed only rice exports. In the late 1960s, the BOT widened the agricultural export product coverage and added commercial papers connected with trade in industrial products to the list of eligible transactions. Some degree of fine-tuning was involved in these operations, as different levels of interest rate discount were offered for different commodities. For example, in regulations issued in 1969, "industries using raw materials of agricultural origin and those which promote agriculture are entitled to the highest benefit while industries using other types of raw materials receive fewer benefits according to their degree of importance. . . . The highest rediscount was that relating to the cement industry . . . followed by the weaving and spinning and the gunny bag industries" (BOT 1970, p. 60).

The rediscount facility has financed working capital and current transactions rather than fixed investment. As a result, the changing priorities by sector or product group, as reflected in the volume of paper rediscounted and in the BOT's stated intentions, have often reflected current market conditions and the BOT's objective of softening the impact of temporarily adverse circumstances. In 1974, because of the slowdown in the textile industry, the BOT offered to rediscount, for the first time, notes arising from payments for imported raw materials and chemicals by textile producers. Producers and traders of various commodities were accorded access to the rediscount window at various times when markets for these products were depressed. The eligibility for rediscount was gradually widened to include small-scale industries and employment-intensive enterprises. In 1984 the BOT began to use the phrase "priority sectors" to describe the categories of products and producers that would be eligible for the concessionary note rediscounting.

Given the variety and changing mix of eligible commercial paper, the distribution of the rediscounting has changed considerably over time. In the period 1964–1970, 36 percent of the value of total rediscounted notes was for agricultural exports, 40 percent was for notes arising from domestic sales of industrial goods, and only 7 percent was for industrial exports. Although the total volume of rediscounting rose over the years,

4. Because of this overlapping of categories, the same producers might have been eligible for accommodation under the "export" and "manufacturing" rubrics, which makes any precise analysis difficult.

the share for agricultural exports fell to 30 percent, that for industrial exports rose to 52 percent, and notes arising from domestic industrial sales virtually disappeared (TDRI 1986, p. 100). While it appears that these changes are consistent with the changing emphasis of development policy, the fit may not be as close as with the measures to promote agricultural credit allocation by the commercial banks, because the frequent fine-tuning of the discount window eligibility and terms (as described in the annual reports of the BOT) was commonly in direct response to short-term market conditions.

Within the separately defined industrial sector, rediscounting in the 1960s saw large shares allocated to the oil refineries, cement and concrete products, and textiles. In the 1970s, the largest shares went to textiles, nonmetallic mineral products, and iron and steel, with the share of the oil refineries reduced to zero. It is unclear, however, whether much meaning should be attached to these numbers, because the "industrial" sector remained relatively small as a recipient of rediscount accommodation, and the separation of "industrial" from "export" recipients is ambiguous.

Comparing the volume of these credits extended by the BOT with the volume of credit extended by commercial banks, one can see that the BOT's priority-sector promotion window provided marginal amounts of credit for industry directly (since 1984, less than 1 percent of commercial bank credit was for manufacturing). The ratio of the volume of BOT rediscounts for export paper to commercial bank export financing has been much larger, reaching as high as 58 percent in 1983, and, as indicated above, has included a significant portion of industrial products. Nevertheless, given the nature of these credits, it is unlikely that the BOT, through this instrument, had any significant effect, and perhaps no effect at all, on the investment decisions taken by the enterprises that subsequently became eligible for concessional rates on working capital. A typical description by the BOT of two of these credit interventions (in 1974) illustrates the point: "During this year, the textile industry was facing [*sic*] with the problems of overstocking and decreasing demand from both at home and abroad. The Bank of Thailand, therefore, granted financial assistance to manufacturers of textiles by rediscounting promissory notes against payments of raw materials and chemicals in stocks. . . . To make available supply of fertilizer at not too high a price, the Bank of Thailand . . . expanded the assistance by temporarily rediscounting promissory notes issued by fertilizer importing companies" (1974, p. 73). There is no case in which the BOT offered to extend rediscount facilities for specific products in advance of the initiation

of domestic production as an inducement to investment in their man-
ufacture.

Purposes and Limits of Credit Allocation

The various forms of public and private credit allocation described
earlier may be summarized in the following categories:

(1) Autonomous private, insider/owner credits, through which the
financial institution is used as a mobilizer of funds for investment in the
owners' own nonfinancial enterprises. Over the years, this allocation
channel has diminished in importance in most banks partly as a result
of regulation and moral suasion by the financial authorities who aim to
transform commercial bank lending in the direction of increasing
neutrality with respect to loan use (agriculture and exports excepted).

(2) Autonomous private, arm's-length credits that are neutral with respect
to end use (agriculture and export excepted) and are market-driven;
sectoral allocation is practiced only as a short-term bank policy.

(3) Directed commercial bank lending, under a combination of mildly
concessional interest rates and mandated sectoral allocation, which
appears to amount to a minor distortion in the allocation of credit in
favor of the agricultural sector, and even smaller discrimination in favor
of exports.

In short, the financial authorities—including most, but not all, minis-
ters of finance—have followed a credit allocation policy that has not
attempted in a major way to direct real allocation, especially within the
industrial sector, that would have been substantially inconsistent with
market forces or that would have introduced substantial inflexibilities
into the economy. This broad noninterventionist approach in the
financial sector has been consistent with the general policies applied in
other areas of economic policy—exchange rates, trade regime, public
sector investment, and incomes and wages—where Thailand has been
among the least intervening among the developing countries. A major
consideration in following a consistent set of policies—financially neutral policies that are consistent with neutral policies in other policy
areas—has been the relatively limited effort made by the Thai government in following the Japanese or Korean example in which the government selects areas for the creation of new comparative advantage and
induces private enterprises to venture into these areas through a variety
of incentives and pressures, including controls over the allocation of
finance. Apart from the agricultural allocation policies discussed earlier,
the one broad exception to nonintervention was the use of tariff in-

creases as import-substitution incentives for "promoted" investments, especially in the 1960s and 1970s. But these incentives were not limited to industry, were never carried to the extent of the Latin American or Indian experiences, and were not supported by a parallel financial allocation system.

Allocation policies aimed at the agricultural sector were initiated in the mid-1970s in response to the widespread perception in Thailand that rural populations were not benefiting equitably from the development process. Thus the allocation measures can be seen as a partial compensation for policies that discriminated against the rural areas. In this complex mix of moderately shaped interventions working in various conflicting directions, the industrial/urban sector is likely to have come out ahead in the balance of intervention effects, although this would not be easy to demonstrate.

Despite the combination of growing concern among the technocratic architects of economic policy over the balance between growth and equity objectives in Thai policy on the one hand and the turbulence of mid-1970s politics driven to some extent by disparities between urban and rural growth on the other, the priority accorded to distributional issues was diluted by the pressing need for economic policy to cope with the effects of the oil shocks and international stagflation. Thus the Fifth National Economic and Social Development Plan (1982–1986) contains both the strongest policy statements and program content with respect to poverty and economic concentration of any plans up to that time as well as a comprehensive policy orientation toward stabilization and structural adjustment. The macroeconomic concerns translated into an intense focus on the importance of efficiency in an open, export-oriented economy. The reexamination of many areas of policy in this context led to calls for reform of credit allocation policies that were now seen as sources of market inefficiencies. The most-extensive criticisms were contained in reports by the World Bank and by the Thailand Development Research Institute (TDRI), an independent think tank. Several reforms that were introduced by the BOT since mid-1990 toward liberalization of capital movements are being extended into the area of credit allocation. The financial authorities share the skepticism of the critics of the practical effectiveness of allocation policies and their efficiency impact on the financial system. The export-financing rate concessions have been cut back and are likely to be phased out; despite their minor effect on Thai export competitiveness, these subsidies have been attacked (for example, by U.S. tuna canners) as an unfair trade practice. Although the financial technocrats appear to have come around to the view that the commercial banks should not be forced to subsidize the rural areas, cutting back on the mandated allocations for agriculture which are designed to benefit "the farmer" would present the government with a more difficult and politically sensitive task. In practice, in recent years the commercial banks have not met their agricultural quotas. The BOT has looked the other way, and it is believed that the banks have been submitting inflated reports on their quota adherence.

III. Credit Allocation and Real Investment

Sizable differences between agricultural and nonagricultural commercial bank credit allocation in relation to sectoral contribution to GDP remained as of 1988, although the gap had narrowed considerably. This narrowing in the gap presumably reflects the impact of BOT policies, some substitution of formal for informal credit in rural areas, and the increasing importance of commercial agriculture, especially the production and processing of agriculture-based export products. In 1981 the ratio of bank loans to value added in agriculture was 9.8 percent, and in mining and manufacturing it was 31.5 percent. In 1988 the ratios had increased to 23.1 percent and 56.8 percent, respectively.

The financial authorities limit their monitoring of commercial bank credit allocation to the banks' performance with respect to the mandated allocations; performance of provincial branches with respect to percentage of credit extended locally within the branch area; and loan portfolio weight in sectors where, as a result of heavy investment, banks need to be restrained from increasing their exposure to nonperforming credits.[5] Because no global targets exist for the distribution of investment within industry as a whole, the question of correspondence between credit distribution and real investment does not arise as a matter of policy.

As the World Bank (1990) concluded in its financial sector study:

> The choice of industrial sector companies in Thailand in need of borrowed capital is essentially limited to the banking segment. The suitability and availability of a given type of loan in any individual case depends, in practice, on the amount required, the size and creditworthiness of the borrower, the purpose for which the funds are required, and whether the borrower is a

---

5. Of course, the BOT regularly monitors loan portfolios to ensure compliance with the full range of statutory safeguards aimed at sustaining the soundness of the financial institutions.

public sector agency or is in the private sector. As a generalization, there is no shortage of funds and no constraint on lending or borrowing, other than that which is dictated by prudential considerations. (P. 106)

The same conclusion regarding the considerations determining allocation—that each loan is determined by the lending institution, based on the merits of the case rather than on sectoral allocation criteria—also applies to the one institution dedicated to industrial lending, the IFCT. This institution is the only one in Thailand providing long-term investment capital credits. The IFCT lends mainly to companies not associated with family-group enterprises related to individual commercial banks. Although it benefits from special legislated relationships with the government and includes the Ministry of Finance and the Krung Thai Bank among its shareholders, along with private banks and publicly held equity, the IFCT is managed like a private institution and has developed a reputation for professional excellence. Except for lending to small-scale enterprises (a low-return or loss-making window), which has been undertaken for social rather than businesslike criteria, the IFCT has provided loan capital to manufacturing enterprises based on considerations of rate of return rather than subsector or product preference. Although the IFCT plays an important role in its market niche, its relative size in the Thai financial system, while growing over the years, remains small.

Finally, mention should be made of the schemes that have been established to channel funds to SMEs. Small (ten to forty-nine workers) and medium-sized (fifty to two hundred workers) enterprises are significant in Thailand's manufacturing sector. In 1979, the only year for which such data are available, SMEs appeared to account for 48 percent of manufacturing value added. It was estimated that in 1984, enterprises employing under two hundred workers accounted for about 60 percent of total manufacturing sector employment (World Bank 1989, pp. 78–79). Since the early 1970s, the government has been promoting special credit programs for SMEs, arguing that credit market imperfections and other institutional weaknesses put SMEs at a competitive disadvantage that should be offset through public policy. The first scheme was the Small Industries Finance Office, an operation that extended very small volumes of credit; but this office fell into serious problems of arrearage. In the 1980s, three new schemes were set up, including the BOT rediscount window, IFCT windows, and the Small Industry Credit Guarantee Fund, which is managed by the IFCT. The funds and guarantees extended by these programs have grown rapidly in the past few years but still amount to only a very small fraction of total financial system credit for the industry.

To develop at least a partial picture of the role of financial resource allocation, I summarize some of the pertinent data in Tables 4.1–4.3. Table 4.1 shows the sources of funds flowing into the private, non-financial "business" sector over the period 1970–1983. Table 4.2 gives the distribution of commercial bank credit for selected years in the period 1970–1990. And Table 4.3 provides a better, but still inadequate, approximation of the institutional credit allocated to the agricultural and manufacturing sectors in selected years between 1970 and 1988 by the major institutional sources: the commercial banks, the BOT, the BAAC, the IFCT, and the finance companies.

Any analyst searching for relationships between recorded credit allocations and the structure or changes in the real Thai economy faces several hazards that could produce meaningless, if not misleading, associations. First, in the past, short-term accommodation extended by the BOT to producers/traders of individual commodities experiencing unexpected price weakness or inventory accumulation typically lasted for a few weeks or months. Such accommodations may or may not show up in series data based on year-end to year-end comparisons. The information published by the BOT in the 1970s shows that the credits outstanding at the end of the year were typically small compared with the year's total flow. The BOT discontinued publishing these data in the 1980s. More significant, the bulk of BOT accommodation has consisted of export paper rediscounting: although it might be possible to allocate these credits by productive sector in some years, a comparable disaggregation of the sizable commercial bank export/import credits is not possible.

Second, informants in the BOT and the commercial banks uniformly describe the sector allocation reports of the latter as unreliable. Little lending is on an identifiable project basis, and no system exists for monitoring the actual use of funds. The general view is that the divergence between reported credit allocation and the actual allocation by borrowers is substantial. Third, commercial bank credits have made up only a fraction, often well under one-half, of total private business absorption of funds, as can be seen from Table 4.1. The frequent and wide year-to-year fluctuations in the relative shares of domestic and foreign funds inflows and in the share of the domestic banking system have resulted from such factors as shifts in investor confidence, waves of foreign investment which reflect regional shifts in industrial location, swings in the liquidity of the banking system and in central bank

Table 4.1. Sources of private (nonfinancial) "business" fund inflows, 1970–1983 (by percentage)

Year	Selected instruments				Selected funding sources			
	Loans	Commercial bills	Share capital	Foreign claims	Households	Commercial banks	Finance companies	Rest of the world
1970	33	15	38	27	38	42	na	27
1971	11	20	55	51	56	14	na	51
1972	6	19	45	40	44	12	na	40
1973	32	37	46	4	45	60	na	4
1974	30	19	28	28	28	44	na	28
1975	26	21	13	41	12	49	na	41
1976	37	20	24	33	23	42	na	33
1977	24	29	22	44	22	61	−19	44
1978	64	21	24	−3	22	51	28	−3
1979	37	19	32	26	32	48	3	26
1980	38	14	6	51	7	22	9	51
1981	31	27	6	34	−3	36	14	34
1982	31	31	19	35	12	35	15	35
1983	32	31	17	25	12	52	7	25

Source: Thailand Development Research Institute 1986, p. 91.
Note: The sum of percentage shares may exceed 100 percent because the values of some omitted instruments and sectors are negative, for example, are net fund outflows. na = not available.

Table 4.2. Distribution of commercial bank credit (by percentage)

	1970	1975	1980	1985	1986	1987	1988	1989	1990
Agriculture	2.1	3.4	5.6	7.4	7.3	6.7	6.6	6.5	6.7
Manufacturing	15.3	19.9	18.4	23.2	22.8	23.6	25.9	25.8	25.1
Exports and imports	31.4	27.4	24.3	15.0	15.1	14.6	13.7	12.6	10.7
Wholesale and retail	21.4	19.5	22.0	23.1	23.3	20.4	19.0	17.7	17.6
Personal consumption	7.8	8.6	7.4	8.6	8.8	9.5	10.4	10.8	10.6
Other	22.0	21.3	22.3	22.7	22.4	25.2	24.4	26.6	29.0
Total	100.0	100.1	100.0	100.0	99.7	100.0	100.0	100.0	99.7

Source: Bank of Thailand statistics.

Table 4.3. Sectoral distribution of institutional credit (billions of baht)

	1970	1975	1980	1985	1988
Agriculture					
Commercial banks	0.6	2.8	12.6	39.4	57.2
BAAC	1.2	4.6	12.5	21.6	26.4
BOT	na	na	na	0.2	1.1
Finance companies	—	—	0.6	1.0	1.3
Total	1.8	7.4	25.7	62.2	86.0
Manufacturing					
Commercial banks	4.3	16.5	41.2	122.6	223.9
BOT	na	na	na	0.4	0.4
Finance companies	—	—	14.1	23.5	33.6
IFCT	0.4	1.3	3.3	6.9	7.1
Total	4.7	17.8	58.6	153.4	265.0
Total: agriculture, manufacturing, and other sectors					
Commercial banks	28.1	83.0	224.3	528.6	860.2
BAAC	1.2	4.6	12.5	21.6	26.4
BOT	—	—	—	0.6	1.5
Finance companies	—	—	14.7	24.5	34.9
IFCT	0.4	1.3	3.3	6.9	7.1
Total	29.7	88.9	254.8	582.2	930.1
Agriculture/manufacturing credit ratios	0.38	0.42	0.44	0.41	0.32
Agriculture/manufacturing value-added ratios	1.63	1.44	1.09	0.76	0.67

Source: Bank of Thailand statistics.
Note: na = not available. — = zero or near zero.

monetary measures, and movements of private funds in response to interest rate differentials or expectations regarding possible changes in the exchange rate. In the 1980s, debt-equity ratios in Thai industry declined as firms adjusted to the cash flow pressures of the early 1980s by retaining profits and issuing shares. Thus the levels and sectoral pattern of fund usage by the private sector have resulted from an interaction of many market forces and investment decisions, many of which would have been independent of a (nonagricultural) credit allocation system if such a system had existed. Another important caveat regarding the flow-of-funds data in Table 4.1 is that these accounts do not capture the financial activity of small-scale unincorporated businesses, which is large in Thailand and is generally underrecorded in all financial and nonfinancial data series.

Fourth, the credit data in Tables 4.2 and 4.3 are recorded by "sector" categories that are not the same as the sectors defined in the national accounts. The reporting system of the commercial banks allocates credit between production sectors (agriculture and so forth) and expenditure categories (for example, consumption), thereby straddling the standard industrial origin and expenditure framework of GDP accounting in a way that does not permit a consistent comparison between the distribution of credit and the distribution of real resources or value added. Fifth, the emergence and rapid growth of finance companies in the late 1970s—note their importance from 1980 on in Table 4.3—adds another ambiguity. The early growth of the finance companies relied on credits from affiliated commercial banks. Since the finance companies were unregulated, these credits in effect enabled the commercial banks to place some funds in a manner that circumvented BOT interest rate ceilings. To the (undetermined) extent that such credits were allocated to industry and agriculture, the sectoral allocations of the commercial banks in Table 4.3 are understatements.

Finally, the causal direction and possible allocative impact between commercial bank allocative preferences and actual sectoral distribution of credit would remain ambiguous as long as banking data are not broken down between short-, medium-, and long-term credit. Short-term credits for working capital and transactions balances are presumably mainly responsive to borrowers' demands, having relatively little impact on the composition of investment compared with medium- and long-term loans. In the Thai case, it would be difficult to pursue this distinction because much de facto term financing has long been carried on the books as short-term rollovers.

The more than doubling of the share of commercial bank credit going to agriculture (Table 4.2) in the period 1975–1985 understates the volume of commercial resources allocated to agriculture as a result of the BOT targets because these accounts do not include the banks' deposits with the BAAC. When BAAC lending is considered, the ratio of agricultural to manufacturing credit rises between 1970 and 1980 from 0.38 to 0.44. During this same decade, a major structural shift took place in which manufacturing value added was rising in relative importance while the value added of the agricultural sector was in relative, but not absolute, decline. Although all sectors were experiencing increases in the ratios of credit to value added, these increases do not correlate with the increases in sectoral value added, the agriculture-manufacturing relationship being a major case in point.

Over the entire period since 1960, only during 1975–1980 did Thai government policies generally move in the direction of increasing market intervention to affect the allocation of resources and of private investment and financial intermediation. As I have indicated, the largest single intervention was to raise the proportion of commercial bank lending to agriculture and then more broadly to "provincial" economic activity not confined to any economic sector as normally defined and measured. The scope for financial repression, for management of interest rate policies that would discriminate among users or broadly subsidize one or more sectors, at the implicit cost of suppressed returns to savers or to financial intermediaries, was limited over this entire time by the overriding policy objective of the monetary authorities to maintain a stable and virtually freely convertible currency. This objective required the maintenance of a relatively high level of foreign exchange reserves. In a regime of convertibility, a large gap between international and repressed domestic interest rates would create a strong incentive for outflows of funds, reducing both international reserves and domestic investment resource availabilities. As Hanson and Neal (1985) noted in a comparative study of ten less developed coontries: "While the Thai financial sector could be counted among the developing world's most market-oriented, and certainly among the most open, the authorities maintained important institutional controls. However, the distortions created by these controls were limited by the overriding objective of maintaining a convertible currency and an open economy" (p. 136).

IV. Toward Further Liberalization

Until the late 1980s, the Thai central bank's principal policy concerns (apart from short-run monetary and exchange rate management) were the stability and solvency of the financial institutions and the use of credit instruments to promote agriculture and exports. From time to time, the BOT has found itself in the position of promoting competition and deconcentration among the commercial banks while simultaneously maintaining policies that reduce competition for the sake of supporting solvency of the weaker banks. Banking legislation in 1979 and passages from the Fifth Plan which were referred to earlier called for deconcentration of bank ownership through dispersal of equity. On the other hand, it has long been BOT policy to promote commercial bank cooperation on interest rates (in effect, a cartel); the BOT feared that price competition for depositors would drive up deposit rates and threaten the solvency of the smaller banks. In addition, existing banks have been protected from competition from new entry for over twenty-five years, with the financial authorities refusing to issue new licenses for either additional domestic or foreign banks.

Standard measures show that concentration in the commercial banking sector is relatively high in Thailand. The concentration is especially conspicuous because the top banks also serve as flagships for family-controlled groups of financial and nonfinancial enterprises. The legislation aimed at forcing dilution of ownership has proved inadequate partly for technical reasons, while the political impetus has greatly diminished since the policy focus of the financial authorities was diverted in the early 1980s from concentration to the problem of financial system solvency and management practices. Concentration among the top commercial banks has been a recurrent target among populist-minded army officers and may well resurface as a political issue in the future.

Notwithstanding the conclusion of most analyses of the operations of the Thai financial sector that there is in fact a substantial degree of competition despite the restrictive features I have discussed, there is no doubt that the efficiency of the system and Bangkok's competitiveness as a future financial center in Southeast Asia would be enhanced if new entry were permitted, if the money market were further developed, and if the existing competitive restraints and institutional segmentation were liberalized. Under the administration of Prime Minister Prem in the 1980s, opinion among Thai economists and in the policy-planning agencies began to swing generally toward liberalization of the financial system along these lines. Even as the BOT was raising agriculture's target percentage, a reaction was setting in against central bank credit allocation either directly or through suasion with the private financial institutions. Within the agriculture allocation sector, the BAAC was moving toward wider interpretation of credit eligibility. Noting that average farm households were revealed by household surveys to be deriving half their income from off-farm activities and that BAAC credit was consequently cut off from half the income-generating activity of its clients, the agriculture bank argued that its loan criteria should be liberalized to include farm household economic activity, whether that activity was agricultural or not.

The central bank's liberalization program unveiled in 1989–1990 moved away from segmentation of the credit market and toward elimination of the moderate financial repression that has characterized the system. Foreign exchange transactions on current account would be freed of most reporting requirements and prior authorizations in a program of gradual dismantling. The flow of foreign funds for capital movements would be freed of all restrictions; some loose controls over capital movements by Thai residents would be retained. Interest rates on deposits were allowed to float freely; loan rate ceilings, which were usually above market rates, would also be gradually eliminated.

The reform program also envisages relaxation on new entry, although this remains a political decision beyond the authority of the BOT alone. Domestic banks have been allowed to open new branches more freely since 1989. New entry of foreign banks might have been achieved that year if the issue had not been clouded by allegations of corruption.[6]

Finally, the liberalization program calls for permitting the banks to engage in a wider range of financial services, thus breaking down the regulatory barriers that had created functional segmentation of the financial institutions. Although all these changes were intended to increase the efficiency of the system and ensure that the Thai system did not fall behind international practice and other regional centers, the liberalization program has been introduced with typical Thai gradualism. The gradual pace was chosen to give the financial institutions time to adjust to a more competitive environment and the BOT time to ensure that its essential prudential responsibilities were not being compromised.

In summary, sectoral credit allocation, significant only for the agricultural sector and of marginal application to industry and other nonagricultural activities, is headed toward greater marginality as an instrument of financial policy. The movement toward further liberalization, interest rate decontrol, and the breakdown of institutional segmentation implies the elimination of the policies that could support fine-tuned sectoral interventions. Whether this evolution of Thailand's broadly noninterventionist orientation is sustained over the long run depends on the development of the country's political system, more problematical than would be the course of economic policy if left relatively technocratic and pragmatic in its adjustments to changing external economic conditions.

I conclude with a few observations with respect to the assertion that the banking system is competitive despite its apparent concentration. The commercial banks have been organized as a cartel for most of the postwar period. The cartel was arranged deliberately by the BOT as a

---

6. The cabinet rejected a proposed granting of licenses to fifteen new foreign banks, fearing intense public pressure against the government as it became widely assumed that the banks in question had been required to make large under-the-table payments.

device to avoid price competition for depositor accounts. Such accounts have been the main source of loanable funds for the banks (in addition to their capital base) because of the absence of a money market in which they could issue debt instruments. The reliance on deposits has led to intense competition for individual and corporate depositors. The central bank long expected that if the search for depositors took the form of competitive increases in deposit rates, the financial condition of the smaller banks in particular would be undermined. Thus in the interests of system stability and maintenance of competitive alternatives to the concentration in the leading banks, the BOT encouraged the Thai Bankers' Association (TBA) to avoid interest rate competition. In this framework of officially sanctioned coordination, the commercial banks have also colluded on service fees and other rates, practices opposed by the BOT. In more recent years, as the central bank has moved to a policy of encouraging greater competition in the financial system, the commercial banks, still focusing on their need to maintain their shares in the depositor market, have continued to be relatively inflexible with respect to making changes in interest rates on either deposits or loans.

Despite these elements of oligopoly, the financial system has been fairly competitive in practice. The cartel has been a loose one; the banks have regularly been unable to agree among themselves over uniform rate changes in response to changes in system liquidity and have had to send the TBA to the central bank to obtain needed movements by imposition. The competition for depositors' funds has been reflected in the spread of bank branches throughout the country. Bank staff salaries have jumped in the past few years partly as a result of interbank personnel "raiding." Individual banks often compete over major projects through their association with, or financial backing of, the rival (nonfinancial) client corporations involved.

A major World Bank study (1990) of the Thai financial sector concluded that the system was relatively efficient and competitive despite its oligarchic characteristics: "Compared to banks in some other countries for which comparable and recent data were available (Indonesia, Morocco, Pakistan, the Philippines, and Turkey), Thai banks are quite efficient and operate on narrower margins" (p. iv). While noting that the lead banks do not hesitate to exercise their visible "social and political power," the study concludes that there is "little firm evidence to substantiate monopolistic abuses," which are generally "believed" to be present because of the sheer size of the top banks relative to the total financial sector.

References

Bank of Thailand (BOT). 1970. *Annual Economic Report, 1970.* Bangkok: BOT.
——. 1974. *Annual Economic Report, 1974.* Bangkok: BOT.
Brown, Ian. 1988. *The Elite and the Economy in Siam, 1890–1920.* New York: Oxford University Press.
Hanson, James A., and Craig R. Neal. 1985. Interest Rate Policies in Selected Developing Countries, 1970–1982. World Bank Staff Working Paper no. 753. Washington, D.C.: World Bank.
Nation. 1986. New Era of Professional Banking (May), p. 39.
Thailand Development Research Institute (TDRI). 1986. *Financial Resources Management.* Bangkok: TDRI.
World Bank (WB). 1989. *Country Economic Memo.* Washington, D.C.: WB.
——. 1990. *Thailand Financial Sector Study.* Washington, D.C.: WB.
——. 1991. *World Development Report, 1991.* Washington, D.C.: Oxford University Press.

CHAPTER FIVE

THE PHILIPPINES

Manuel F. Montes and Johnny Noe E. Ravalo

The Philippine financial system has been described as quite sophisticated for its level of development (World Bank 1980). It has a well-organized money market, long experience in experimenting with financial instruments, and professional staffing. The country's savings rate is also relatively high by developing-country standards. By these conditions, the Philippine financial system seems comparable with that of almost all other countries in Asia, including Japan, Korea, and Taiwan.

Despite its apparent sophistication, however, the financial system has been deemed a failure in several important senses, including poor resource mobilization, a high degree of instability, and deficient provision of long-term funds. The standard explanation for these financial market failures is that they are consequences of financial repression.[1] Most analyses of financial repression in the Philippines have followed the McKinnon-Shaw framework (Tolentino 1989);[2] Table 5.1 provides a summary of the features of that framework which have been identified in the Philippine financial system.

While such analyses of financial repression are enlightening, they fail to capture the underlying political and organizational factors which contribute to financial repression in the first place and which influence

---

1. See, for example, Lamberte 1985 and the references therein; see also Fry 1988.
2. Tolentino (1989) characterizes the reforms of the early 1980s as follows: "It is not surprising that the package of reforms prescribed for the Philippines contained the classical elements of financial liberalization. The Philippines, after all, had adopted and even developed innovations for the supply-leading strategy of financial development lock, stock, and barrel up [sic] the late 70s" (p. 326).

Table 5.1. Repression theory

Government intervention	Harmful effects
Interest rate ceilings	Subsidizes government and established borrowers and rations out small, unknown borrowers
	Encourages capital-intensive projects
	Reduces return on savings, discourages domestic resource mobilization, and reduces domestic investment rate
High reserve requirements	Provides financial resources to government at lower-than-market rates
Bank regulation, credit allocation, and legal differentiation of financial institutions	Guarantees monopoly margins for financial institutions
	Subsidizes credit for favored enterprises
Government provision of credit, and rediscounting for development purposes	Provides special access to credit for government corporations
	Results in inefficient allocation of credit

both the nature and consequences of financial market liberalization. For much of its postwar political history, the Philippines has been characterized by a weak and porous central government. This was particularly apparent during the Marcos period. The Marcoses held a personal stake in a number of crony enterprises and used their discretionary control over state financial institutions and the regulatory structure for both political and personal purposes; in short, the boundary separating the public and private sectors broke down completely (Haggard 1990).

As a result, financial repression in the Philippines must be comprehended within a broader political economy framework in which particular policies are seen as efforts to protect a vector of relationships among important players in the private sector, especially in the banking sector itself. The elements of financial repression helped to maintain these relationships; insiders were party to high profits (for families whose principal business was banking) or cheap credit (for families whose interests lay primarily in the real sector). These relationships also manifested themselves in the structure of the industry, the nature of bank-customer interactions, and the extensive interlocking directorates that linked the banking and manufacturing sectors (Makil, Reyes, and Koike 1983).

As this chapter will show, financial liberalization did not eliminate these relationships. Given the structure of the industry and the pervasive nature of the political relationships just outlined, policy changes proved ineffectual in achieving their stated objectives. For example, liberalization did not succeed in raising rates to depositors and had little effect on the degree of concentration in the industry, which facilitated not only anticompetitive behavior but strong political influence over policy.

In some senses, these relationships appear to approximate the definition of a "quasi-internal organization" (QIO) as described by Lee and Haggard in their introduction, especially in the close relationship that existed between a small number of banks and the monetary authorities and regulators. Why did such a system fail so miserably in the Philippines, whereas it appeared to yield results in Korea and Taiwan? A full answer is beyond the scope of this chapter.[3] Yet three factors appear to have been important.

First among these factors is the recurrence of severe macroeconomic problems that not only impeded financial deepening but also gave rise to banking practices that impeded long-term lending. Second, private sector actors had long-standing sources of economic and social power, while the bureaucracy and other organs of the state, including the state-owned banks, were relatively weak. Thus, in contrast to other countries, the exercise of influence did not lead to the extensive use of preferential credit as an instrument of industrial policy, though because of the higher rates of return on capital that resulted from the protection, the protected sectors received a larger share of credit and thus, in effect, received preferential treatment during the period of financial repression. But the power of the private sector was visible with respect to financial policies that affected the banking sector itself, where state–private sector relations have often resembled a model of "capture." Such a close relationship is completely antithetical to the government independence required for a QIO to operate effectively. Finally, the power of the private actors also affected the broader incentives in the system, including those associated with the country's exchange rate and trade policies. In contrast to Korea and Taiwan, the Philippines lacked the external check on its policies that was provided by an export-oriented development policy; financing thus flowed toward protected sectors, even though protection had a negative effect on total productivity growth.

3. Hutchcroft (1993), however, has offered an explanation in the companion volume to this one.

I. A Brief History of the Philippine Financial System

Summary of Conditions before 1972

The private sector's participation in the Philippine financial system begins in the early nineteenth century during the Spanish era, when a charitable and savings institution provided banking services and, later on, the local paper currency. It is difficult to classify this bank, which became the present Bank of the Philippine Islands, as either private or public. On the one hand, it was associated with the Catholic Church, an institution that answered to a higher authority; on the other hand, it had the most extensive earthly network in the Philippine colonial administration. For such an institution, anti-usury was not just a matter of the state's commandeering of capital resources but also a matter of faith.

Following the American occupation in 1898, the private banking system expanded along with the growth of international trade. By 1941, there were seventeen banks (eleven domestic and six foreign) with twenty-two provincial branches and fifty-four provincial agencies (Sicat 1983, p. 285). Characteristically, the American period also saw the establishment of the government-owned Philippine National Bank, which financed the expansion of sugar mills for export and almost immediately went bankrupt (Hutchcroft 1993).

Although World War II interrupted the expansion of the system, the end of the war saw the granting of independence by the United States and the emergence of a small financial system consisting of about seven commercial banks, three savings banks, and a small stock exchange (Tan 1980, p. 1).[4] The Central Bank of the Philippines was created in 1949 with support from the United States in the midst of a full-blown balance-of-payments crisis and provided the basis for a Philippine monetary policy that was administratively independent of the U.S. Treasury Department. With these institutions, the financial market began a new phase of development, attempting to keep pace with the increasing financial and commercial needs of the growing economy, permitting a shift from the dominance of tangible assets toward financial claims (including insurance claims), and enabling an increase in the range of financial instruments (Hooley and Moreno 1974, p. 95).

During the 1960s, the central bank adopted aggressive but highly selective financial policies. It supported the establishment of new private banking institutions by providing subsidies on their initial capital and

---

4. The small prewar banks did not survive the war, but the government-related Philippine National Bank and the private bank controlled by the Catholic Church were rehabilitated.

operational funds via the rediscount window. The main recipients were rural banks, although all banks could potentially avail themselves of such rediscounting privileges (Tan 1980, p. 19).

Throughout this period, the central bank dutifully regulated financial institutions under its purview, implementing the anti-usury laws and fulfilling its quantitative import-restricting task. There was a rapid growth of nonbank financial institutions, notably insurance companies, that were not regulated by the central bank. There was also a rapid increase in demand for investment funds during the period of economic growth induced by the import-substitution policy. Despite all this, the growth of the financial system continued to revolve around growth of the commercial banks, which became the main investment intermediaries (Patrick and Moreno 1982, pp. 10–11).

The 1972 Reforms and the Following Years

The reforms recommended in 1972 by a joint International Monetary Fund (IMF) and Central Bank of the Philippines (CB) commission focused on the CB's increasing loss of control over the financial system, which had developed processes and institutions beyond those provided for in the General Banking Act of 1949. The lively private money market, which was not under CB supervision, had circumvented the anti-usury law, offering interest rates well above the legal interest rate ceilings and providing large, established business enterprises with liquidity at more attractive rates of interest. It was, however, also a market where institutions with fiduciary obligations sold their paper. For example, in the early 1970s, the failure of two banks—the General Bank and the Continental Bank—was associated with their active participation in the money market. In both cases, management carried out term transformation of money market funds into long-term projects of the banks or their owners.

Under the 1972 reforms, the CB was basically given the authority and responsibility over the entire financial system and not just the monetary system. As a part of the reforms, the Usury Law was repealed and the CB empowered to set all interest ceilings, and the number of types of banks was reduced from five to three. In addition, the commission proposed the diffusion of bank ownership, limiting the control of any party (and up to third-degree consanguinity) to no more than 20 percent.[5] A lasting legacy of the 1972 reforms was the virtual end, not as a matter of law but as a matter of policy, of the granting of new commercial banking

5. This proposal was not implemented and continues to be an issue.

licenses. These licenses were granted liberally in the 1960s, but only two new commercial banks have been licensed since 1970: the Union Bank in the late 1970s and the Asian Bank in 1989.[6]

The 1970 balance-of-payments crisis forced the Philippine government to adopt a conservative macroeconomic stance in the first part of the 1970s which was initially monitored under an IMF standby arrangement. With the sudden availability of private international funds from petrodollar recycling and unequivocal support from the Bretton Woods agencies after the 1976 IMF–World Bank (WB) annual meeting in Manila, this conservative stance gave way. The increase in net borrowing from abroad—both private and official—was assisted by extensive tie-ups between the local financial system and the international banking community (Santiago and Tagle 1981).

Even with the economic recovery in the mid-1970s, criticism about the limited extent of intermediation continued. Antonio Ozaeta, a leading banker of the period, aired the apparently paradoxical behavior of commercial banks: "The term funds of the commercial banks, consisting of term deposits, capital and reserves, rose from 18 percent of total assets in 1974 to 27 percent in 1978. If we include savings deposits, 45 percent of their total resources can be construed as potentially available for medium-term lending. Yet we find that less than 2 percent of their total volume of credit actually went to intermediate and long-term loans" (Ozaeta 1980, p. 170). By 1990, this discrepancy had widened; the sum of time and savings deposits constituted 86 percent of total deposit resources (which is up from 67 percent in 1980), whereas the proportion of long-term loans had fallen from 12 to 10 percent in the same period. Figure 5.1 shows the distribution of both deposit resources and loan maturities in the banking system.

The paucity in the supply of long-term lending has been blamed, along with the regime of interest rate ceilings, on generous short-term CB rediscounting policies (Remolona and Lamberte 1986, Lamberte 1985). This explanation, which utilizes the McKinnon-Shaw framework, ignores the fact that access to rediscounting has been highly skewed among existing banks (Hutchcroft 1993). The explanation also does not address the basic discrepancy between the existence of long-term private deposit resources and the predominance of short-term lending.

Our explanation for the low supply of long-term lending is that much of the short-term credit outstanding in the private sector could, in fact, be classified as effectively medium- or long-term because of the policy of

6. Bankruptcies, mergers, and acquisitions, however, have changed the list of banks.

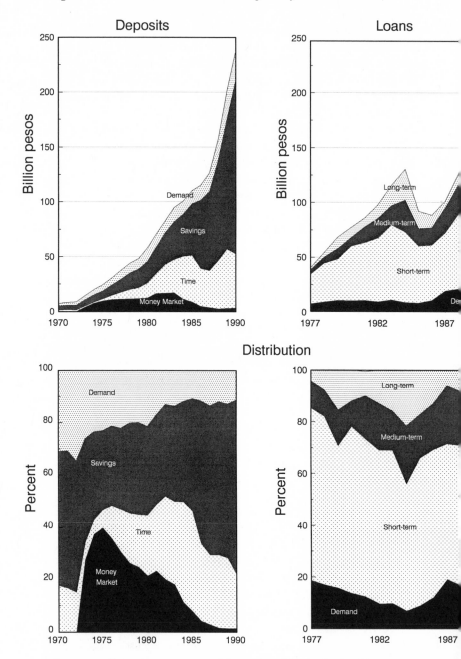

Figure 5.1. Deposit resources and loan maturities in the banking system

rolling over loans. Tables 5.2–5.5 provide an indirect indication of the rate of rollover of loans in the commercial banking system. There is an inordinate difference between the change in total credits outstanding and the total amount of credits granted by commercial banks. A comparison of the data in Table 5.2 with that in Table 5.3 reveals that total credits granted by commercial banks between 1960 and 1973 exceed the change in credits outstanding by four to eight times over this whole period (in fact, the level of outstanding credit is comparable with the amount of credits granted). Because the rate of loan write-off has not been high except in the 1980s,[7] only a high rate of repayment and subsequent regranting of loans can reconcile the high level of loan grants to the rather small increases in loans outstanding.[8]

Because data on the rate of repayment of loans are not available, we assumed that only 80 percent of loans granted are actually disbursed and that all these are disbursed in equal amounts over five years to get an idea of the extent of the rollover process based on the annual data (this is tantamount to assuming that all loans granted are medium-term loans).[9] Table 5.4 reveals that the ratio of the assumed disbursements to change in outstanding credit is considerably larger than 1.0, and the numbers can be roughly interpreted as the number of times loans are rolled over in a year. Table 5.5 uses this proportion to demonstrate implied average maturities, for which the grand average is forty-one days, implying that on average, loans are rolled over nine times a year.[10]

This pattern of intermediation can be explained by the perverse interaction between macroeconomic crisis and the strategy of banks in managing risk in crisis-prone environments. As Fried and Howitt (1980) suggest, macroeconomic crises present themselves as drastic increases in

7. This has not yet occurred in private banks. A similar calculation for the period 1985–1988 reveals the same large difference between the change in the outstanding balance and loans granted.

8. The only other possibility not ruled out by the data is for a very high rate of client shifting within the operations of the formal commercial banks. This is not likely, however, given the inability of the commercial banks to service all but the largest enterprises in the country and the importance of stable client relationships in the banking sector. A comparison of the mining column in Tables 5.2–5.5 shows that only a few mining companies have access to commercial bank credit. The size of the increase in credit outstanding is minuscule compared with the total credits granted for the same year. In 1972, for example, P 563 million in credits was granted, while total credits outstanding increased by only P 102 million; for all other years, the mismatch between the increase in credits outstanding and credits granted is even higher.

9. Without these assumptions, the rate of turnover for each year and each industry would be higher.

10. Because we are using only annual data, the data do not permit us to calculate average maturities longer than one year.

Table 5.2. Change in total credits outstanding of commercial banks, classified by industry, 1960–1973 (millions of pesos)

Year	Grand total (private and public sectors)	Total private sector	Sector										
			Agriculture	Mining	Manufacturing	Construction	Public utilities	Services	Trade	Banks and financial institutions	Property loans	Consumer loans	Government
1961	579.3	575.8	74.8	0.8	257.8	7.4	20.6	7.8	156.6	25.7	19.1	5.2	3.7
1962	447.1	455.9	68.3	2.6	160.8	6.8	13.4	14.8	183.5	7.0	3.2	-4.5	0.3
1963	883.6	832.8	177.3	7.6	137.3	22.2	22.6	16.4	366.9	52.2	9.7	20.6	41.8
1964	601.3	608.7	142.6	7.1	123.7	25.1	18.6	7.7	259.1	17.1	2.7	5.0	-37.4
1965	506.1	520.2	114.7	-7.8	37.6	7.1	10.0	-0.8	282.3	50.1	10.6	16.4	15.0
1966	133.3	142.9	50.3	10.6	75.4	4.8	15.7	15.3	-50.0	-39.7	17.7	42.8	-8.7
1967	847.0	826.8	123.9	5.9	54.6	19.6	22.4	44.9	417.0	82.4	32.9	23.2	10.2
1968	972.4	397.4	267.7	-11.4	119.2	1.0	5.5	40.4	-83.9	-55.5	71.2	43.2	585.0
1969	610.0	497.6	140.6	2.9	-20.5	6.0	-26.4	-1.3	124.1	91.3	107.4	73.5	112.4
1970	1,167.4	1,176.0	104.3	5.7	320.9	15.3	28.7	68.7	426.9	175.6	12.8	17.1	-8.6
1971	1,644.6	1,617.1	64.3	47.0	376.8	12.9	38.0	52.2	570.7	-72.9	83.7	444.4	27.5
1972	2,348.9	2,057.8	-4.6	101.8	1,129.1	62.1	133.6	94.9	519.5	213.7	103.7	-296.0	291.1
1973	5,371.1	5,697.7	469.8	41.0	2,493.3	142.6	2.5	-4.2	2,242.8	63.6	13.7	232.6	-326.6

Sources: Central Bank of the Philippines, various years.

Table 5.3. Total credits granted by commercial banks, classified by industry, 1960–1973 (millions of pesos)

Year	Grand total (private and public sectors)	Total private sector	Agriculture	Mining	Manufacturing	Construction	Public utilities	Services	Trade	Banks and financial institutions	Property loans	Consumer loans	Government
								Sector					
1960	2,849.1	2,844.2	499.8	36.7	886.4	45.6	65.3	41.0	1,077.8	71.9	38.9	80.8	4.9
1961	4,133.6	4,120.2	659.3	51.2	1,436.7	62.1	112.5	48.9	1,478.9	127.5	44.6	98.5	13.4
1962	4,916.4	4,915.6	786.1	50.0	1,791.9	77.5	115.1	61.5	1,709.1	170.5	60.8	93.1	0.8
1963	6,826.3	6,739.2	1,052.0	58.8	2,092.9	124.9	175.4	87.3	2,545.6	372.7	90.5	139.1	87.1
1964	7,349.7	7,349.4	1,105.9	70.3	2,238.3	114.5	148.5	94.5	2,773.5	571.0	85.2	147.7	0.3
1965	7,766.7	7,754.2	1,141.6	51.1	2,287.8	142.8	144.4	83.8	3,022.6	650.7	91.8	137.6	12.5
1966	8,165.6	8,164.1	1,260.9	70.6	2,615.4	132.7	168.7	161.6	2,627.3	803.2	120.5	203.2	1.5
1967	9,753.6	9,753.3	1,551.0	60.6	2,963.6	151.6	200.7	169.1	3,413.2	826.9	179.3	237.3	0.3
1968	15,335.8	14,752.0	1,652.0	95.1	3,583.3	191.8	257.7	250.4	6,782.7	1,495.4	221.1	222.5	583.8
1969	16,389.5	15,601.3	1,772.0	93.0	3,656.2	223.8	172.3	263.9	7,130.0	1,717.3	247.8	325.0	788.2
1970	21,951.7	21,023.0	2,194.5	95.7	4,055.8	186.0	277.3	365.5	9,795.2	2,774.9	410.1	868.0	928.7
1971	28,820.4	28,481.0	2,513.5	321.9	5,966.2	227.0	464.4	494.7	12,001.3	4,829.7	502.7	1,159.8	339.4
1972	32,689.4	32,184.0	2,551.2	562.5	7,391.3	364.5	184.5	549.5	13,872.7	4,693.4	514.4	870.0	505.4
1973	46,684.6	45,757.7	2,827.9	835.3	10,359.0	367.5	854.6	590.4	22,380.1	5,776.0	795.9	971.0	926.9

Sources: Central Bank of the Philippines, various years.

Table 5.4. Eighty percent of credits granted disbursed over five years as a proportion of change in outstanding credits, classified by industry

Year	Grand total (private and public sectors)	Total private sector	Sector										
			Agriculture	Mining	Manufacturing	Construction	Public utilities	Services	Trade	Banks and financial institutions	Property loans	Consumer loans	Government
1965	9.80	9.50	6.62	-5.77	41.90	11.76	11.13	-75.20	6.53	6.04	5.63	6.01	1.22
1966	42.04	39.10	17.01	4.54	23.40	19.75	7.66	5.11	-40.57	-10.35	4.06	2.69	-1.88
1967	7.53	7.69	7.89	8.44	35.75	5.44	5.98	2.12	5.52	6.26	2.76	5.96	1.60
1968	7.96	19.23	4.01	-4.88	18.37	117.34	26.76	3.01	-35.51	-12.53	1.57	3.51	0.16
1969	15.06	18.01	8.40	20.44	-117.90	22.47	-5.72	-114.31	29.62	9.63	1.28	2.45	1.97
1970	9.81	9.43	12.93	11.65	8.41	9.26	6.00	2.82	11.15	6.94	14.73	17.37	-42.84
1971	8.97	8.87	24.09	2.27	8.59	12.16	5.78	4.73	10.97	-25.56	2.98	1.01	15.36
1972	7.85	8.71	-371.59	1.84	3.49	3.07	1.62	3.24	15.27	11.61	2.93	-1.86	1.73
1973	4.37	4.02	4.04	7.45	2.02	1.54	125.00	-86.25	4.65	49.79	28.86	2.88	-1.71

Note: Calculated from data in Table 5.3.

Table 5.5. Implicit maturity of loans granted by commercial banks (no. of days)

								Sector					
Year	Grand total (private and public sectors)	Total private sector	Agriculture	Mining	Manufacturing	Construction	Public utilities	Services	Trade	Banks and financial institutions	Property loans	Consumer loans	Government
1965	37	38	55		9	31	33	71	56	60	65	61	300
1966	9	9	21	80	16	18	48	172	66	58	90	135	229
1967	48	47	46	43	10	67	61	121			132	61	
1968	46	19	91		20	3	14				233	104	185
1969	24	20	43	18		16	61	129	12	38	285	149	
1970	37	39	28	31	43	39	63	77	33	53	25	21	
1971	41	41	15	161	43	30	225	113	33		122	360	24
1972	47	42		199	104	119	3		24	31	125		211
1973	84	91	90	49	181	238			78	7	13	127	
Mean	41	39	43	65	47	62	56	76	34	28	121	113	105

Note: The implicit loan maturity figure is based on the ratio of loans granted to change in outstanding credit. It is assumed that 80 percent of total credits granted is disbursed in equal amounts over five years, starting from the year noted. Blank cells are those in which the change in outstanding credits is negative or fractional.

the cost of funds, forcing banks to call in their loans. Such crises are also frequently accompanied by devaluations that invalidate the cost assumptions of loan projects. As bankruptcies mount, however, the paradoxical behavior of the conservative commercial banks in lending short-term is validated.

This rollover system of lending is associated with a particular set of social relationships. Rollovers are subject to the uncertainty of not being renewed, especially during liquidity crises. During normal times, an implicit contract between the lender and the borrower establishes the effective maturity of the loan, taking into account macroeconomic risk and the relative political influence of the loan supplier which serves as an indicator of the potential for a government bailout.

The importance of an informal contract in rollover short-term lending might be interpreted as another example of how repressed interest rates encourage nonprice rationing of credit. This would be a legitimate interpretation if the vast majority of loans were effectively lent at or below the statutory ceiling rates. Rollover instruments, however, are especially susceptible to renegotiation based on current conditions; in any case, since the early 1970s, interest regulations did not apply to the money market.

More important, it is not clear that the interest rate on the loan instrument actually reflects the true cost of the loan to the borrower. The practice of requiring compensating balances and imposing uncompetitive closing costs (this is especially easy if banks do not compete for clients) are well known.[11] Thus, the inefficiency associated with credit rationing was not due to interest ceilings, which were not in any case effective on the loan side. Rather, the rationing occurred even without government-mandated price repression, a point that is made by Stiglitz and Weiss (1981).

The availability (or pervasiveness) of rollover lending provided a flexible loan instrument for accommodating differences in connectedness and risk of the loan. A borrower from a "friendly" group could reasonably expect a continuing rollover of her loan at comparable terms. While keeping an eye on the probability of the onset of an overall liquidity crisis and the prospect of her credit bank receiving government support in such an event, this borrower could prudently borrow ostensibly only for working capital but then "divert" some of the loan either for fixed capital investment or for start-up of related ventures by the same

---

11. This is another example of data that could potentially be available, even on a historical basis, from the CB's examining section to study whether effective lending rates were actually close to market-determined rates.

company. On the other hand, a borrower with more tenuous connected-ness or one with a riskier project could still be accommodated through the same instrument but kept on a shorter lease by the lending bank at the point of rollover.

The 1979 Review and the 1980s

Based on the findings of a joint WB-IMF mission in 1979, the Philippines embarked on a financial liberalization program through the Universal Banking Act of 1980. The 1979 study made two recommendations: deregulation of interest rates (that is, taking away from the CB the power to set ceilings on the interest rate), and the introduction of "universal banks" with the power to engage in all financial activities.

The joint WB-IMF mission laid the blame for the inadequacy of long-term finance on the interest rate structure, the tax structure, and the legislated specialization of financial institutions. Consequently, the mission recommended that specialization among financial institutions be weakened. This meant giving quasi banks the option of providing basic bank services, particularly the right to solicit deposits. It also meant encouraging the conversion of existing commercial banks to "universal banks" that could not only lend but take equity positions as well. The mission also recommended an increase in the capitalization of banks and once again advised that ownership be broadened. To protect the bank from sudden liquidity problems brought about by the proposed shift in loan maturities, it was suggested that the CB establish a lender-of-last-resort facility and develop a parallel active capital market.

At the onset of the 1980s, therefore, the Philippines began an explicit era of financial liberalization and a public policy to create "bigger and stronger" banks. The larger size of the banks was expected to result in more efficient banks because they would avail themselves of economies of scale and scope. By eliminating the legislated specialization, competition was expected to be heightened, with banks competing across the broad range of financial institutions but subject to certain regulatory safeguards. It was intended that the problem of term financing would be addressed automatically by the bigger banks because their potential portfolio holdings would make it easier, together with the banking privileges under unibanking, to transform short-term, volatile deposits into long-term, low-risk loans. By 1985, government intervention in setting the interest rate was completely eliminated, the specialized credit programs had been cut in half, and the remaining programs were charging close to market rates. In addition, special rediscounting and subsidies to rural banks had been withdrawn.

The timing of the financial liberalization appeared auspicious, for the government was poised to initiate a variety of other reforms as well, including trade liberalization. But in quick succession, the economy was hit with a series of shocks. In 1981, the money market's role in term transformation collapsed abruptly when Chinese businessman Dewey Dee fled the country, leaving over $80 million in liability adrift in the money market, mostly in short-term commercial paper. This led to the bankruptcy of three major investment houses, which, in turn, compelled the CB to orchestrate equity and deposit infusion from government corporations into three commercial banks.

Macroeconomic problems also erupted, compounded by the deteriorating political situation. After the second oil shock, the Philippines doubled its rate of external borrowing to finance increased deficits, which were run as part of a countercyclical macroeconomic policy designed to carry the country through the recession of the early 1980s. In October 1983, however, a balance-of-payments crisis sparked by the final political crisis of the Marcos regime, led to the failure of 146 rural banks, 32 savings banks, and 4 commercial banks. Both the government-owned Philippine National Bank (PNB), the largest commercial bank, and the Development Bank of the Philippines (DBP), through which much of foreign borrowing were channeled, became technically bankrupt. To rehabilitate these institutions and maintain an orderly relationship with foreign creditors, the Treasury of the newly installed Aquino government accepted 59 and 90 percent of the assets of PNB and DBP, respectively. The assets written off represented 13 and 16 percent of total banking system assets of PNB and DBP in 1985.

There is no evidence that these failures can be traced to the financial liberalization; the liquidity crisis and sharp depreciation of the peso, which invalidated all loan projects viable at the old rate (Montes 1987), were responsible. As a result, the financial liberalization period of the 1980s coincided with a contraction of real assets of the financial system (excluding those of the CB) from P 247.7 billion in 1980 to P 161.0 billion by 1988 (Table 5.6). Even after the liberalization episode, however, the system remained characterized by low interest rates on deposits and limited long-term lending, with an imperceptible change in the mobilization of savings. Low deposit rates have been explained by the existence of an oligopoly in the banking system (Remolona and Lamberte 1986), an explanation we have emphasized here. This approach acknowledges the possibility that removing deposit ceilings is no guarantee that market participants will behave in a more competitive fashion; much depends on market structure.

Table 5.6. The assets of the financial system (billions of pesos)

	1970	1975	1980	1983	1985	1988[a]
Central bank	6.0	26.0	65.4	130.4	251.6	349.9
Banking system	18.8	69.9	188.8	331.5	394.3	360.1
Commercial banks	14.1	53.2	138.2	247.9	285.7	299.3
Private	8.3	35.1	85.1	141.7	165.7	224.6
Government	4.6	18.1	34.6	65.2	76.1	38.8
Foreign	1.2	—	18.7	41.0	43.9	35.9
Thrift	0.9	2.1	10.6	16.1	15.1	24.9
Savings	0.7	1.4	7.4	7.4	6.8	14.2
Private development	0.2	0.4	1.6	4.1	5.1	6.7
Stock savings/loans	—	0.3	1.6	4.1	3.2	4.0
Rural banks	0.7	2.8	5.6	9.5	8.6	10.7
Specialized government banks	3.1	11.8	34.2	65.3	84.9	25.2[a]
Nonbank intermediaries	6.1	26.8	58.9	92.0	105.6	140.2
Insurance companies	5.9	11.9	29.5	44.6	60.8	98.3
Government (including Social Security System/Government Service Insurance System)	4.0	7.7	19.5	30.9	42.7	68.6
Private	1.9	4.2	10.0	13.7	18.1	29.7
Investment institutions	—	10.3	25.6	25.2	23.8	21.4
Trust operations	—	2.6	1.7	1.5	1.6	1.8
Other intermediaries	0.2	2.0	2.1	20.7	19.4	18.7
Total	30.9	122.7	313.1	553.9	751.5	850.2
In real terms (GNP deflator 1980 = 100)	105.8	209.4	313.1	412.4	316.8	282.4
Total excluding central bank	24.9	96.7	247.7	423.5	499.9	500.3
In real terms	85.0	165.1	247.7	315.3	211.1	161.0

Sources: World Bank 1988, annex 4; Central Bank of the Philippines 1988.
[a] After transfer of part of the assets and liabilities to the government.

Financial liberalization was also supposed to give banks access to subsidized sources of funds such that they would not compete for deposits and would thereby contribute to savings mobilization. Financial liberalization and freer interest rates (and higher nominal rates, particularly during the foreign exchange and political crisis of 1983–1985), however, did not lead to marked improvement in savings mobilization. The reason for this is that during this period, a strong tide of capital flight offset much of the positive effect that a reasonable increase in domestic interest rates might have had on savings mobilization. But deposits increased rapidly after 1988, when the uncertainty from the crisis receded (see Figure 5.2, panel B, and Figure 5.3, panel C, for the trend in nominal and real deposits, respectively).

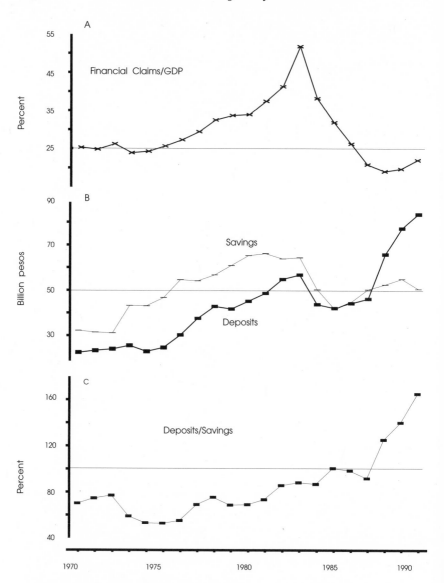

Figure 5.2. Financial claims, savings, and deposits

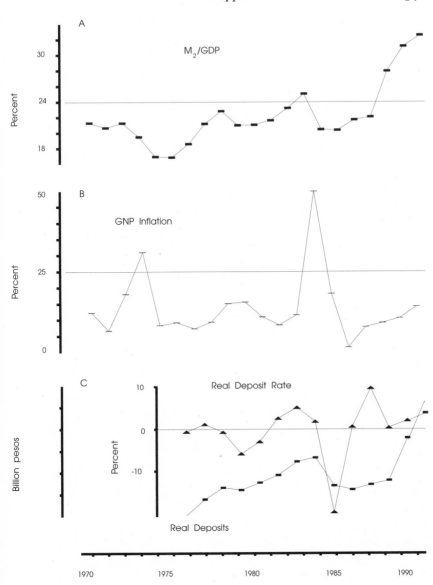

Figure 5.3. Financial development

The 1988 World Bank Financial Sector Review

Working within an intellectual atmosphere in which the utility of regulation and interest rate ceilings was better understood, a World Bank mission carried out another wide-ranging review in 1988.[12] The report is notable for pointing out the weak features of the financial system's legal underpinning which had been exposed during the post-repression era. For our purposes, we need only point to some of these features:

(1) Fiduciary controls on insider abuse of bank resources—more specific, controls against the overexposure of banks to "directors, officers, stockholders, and related interests"[13]—were characterized as ineffective because the secrecy of bank deposits extended to situations where a probable criminal act had been committed. The inviolability of secrecy in the Philippines exceeded that in U.S. jurisprudence.

(2) CB staff had been subject to lawsuits from bank owners/officers after issuance of cease-and-desist orders. It was recommended that CB staff be immune from such suits.

(3) The system of loan foreclosure and recovery of collateral assets was ineffective. Philippine law permits owners one year in which to file suit, including injunction, against foreclosure. During this one year, the asset could be depreciated substantially. It was suggested that these laws be amended to permit easier recovery of foreclosed assets.

(4) The Securities and Exchange Commission (SEC) had inadequate power to police the sale of commercial debt instruments and no reliable credit-rating service existed; these conditions invited abuse. Thus, the strengthening of the SEC was recommended.

These suggestions are indicative of the relative weakness of the state and the political difficulties of enforcing regulation in the face of private sector resistance.

The World Bank report also identified the lack of competitive behavior among the banks as an important feature needing reform. The recommendations were to dispose of the "weak banks" (that is, banks carrying a significant proportion of bad loans) as quickly as possible; allow freer branching; and ease entry into the industry. The delay in the disposition of weak banks is not simply a question of the government's difficulties in finding buyers for the weak banks; the state also did not have the capability to "referee" the distribution of the gains generated by

12. The report is titled *Philippines: Financial Sector Study*, Industry and Energy Operations Division, Country Department II, World Bank, August 23, 1988.
13. DOSRI is the Philippine acronym for these interests.

the disposal of these assets among the private actors. The government had problems dealing with issues such as deciding which business group should have access to the branch networks of banks, given that freer branching among banks devalued the worth of branch networks. Other components of the proposed reform directly raised the issue of whether there would be new players in the banking system and whether some existing players would be allowed to capture a larger market share.

Until resolutions to these conflicts are found, the existence of weak banks provides the rationale for continuing the high fees for bank services and low interest rates for deposits. These, in turn, tilt the incentive against a quick disposition of weak banks and help maintain the "gentlemanly competition" in the banking system.[14]

II. The Structure of the Financial System

The Size and Mobilization of Funds

The total resources of the Philippine financial system expanded by more than twenty times between 1946 and 1961 in terms of current pesos (Sicat 1983, p. 287). The pattern of growth in the last fifteen years, however, has been less robust. Between 1980 and 1988, the total assets of the financial system in 1980 prices declined from P 313.1 billion to P 282.4 billion (Table 5.6). Moreover, the proportion of assets accounted for by the CB doubled over the period from 21.2 percent to 42.9 percent. Between 1975 and 1988, the real value of non-CB assets in the financial system actually declined from P 165 billion to P 161 billion. Figure 5.2, panel A, demonstrates the loss in financial development associated with the macroeconomic crisis of the mid-1980s by showing the ratio of "claims" (excluding foreign assets) to GDP on the asset side from both the monetary survey and the banking system. After a steady growth of financial assets in the 1970s, the financial system at the beginning of the 1990s was less deep than in the mid-1970s.

Because the Philippine financial system is dominated by the commercial banking system (which accounts for 75 percent of loans granted), our analysis concentrates on the operations of the commercial banking system. Conventionally, the development of a financial system is measured primarily by the ratio of M_2 to GDP. Between 1970 and 1987, this ratio remained within a narrow range in the Philippines, following

14. See Hutchcroft 1993 for a description of the role of the Bankers Association of the Philippines in helping to maintain these fees.

a meandering pattern, despite the fact that GDP grew steadily until the 1980s (Figure 5.3, panel A). Fairly rapid increases in the ratio are evident during periods of strong growth; precipitous drops occur during balance-of-payments crises. There has been a sharp increase in the ratio since 1987, with the economic recovery, even though government borrowing from the financial system also increased in this period.

Several authors have noted that the ratio of M_2 to GDP for the Philippines has lagged those of neighboring countries, despite being at approximately the same levels in the 1970s.[15] Both the high rate of inflation and the explicit and implicit taxation of financial assets have been identified as the main culprits for the slow pace of financial deepening (Chamley and Hussain 1988). These two particular factors are, however, highly correlated with the Philippines's macroeconomic crises, which we believe have been the main determinants of the current low level of the M_2/GDP ratio. Periods of crisis are correlated with declines in the ratio. As shown in Figure 5.3, panel A, the M_2/GDP ratio fell between 1972 and 1974 (the first oil shock and the imposition of martial law), in 1978 (that is, the second oil shock), and again after 1983 (the crisis years sparked by the assassination of political opposition leader Benigno S. Aquino). The strong growth years of 1988–1989 show a sharp increase in the ratio. And in late 1989, the Philippine economy began showing signs of entering another foreign exchange crisis.

Real rates of return on financial assets, reflecting both the responsiveness of nominal interest rates and the vagaries of the inflation rate, also help to explain the shallowness of the financial system. Panel C of Figure 5.3 suggests a close correlation between the real rate of return on financial assets—in this case measured as the real deposit rate[16]— and M_2/GDP and core deposits (that is, the sum of demand, savings, and time deposits in deposit money banks). The timing of the turning points in this graph is, however, questionable, suggesting that the real deposit rate is, in fact, endogenous to financial development and deposits.[17]

There is at least a suggestion that the different types of financial assets are poor substitutes for each other and that higher yield rates cannot be

---

15. See, for example, Tan 1989. Note, however, that Tan uses the M_3/GDP ratio in her comparisons, although it is not likely that the M_2/GDP figures will be significantly divergent.

16. The treasury bill rate, the most dominant single interest rate in the Philippine financial system, was also used. The graphical result is almost identical to the real deposit rate.

17. The series available to us is too short to carry out a credible causality test.

expected to mobilize further financial savings. Figure 5.3 suggests that real deposit rates have risen slightly, with noticeable variability; yet real core deposits have risen steadily between 1976 and 1987, except for the crisis years 1978–1979 and 1983–1985.

The most suitable explanation for these trends has to do with market segmentation and the dualistic structure of the formal and informal markets. With bank deposits being practically the only form of savings available to the common saver,[18] there is little choice but to keep money in time deposits, despite unfavorable movements in the real return rate. Tan (1989) proposes that deposit markets are segmented between small depositors—who receive low, even negative, real interest rates—and big depositors—who enjoy high rates because banks compete for their deposits. Savers with larger volumes had access to the money market with competitive rates of interest, and some, because of their ethnic background, always had access to the informal market (see the discussion of the informal market below).

To get a numerical perspective on this, we can compare the movements of real national savings versus real core deposits between 1970 and 1990. Figure 5.2, panel B, suggests that these two variables moved coincidentally with each other. Up until the 1983 crisis, both were on a general upward trend, with deposits decreasing marginally in 1974 and 1979. After 1986, core deposits actually exceeded the level of national savings (note that the latter is a flow variable and the former is a stock variable). These coincidental movements indicate a high proportion of savings flowing through the formal system.[19]

By taking the ratio of the stock of core deposits to the flow of national savings, we can infer a rather rough measure of the intermediating role of the formal financial system (Figure 5.2, panel C). This ratio has been generally increasing since 1975 (it exhibits both a positive and stronger trend than M_2/GDP). This is quite paradoxical in light of all of the criticism poured on the poor savings mobilization performance of the financial system.

It appears that, at least since 1972, the increase in core deposits has matched the growth in savings. Deposit mobilization could have been higher if there had been no macroeconomic and especially balance-of-payments uncertainty. This is, however, unlikely given that even when

18. Government securities naturally tend to be in large-amount blocks. The treasury bill, for example, has a current minimum of P 50,000 at face value which can be purchased only through banks and not directly from the CB.

19. There are also indications of some underestimation of savings owing to the underestimation of income of overseas workers (Vos 1990).

deposit rates of interest have been repressed, core deposits have appeared to keep pace with savings.[20]

The 1973 banking reform has been criticized on the ground that instead of extending CB supervision over the money market, the government should have lifted all ceilings on interest rates.[21] Our observation that a rising proportion of savings shows up as core deposits, in spite of the fact that the traditional measures of financial development have shown little development, suggests that such a policy would have had limited impact on the supply of investable funds. The more important aspect is how the financial institutions would utilize these resources. This points to the key role played by the financial system in allocating bank cash flows and its role in international capital flows, which in the case of the Philippines also takes the name of "capital flight" (Vos 1990).

The intermediation ratio, that is, the ratio of loans to core deposits, over the past twenty years is shown in panel A of Figure 5.4. To find out how available core deposits are allocated to the private sector, we included only claims on the private sector in the numerator.[22] Figure 5.4 dramatizes the disintermediation that has coincided with the period of financial liberalization. The intermediation ratio has generally remained above 1.5, which was certainly the case between 1973 and 1983. The ratio has not changed much despite the two oil shocks in the 1970s and the liberalization program in 1980. As panel C confirms, real deposit money bank claims on the private sector rose continually until 1983. The free-fall of real domestic credit relative to the drop in real core deposits induced a plunge in the intermediation ratio after 1983. In fact, by 1986, the ratio had fallen to less than 1.0.

Thus, the 1980s has seen an important shift away from loans to the private sector in the portfolio holdings of deposit money banks. Some of these core deposits have undoubtedly found their way into foreign asset holdings, which increased dramatically in nominal terms in the 1980s. In real terms, however, these balances have not increased significantly (Figure 5.4, panel C), which suggests some kind of an adjustment mechanism in operation. An important portion of core deposits has flowed

20. Assuming that the government did not engage in Singapore-style intervention.
21. See, for example, Yap et al. 1990.
22. The bias will materialize when part of the loans to the government and other official entities were extended by the application of "appropriate" pressure from "appropriate" channels. This is strictly not part of the intermediation process but largely a reflection of the politics involved. Finally, loans to other financial institutions tend to be very short-term maturity loans (that is, interbank loans) that are significant only in that they were recorded the day the financial statements were submitted. Their appearance is consequently more a matter of coincidence rather than a part of regular bank policy.

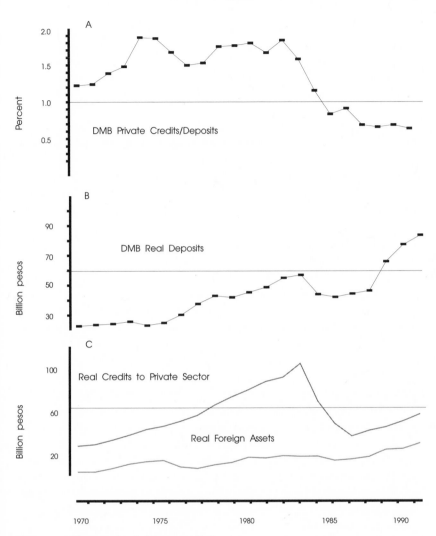

Figure 5.4. Deposit banks' intermediation

into investment in government securities (see below). Higher yields on government securities—a result of interest rate liberalization, coupled with a sudden increase in 1985 in the government's responsibility for servicing the foreign debt—accounted for the increase in investment in government securities.[23]

23. There was no significant reduction in reserve requirements during the liberalization process.

A third important adjustment mechanism is that in the face of poor private sector financeable projects, the banking system was adjusting its asset base downward.[24] If this is the case, it is not surprising that banks are indifferent to savings mobilization.

Informal Credit Markets

In the Philippines, one can identify at least two informal credit markets: the small-scale market to and among households and peasants,[25] and the Chinese network. Just as in other Asian contexts, the informal market is concentrated in providing credit for agriculture and trade and, to a lesser extent, working capital for industrial enterprises. Like other informal arrangements, data on these markets are difficult to obtain. Although it is hard to determine the size of the informal markets accurately, some have suggested that it could be as large as three-fourths the formal financial market (Bautista and Magno 1990). What is important for our purpose is to describe the relationship between these informal and formal markets.

It is no surprise that both the rates of return and the transactions costs are higher in the small-scale market. The small-scale market, while not insignificant, is limited in scope because funds do not cross large geographical or sectoral boundaries.[26] Government intervention, which consisted of subsidizing the creation of rural banks since the 1960s and the shift into high-yielding rice varieties in the 1970s, has had marginal effect on the robustness of the informal, rural credit market.

The Chinese network is known to be a source of start-up capital for small Chinese businesses; casual tales about its nature support the view that it is a prototypical internal market, depending not on the law but on familial relationships to enforce obligations. Chinese businesspeople are able to borrow from Chinese creditors on the basis of their reputation. Historically, many of the large landowning, non-Spanish families originated as moneylenders.

It is general knowledge, but not formally researched, that a significant portion of the wealth of long-lived, Binondo-based Chinese clans is kept in very liquid form, ready to be lent or used at a moment's notice.[27] In

24. An increasing amount of literature argues that the transmission mechanism may occur not only through bank liabilities but through bank assets as well. See, in particular, Blinder 1987 and Friedman 1983.
25. See, for example, Lava et al. 1989.
26. See Lava et al. 1989 for case studies on this market.
27. Binondo is a locality in downtown Manila which has been the traditional haven of both the roots of Philippine business and the aforementioned clans of Chinese descent. It is not surprising, therefore, to find that many commercial banks had their roots in Binondo and

fact, it was fashionable in the media during the last years of the Marcos regime to refer formally to the financial powers of Binondo as the "Binondo Central Bank." The Chinese are also important suppliers of credit in the small-scale market.

Two of the largest and most discreet commercial banks are Chinese-controlled; in the 1980s, a few important Chinese entrepreneurs also obtained dominant control over other large commercial banks. It is no surprise that the clearing facilities of these banks (and the other non-Chinese banks) are useful for the Chinese network, which extends beyond the national boundaries. There are no customary arrangements such as deposit assignment by which resources in the formal market can be applied directly to informal lending. Lending practices in the Chinese sector of the private banking system, however, make it difficult to mark out the boundary between the extensive informal lending network and the formal banking system.

The Dewey Dee scandal in 1981 shed momentary light on the nexus between the informal Chinese way of doing business and the formal market. Chinese families and banks were reputed to be the most bitter losers in the (formal) money market, as they were left holding paper floated by the companies associated with Dewey Dee. The money market undoubtedly played an important role in assisting participants in the informal market to manage their liquidity. At the same time, Chinese holders of the paper had believed that the reputation of Dewey Dee's family reduced the risk of being overexposed to this particular family.

The formal financial system serves as a depository and a source of funds for moneylenders in the informal markets. Bautista and Magno (1990) provide evidence that rural moneylenders use accounts in the banking system to maintain their lending resources. Agabin (1988) demonstrates that moneylenders engaging in domestic agricultural trade are considered prime customers of commercial banks, providing excellent collateral, including their stock of agricultural commodities.

Size and Concentration in the Private Banking System

The question of collusion and cartelization is a key issue in discussions of financial reform. During the years of financial repression as well as after the period of financial liberalization, it was fashionable to describe

---

were or are still funded by any of a number of the major families of Chinese descent. Talk on the streets reveals that the bulk of the funds in the informal market are indeed Binondo-based, usually lent at a fascinating coupon rate of 20 percent, collectible from anywhere between one day to one week.

the banking industry as being controlled by a cartel (Tan 1989). A compelling empirical test of the hypothesis has yet to be carried out, however. The subsequent discussion suggests that although it will not be difficult to provide evidence of collusive behavior among participants within the banking system, it will be more difficult to prove that such behavior is "uncompetitive" in the economic sense.

Since 1953, while the ratio of net earnings to net worth among private banks stayed within the 10–15 percent range (Figure 5.5, panel A), or about 4–5 percentage points higher than the inflation rate, maximum returns to the leading banks were often double that. The market leaders such as Bank of the Philippine Islands, China Banking, and Far East Banking and Trust Corporation enjoyed almost three times the industry's average return over the period 1960–1989. The data indicate two general types of financial institutions: those which are operated by their owners to provide financing for their nonfinancial enterprises (and which tend to exhibit lower returns) and those whose owners are primarily engaged in financial services.

Bank concentration has been increasing in the Philippines. Panel B of Figure 5.5 shows the percentage share of each type of bank ownership to total banking industry assets, and panel C traces the time path of the three-bank concentration ratio at both ends of the market. The three largest private domestic banks controlled roughly 20 percent of total private domestic bank assets in both the 1960s and the 1970s. If the government-owned Philippine National Bank, perennially the largest bank (in terms of assets, it is larger than Citibank, Manila) is included, then the largest four domestic-based banks controlled almost one-half of the system's resources during the 1960s, when banks were mushrooming, and through the 1970s, when the number of banks declined.[28] Since liberalization, the concentration index has been on an upward trend. With the percentage share of government-owned banks decreasing, the dominant position of the private domestic banks has increased.

But beyond an analysis of concentration indices in the financial system lies the question of the banks' behavior in terms of economic competition. Based on the historical experience reviewed in the first section, it is not clear that reducing the number of large banks to five or six, even though this could conceivably reduce the unit cost of producing financial services, encourages competitive behavior. Moreover, the entry of foreign participants will not necessarily provoke financial institutions

---

28. Industrial organization economists tend to consider three-firm or four-firm ratios of over 75 percent as more indicative of market power.

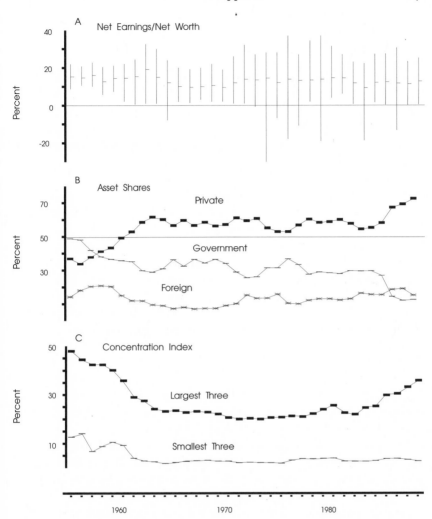

Figure 5.5. Earnings and concentration

to contest one another's existing markets. As suggested in the 1988 World Bank mission recommendations, a necessary condition for such competition is the strengthening of the state's ability, through legal reform, to break down anticompetitive collusion and regulate insider use of resources.

Cost competitiveness is another matter. We have already commented on the dynamic portfolio behavior of Philippine banks. The high intermediation margin of Philippine banks has been the subject of much analysis (World Bank 1980, 1988). About half this cost originates from taxation and remaining portfolio restrictions. In the present juncture, high margins on financial services, determined informally through the Bankers' Association of the Philippines, help to prop up those banks that are technically insolvent as the result of the mid-1980s liquidity crisis.

Both during and after the period of financial repression, the management of competition among the banks has been an underlying concern of the private sector and the monetary authority. During the period of repression, interest rate regulation inhibited competition for deposits but at the same time permitted wide latitude in portfolio allocation, loan rate setting, and risk sharing. (Nevertheless, as we have seen, the rise of the unregulated money market was not prevented.) After financial liberalization, the private bankers' association has regulated deposit rates, thus helping to prop up weak banks, while compelling the government to pay market rates for its domestic borrowing. This illustrates how both repression and the nature of the subsequent liberalization have reflected the capacity of private interests to define the regulatory and policy agenda to their benefit. It is to that policy agenda which we now turn.

III. The Nature of Financial Policy

The Nature and Objectives of Government Intervention

Financing for the country's traditional exports (that is, agricultural, timber, and mining exports) and import-substituting industries has constituted the principal demands on the formal financial institutions, and government financial policy has supported this role. Import substitution began almost inadvertently[29] in the 1950s in response to a foreign exchange crisis that had been building since 1947; the central bank became the government's instrument for rationing foreign exchange earnings according to an essentiality criterion that provided protection for nonessential products and the establishment of domestic industries to assemble these goods. Since then, import substitution has never been an orderly process embedded in successive longer-term development plans.

When the martial law era began in 1972, technocrats ascended to the highest levels of government, and the Bretton Woods agencies strongly

---

29. This is the adjective used by Golay (1961).

influenced agenda setting in the area of economic policy (Montes 1989); export orientation as an intention was not only reaffirmed but also fortified in the country's development plans. When the martial law government was overthrown in 1986, the new Aquino government reaffirmed the intention to initiate an export orientation. Nevertheless, the trade regime has maintained its inward orientation in practice.

The ability of the government to implement its priority "intentions" has depended on its access to foreign financing and the extent to which domestic prices diverged from market values. Low tax and revenue effort has made foreign financing indispensable (Montes 1989). There are three periods in which the availability of foreign financing provided the government with more influence over economic development: in the 1930s, with the sugar export resources of the Philippine National Bank and the National Development Company; in the 1950s, in the utilization of war damage payments through the Rehabilitation Finance Corporation, which subsequently became the Development Bank of the Philippines; and in the 1970s during the international debt boom.

The belief in social planning is deeply held, but as a means of determining future action, social planning is practiced little. Overall economic plans encompass general intentions that can be consistent with almost any priority list (Montes 1988). Priority lists are very much the outcome of lobbying by the preeminent family groups in an affected industry. During the martial law regime, government financial resources were provided to a handful of individuals supportive of the regime (Montes 1989).

Interest Rate Policy and Credit Allocation

In 1973, the anti-usury law was rescinded, and the Monetary Board was given the authority to change the interest ceiling. The board proceeded to change the interest rate four times during the 1970s, but even then a positive real interest rate on deposits was never achieved (though large lenders could always obtain positive rates in the money market). In 1981, the Monetary Board's authority over interest ceilings was totally rescinded. Since then, interest rates have not been controlled by the government and are determined in an institutional setting that can be called a "market." The Bankers' Association of the Philippines, however, has managed to sustain an oligopolistic pricing mechanism on deposit rates.

Except during the periodic balance-of-payments crises and the allocation for agricultural and agrarian reform, the government has not directly allocated credit through the private banking system. Its role in credit allocation has ensued through (1) the Philippine National Bank, which has represented almost 50 percent of commercial bank assets until the late 1980s (PNB's lending also represented a significant proportion of gross investment), and the Development Bank of the Philippines (DBP), and (2) the provision of subsidized rediscount windows during the debt boom.

It is notable that the DBP distribution of lending is not very different from that of commercial banks (Table 5.7). It is difficult to observe the smoking gun of selective credit allocation at these aggregate categories, though it does occur at the individual project level. It is nevertheless true that for the whole system, both private and government institutional lending did not occur in the same proportions as the sectoral distribution of GDP. Comparison of the data in Table 5.8, which show the real resources that flowed from the commercial banks (using implicit price deflators of GDP sectors), with the data in Table 5.9, which show the sectoral distribution of GDP, indicates that although both manufacturing and agriculture each accounted for about one-fourth of GDP, manufacturing captured 40 percent of the financial resources, whereas agriculture's share is only 15 percent, despite the special government programs to agriculture during the period. Part of this difference relates to the fact that manufacturing is relatively more capital intensive than agriculture. But even in the case of manufacturing, working capital financing represents the bulk of lending; thus the difference at least says that commercial banks are small players in agricultural financing. Also, given that working capital finance relates strongly to the import of intermediate inputs, the difference suggests that agriculture is relatively less import dependent.

The lending policies of government institutions are based on a priority list. Within the priority list, access to credit is strictly rationed according to the viability of the project rather than a plan criteria. Political connection was understood to be a critical ingredient of project viability. Thus it was an exercise in financial imprudence for any bank, whether private or government, to maintain a large exposure to clients from unknown families, which is why the Chinese informal network had always been relatively more dynamic.

When foreign financing was especially plentiful in the 1970s, the borrowing by (mostly new) government corporations and the provision of a government guarantee became the most potent instruments of selective credit control (SCC). In the debt boom (which had an almost surreal mini-boom in the late 1970s when the Marcos government managed to accelerate short-term borrowing from private international

Table 5.7. Distribution of loans and equities approved, Development Bank of the Philippines, FYI955–1956 to FYI988 (by percentage)

Year	Total	Agricultural	Industrial	Real estate	Government	Educational assistance	Rural bank equity	Advances/subsidies to private development bank	Financial rehabilitation
1955–1956	100.00	32.68	24.45	33.29	7.00	0.61	1.97	0.00	0.00
1960–1961	100.00	19.29	70.79	2.96	2.37	0.00	2.55	2.05	0.00
1965–1966	100.00	36.51	36.51	6.50	7.63	0.00	4.68	8.15	0.00
1970–1971	100.00	46.63	17.15	17.34	3.08	0.00	3.66	12.14	0.00
1974–1975	100.00	20.83	28.38	40.01	1.29	0.00	0.37	9.12	0.00
1975–1976	100.00	32.83	42.18	17.49	2.23	0.00	0.43	4.84	0.00
1976	100.00	30.02	38.83	21.30	1.88	0.00	0.32	1.76	0.00
1977	100.00	17.47	60.21	8.76	2.59	0.06	0.21	2.04	0.00
1978	100.00	14.77	55.40	14.33	2.09	0.07	0.00	1.67	0.00
1979	100.00	11.94	51.97	8.50	2.22	0.07	0.00	1.66	0.67
1980	100.00	9.78	53.75	15.84	0.63	0.07	0.00	2.28	0.00
1981	100.00	8.32	49.29	10.68	0.97	0.04	0.00	1.93	0.00
1982	100.00	8.04	38.51	12.86	1.19	0.09	0.15	2.83	0.00
1983	100.00	1.95	52.46	19.09	1.05	0.11	0.10	2.82	0.00
1984	100.00	1.02	10.02	8.12	0.00	0.06	0.01	0.46	0.00
1985	100.00	36.68	13.94	45.72	0.00	3.66	0.00	0.00	0.00
1986	100.00	26.64	62.50	10.34	0.00	0.47	0.00	0.00	0.00
1987	100.00	63.69	4.19	30.95	0.00	1.17	0.00	0.00	0.00
1988	100.00	16.64	56.75	7.75	0.00	0.00	0.00	0.00	3.71

Source: National Statistical Coordination Board 1989, table 16.13.

Table 5.8. Real flow of financial resources from commercial banks (millions of 1972 pesos)

End of period	Total	Agriculture, fishery, and forestry	Mining and quarrying	Manufacturing	Electricity, gas, and water	Construction	Trade	Transport, storage, and communication	Financing, insurance, and business services	Real estate	Community, social, and personal services
1979	5,736	956	697	1,968	178	195	-38	247	1,122	282	190
1980	3,125	1,490	505	1,777	-40	227	-824	66	613	-136	-461
1981	2,933	-315	-84	-225	99	395	1,113	211	834	562	45
1982	3,411	520	884	1,066	27	283	241	150	-9	114	254
1983	3,420	617	952	1,438	-127	186	-427	103	580	-2	383
1984	868	-968	1,099	-556	333	245	803	133	-215	103	-402
1985	-4,227	-4	-1,532	-1,471	-118	-145	-731	-138	387	-357	-75
1986	-652	663	-231	-13	-69	-375	-47	-86	-198	-104	-6
1987	1,866	-260	-55	2,276	-29	-90	47	49	-328	87	177
1988 (Q1)	3,075	190	-22	1,467	31	-107	781	103	101	137	218
Total	19,555	2,889	2,211	7,726	286	816	918	838	2,886	687	323
Percentage	100.0	14.8	11.3	39.5	1.5	4.2	4.7	4.3	14.8	3.5	1.7

Sources: Central Bank of the Philippines, various years.

Table 5.9. Distribution of real gross domestic product (by percentage)

End of period	Total (millions of pesos)	Agriculture, fishery, and forestry	Mining and quarrying	Manufacturing	Electricity, gas, and water	Construction	Trade	Transport, storage, and communication	Financing, insurance, and business services	Real estate	Community, social, and personal services
1978	82,784	26.1	2.2	25.5	0.9	7.2	12.9	5.4	7.4	7.2	5.1
1979	87,962	25.7	2.4	25.3	1.0	7.7	13.1	5.2	7.5	7.1	5.1
1980	92,568	25.6	2.4	25.0	1.0	7.7	13.2	5.3	7.7	7.1	5.1
1981	96,207	25.6	2.3	24.9	1.0	8.1	13.2	5.2	7.2	7.1	5.3
1982	98,999	25.6	2.0	24.8	1.1	8.2	13.2	5.2	7.3	7.1	5.4
1983	99,921	24.9	2.0	25.1	1.2	7.7	13.9	5.3	7.6	7.0	5.3
1984	93,927	27.1	1.9	24.8	1.4	6.2	15.0	5.4	5.5	6.8	5.9
1985	89,904	29.2	2.0	24.0	1.6	4.7	15.6	5.5	4.8	6.8	5.8
1986	91,180	29.7	1.7	23.8	1.9	3.7	15.7	5.6	5.3	6.6	5.9
1987	95,463	28.1	1.6	24.3	2.0	4.2	15.9	5.5	6.1	6.4	6.0
1988 (Q1)	101,534	27.4	1.6	24.9	2.0	4.3	15.6	5.4	6.1	6.3	6.5
Total (1979–1988)	947,665	26.9	2.0	24.7	1.4	6.3	13.1	5.4	6.5	6.8	5.6

Source: National Statistical Coordination Board 1989.

banks after the second oil shock), it became a burden and an achievement on the part of the government to inveigle private banks to utilize the available rediscount windows fully.

IV. Credit Allocation and Real Investment

As shown in Figure 5.1, the weight of private lending has been in short-term loans, and the financial system never really obtained an adequate amount of long-term funds to support real investment. By the end of the 1980s, 50 percent of the loans provided in the system continued to have a short-term maturity, which is another indication of the paucity of long-term finance. Beyond their internal cash flow, those businesses carrying out large capital investments either relied on government credit programs or utilized their long-term relationships with large private banks, which either provided the resources or led in the private syndication of the loans. In either case, government support—in terms of being on the Board of Investments priority list and in terms of being politically important—was critical in raising private financial resources for large projects.

One example is the petrochemical venture for which the Lopez family obtained private syndicated financing in 1971. The reliance on private financing for the petrochemical project is an indication of both the limited government resources during the period after the 1970 balance-of-payments crisis and the increasingly strained relationship between President Marcos and Vice President F. Lopez. When the Lopez family ran completely afoul of the Marcos martial law regime in 1972, they lost control of their enterprises, and the petrochemical venture was suspended (Montes 1989). (After the overthrow of the Marcos government, the Lopezes regained control of most of their enterprises.) If the original project had relied heavily on government financing, it would have been counted as a case of selective credit allocation.

To provide an indication of how the private financial sector responded to the trade regime, we managed to identify loan data that were matched with information on the distribution of industrial protection. CB data on commercial bank loans outstanding by industry for the period 1960–1974 were used to test the efficiency of credit allocation during the period of financial repression.[30] We then associated these

30. The raw data are taken from table 21 of Central Bank of the Philippines 1974, pp. 59–64.

Table 5.10. Financial resources and the trade regime, simple correlation matrix

Correlations over manufacturing industries, 1960–1974

	EPI	TFP	PLOUTS	KAP_GR	DLOUTS	PRPOUT	REALOUT
EPI	1.0000	−0.0508	0.1543	0.0375	−0.0620	0.1895	0.2324
TFP		1.0000	−0.0352	0.0655	0.0391	0.0546	0.0422
PLOUTS			1.0000	0.1085	0.6775	0.7368	0.6595
KAP_GR				1.0000	0.0581	0.0359	0.0502
DLOUTS					1.0000	0.0576	0.1823
PRPOUT						1.0000	0.8960
REALOUT							1.0000

Notes: Variable names are as follows:
EPI = (1 + effective protection rate)
TFP = rate of growth of total factor productivity
PLOUTS = proportion of total credit outstanding from commercial banks
PRPOUT = proportion of total real output from industry
KAP_GR = growth rate of the capital stock
DLOUTS = change in outstanding loans from commercial banks
· REALOUT = value added by industry divided by manufacturing price
Industries for which a complete set of variables was available include food, textiles, apparel, leather, footwear, wood products, wooden furniture and fixtures, paper products, industrial chemicals, petroleum products, plastic products, nonmetallic products, steel, fabricated metals, machinery, electrical machinery, and transportation equipment. Industries excluded because of missing data include sugar, beverage, tobacco, glass, other chemicals, and rubber products.

credit allocation data with the industry-by-industry effective protection rate for imported intermediates reported in Hooley 1985, p. 128, which provides data for the same period.[31]

The relationships between commercial bank lending, the distribution of protection, the rate of growth of the capital stock, and the rate of growth of total factor productivity are explored in Tables 5.10 and 5.11. Table 5.10 lists the variable definitions and reports the simple correlations between these variables. The strongest correlations in the time series, cross-sectional data are between the proportion of output and the proportion of loans received; there is a relatively stronger correlation between the proportion of commercial bank loans outstanding and the rate of growth of the capital stock and weak correlations between the other variables.

The data were used to estimate a simple structural model, detailed in Table 5.11, which was assumed to describe this pattern of correlations. The model was meant to analyze the following questions and provided the following answers based on the estimation results:

31. Both data sets suffer, however, from problems of aggregation.

Table 5.11. Effect of protection on commercial bank lending and productivity growth

Three-stage least squares estimates of the model:

(1) TFP   = a_1 KAP_GR + a_2 EPI + u_1
(2) KAP_GR = b_1 PLOUTS + b_2 EPI + u_2
(3) PLOUTS = c_1 TFP   + c_2 EPI + u_3

Instrumental variables: DLOUTS, PRPOUT, REALOUT

Note: When constant terms were included, they were insignificant, reduced the signifi-cance of the EPI variable, and considerably increased the significance of the other explana-tory variable. Signs were the same. A scale variable such as PRPOUT or REALOUT directly on the right-hand side gave insignificant estimates except for the equation for PLOUTS. The signs were the same.

Coefficient estimates for equation 1: TFP

Number of observations = 255				Sum of squared residuals = 3.285		
Mean of TFP	= −0.00178			Disturbance std. dev.	= 0.11351	
S.D. of TFP	= 0.09681			Durbin-Watson statistic	= 1.8860	

Variable	Coefficient	Std. error	T-ratio	Probltl≥x	Mean of X	Std.D. of X
KAP_GR	0.261140	0.416069E-01	6.276	0.00000	0.77192E-01	0.25520
EPI	−0.218973E-03	0.757194E-04	−2.892	0.00383	102.85	13.276

Coefficient estimates for equation 2: KAP_GR

Number of observations = 255				Sum of squared residuals = 16.395		
Mean of KAP_GR	= 0.07719			Disturbance std. dev.	= 0.25356	
S.D. of KAP_GR	= 0.25520			Durbin-Watson statistic	= 1.8055	

Variable	Coefficient	Std. error	T-ratio	Probltl≥x	Mean of X	Std.D. of X
PLOUTS	0.310172E-01	0.390355E-02	7.946	0.00000	1.5557	1.3465
EPI	0.280582E-03	0.164156E-03	1.709	0.08741	102.85	13.276

Coefficient estimates for equation 3: PLOUTS

Number of observations = 255				Sum of squared residuals = 36243.366		
Mean of PLOUTS	= 1.55569			Disturbance std. dev.	= 11.92186	
S.D. of PLOUTS	= 1.34652			Durbin-Watson statistic	= 1.6618	

Variable	Coefficient	Std. error	T-ratio	Probltl≥x	Mean of X	Std.D. of X
EPI	0.179604E-01	0.682746E-02	2.631	0.00852	102.85	13.276
TFP	122.254	19.5036	6.268	0.00000	−0.17843E-02	0.96811E-01

(1) What role did commercial bank lending and industrial protection have on capital investment (see equation 1 in Table 5.11)?

The results here are not unexpected, though the significance of the coefficients is notable given the rather weak, simple correlations. Both protection and a larger proportion of commercial bank lending to a sector were associated with more capital investment in that sector. Thus, as we would expect, financial repression was used to further the objectives reflected in the structure of protection. Without making too much of the aggregate data used, the results also suggest that credit diversion was not a major problem for commercial bank lending (the government-owned PNB provided one-half of these resources during the period of the data set).

(2) How did capital investment and industrial protection affect the rate of growth of total factor productivity (see equation 2 in Table 5.11)?

Capital investment had a positive effect on total factor productivity (TFP) growth, but industrial protection had a negative and significant effect on productivity growth. Based on the overall effect of the simultaneous three-equation model, that is, going beyond the simple coefficient of this equation, we can infer that an increase of protection of 1.0 percent reduces productivity growth by 1.33 percent. Thus the two policy instruments worked at cross-purposes; commercial bank lending contributed to higher investment and higher TFP growth in the sectors that received it, but this positive effect on TFP growth was partly offset by protection.

(3) What role did total factor productivity growth and industrial protection play in the distribution of commercial bank lending (see equation 3 in Table 5.11)?

The estimated model suggests that higher productivity growth was rewarded with a larger proportion of commercial bank lending and that a more protected industry enjoyed a larger proportion of commercial bank lending. There are, however, offsetting effects: protection decreases efficiency, as represented by total productivity growth (which is enhanced by more capital), but it also increases lending to the sector, which leads to more capital being invested in the sector. The net effect of protection on bank lending through the model is positive, with an elasticity close to 1.

As we have suggested, aside from the informal arrangements regarding the rollover of loans in the private sector, public financing was the main identifiable source of investment finance. Roughly in line with government priorities, the DBP lent 43 percent of its resources to manufacturing and provided 12 percent to agriculture. The PNB was also a significant source of long-term finance, with greater emphasis on lending for agricultural purposes. The CB itself operated special lending programs through its rediscount windows from the late 1950s. It was really in the agricultural sector, where the private formal banking system did not have much of a presence in the first place, where most directed lending occurred during the 1970s.

What is important is that the proportion of loan portfolios going to manufacturing of both the commercial banks (in which the government-owned PNB was an important part) and the government development bank did not differ significantly; only in terms of the maturity of the lending, with the development bank providing longer-term loans, have the portfolios differed. The convergence did not occur as a result of government controls but through the interaction of the rates of return provided by the trade regime with customer niches in both the private and the public sectors.

The Philippine record on resource mobilization is mixed, with a high degree of observed domestic savings appearing as deposits despite an unstable trend in financial deepening over the longer term. But in recent years, deposit mobilization has remained strong even in the face of lower real deposit rates and the noticeable shift in financial portfolios to government and foreign debt instruments.

The Philippine government has been an important provider of long-term ventures, which have seldom survived the periodic liquidity crises. This is not surprising as the government's leverage in goal setting and discipline has never been strong. In the Philippines, development plans have been cheerleading exercises rather than targets for which specific resources are identified and against which performance is measured. In this important regard, the role of government in the Philippine economy differs from the QIO structure in Korea.

This chapter is not a second-best argument in favor of utilizing the financial system to rectify the distortions existing in the real sector. For such a policy to be effective, the government must have the capability—consisting of sufficient dominance over the private sector—and the audaciousness to pursue clear objectives. The social intentions of the various Philippine government administrations have never been well defined and independent of interests of influential private sector elements, including the banking sector itself. Our econometric evidence suggests that the financial system responded to the trade regime, which implies that as long as the trade regime is distorted, financial liberalization will only magnify the distorted pattern of allocation which is inherent in the overall industrial stance.

The government, whose leverage ebbed and flowed along with its access to foreign financing, never seems to have taken seriously its own stated goals of expanding exports. Moreover, it never attempted to use the financial system, even in the period where government played a large role in it, to buttress industrial policy goals. Nor was it politically or administratively capable of commandeering private financial resources to realize its objectives.

Our findings suggest some of the risks associated with financial liberalization. First, in the absence of a stable macroeconomic environment, financial liberalization will not realize its objectives. But we also find that in the absence of adequate political independence and regulatory capacity on the part of the state, financial liberalization can lead to the dominance of private interests just as easily as can a strategy of financial repression.

References

Agabin, Meliza. 1988. *A Review of Policies Impinging on the Informal Credit Markets in the Philippines.* Quezon City: Social Weather Station.
Bautista, Ernesto, and Marife Magno. 1990. Overtime Changes in the Structure and Operation of Rural Informal Credit Markets in the Philippines. Paper presented at the seminary workshop on Rural Savings and Informal Credit in the Context of Financial Liberalization, sponsored by the Central Bank of the Philippines Agricultural Credit and Policy Commission and the Philippine Institute for Development Studies, Manila, June 7–8.
Blinder, Alan. 1987. Credit Rationing and Effective Supply Failures. *Economic Journal* 97:327–52.
Central Bank of the Philippines. 1974. *Twenty-Five Years of Economic and Financial Statistics in the Philippines.* Manila: Central Bank of the Philippines.
——. 1988. *Factbook: The Philippines Financial System.* Manila: Central Bank of the Philippines.
——. Various years. *Statistical Bulletin*, various issues. Manila: Central Bank of the Philippines.
Chamley, Christophe, and Qaizar Hussain. 1988. The Removal of Interest Ceilings and Other Regulations on Financial Assets in Thailand, Indonesia, and the Philippines: A Quantitative Evaluation. Washington, D.C.: World Bank. Unpublished manuscript.
Fried, Joel, and Peter Howitt. 1980. Credit Rationing and Implicit Contract Theory. *Journal of Money, Credit, and Banking* 12(3): 471–87.
Friedman, Benjamin. 1983. The Roles of Money and Credit in Macroeconomic Analysis. In *Macroeconomics, Prices, and Quantities: Essays in Memory of Arthur M. Okun*, ed. James Tobin. Washington, D.C.: Brookings Institution.
Fry, Maxwell J. 1988. *Money, Interest, and Banking in Economic Development.* Baltimore: Johns Hopkins University Press.
Golay, Frank H. 1961. *The Philippines: Public Policy and National Economic Development.* Ithaca: Cornell University Press.
Haggard, Stephan. 1990. The Political Economy of the Philippine Debt Crisis. In *Economic Crisis and Policy Choice: The Politics of Adjustment in Developing Countries*, ed. Joan M. Nelson. Princeton: Princeton University Press.
Hooley, Richard. 1985. *Productivity Growth in Philippine Manufacturing: Retrospect and Future Prospects.* Philippine Institute for Development Studies Monograph Series no. 9. Makati: Philippine Institute for Development Studies.

Hooley, Richard, and Honorata Moreno. 1974. *A Study of Financial Flows in the Philippines.* Quezon City: Institute of Economic Development and Research.

Hutchcroft, Paul D. 1993. Selective Squander: The Politics of Preferential Credit Allocation in the Philippines. In *The Politics of Finance in Developing Countries,* ed. Stephan Haggard, Chung H. Lee, and Sylvia Maxfield. Ithaca: Cornell University Press.

Lamberte, Mario B. 1985. Financial Liberalization: What Have We Learnt? *Journal of Philippine Development* 12:274–89.

Lava, Aida, Dennis Arroyo, Rosario de Guzman, and Joselette de los Santos. 1989. *Case Studies on the Monitoring of Informal Credit Markets.* Working Paper Series no. 89–13 (July), Philippine Institute for Development Studies.

Makil, Perla Q., Leonora A. Reyes, and Kenji Koike. 1983. *Philippine Business Leaders.* Tokyo: Institute for Developing Economies.

Montes, Manuel F. 1987. *The Philippines: Stabilization and Adjustment Policies and Programmes.* Helsinki: World Institute for Development Economics Research (WIDER).

———. 1988. The Business Sector and Development Policy. In *National Development Policies and the Business Sector in the Philippines,* ed. Manuel F. Montes and Kenji Koike. Tokyo: Institute for Developing Economies.

———. 1989. Financing Development: The "Corporatist" versus the "Democratic" Approach in the Philippines. In *The Political Economy of Fiscal Policy,* ed. Miguel Urrutia, Shinichi Ichimura, and Setsuko Yukawa. Tokyo: United Nations University.

National Statistical Coordination Board. 1989. *Philippine Statistical Yearbook.* Manila: National Statistical Coordination Board.

Ozaeta, Antonio. 1980. Towards a More Responsive Financial System. In *Fookien Times Philippines Yearbook.* Manila: Fookien Times Yearbook Publishing.

Patrick, Hugh T., and Honorata Moreno. 1982. *The Evolving Structure of the Philippine Private Domestic Commercial Banking System from Independence to 1980: In Light of Japanese Historical Experience.* Tokyo: International Development Center of Japan.

Remolona, Eli M., and Mario B. Lamberte. 1986. Financial Reforms and the Balance-of-Payments Crisis: The Case of the Philippines, 1980–83. *Philippine Review of Economics and Business* 23:101–41.

Santiago, Ben, and Roberto Tagle. 1981. A Review of the Economics of Unibanking. Undergraduate thesis, School of Economics, University of the Philippines, Manila.

Sicat, Gerardo. 1983. *Economics and Development: An Introduction,* 1st ed. Quezon City: University of the Philippines Press.

Stiglitz, Joseph E., and Andrew Weiss. 1981. Credit Rationing in Markets with Imperfect Information. *American Economic Review* 71(3): 393–410.

Tan, Edita A. 1980. Philippine Monetary Policy and Aspects of the Financial Market: A Review of the Literature. In *PIDS Survey of Development Research.* Manila: Philippine Institute for Development Studies.

———. 1989. Bank Concentration and the Structure of Interest. Discussion Paper no. 8915 (October), School of Economics, University of the Philippines.

Tolentino, V. B. J. 1989. The Political Economy of Credit Availability and Financial Liberalization: Notes on the Philippine Experience. *Savings and Development* 4:321–34.

Vos, Rob. 1990. Private Foreign Asset Accumulation: Magnitude and Determinants. ISS Working Paper Series on Finance and Development, no. 33. The Hague: Institute of Social Studies.

World Bank (WB). 1980. *The Philippines: Aspects of the Financial Sector.* Washington, D.C.: WB.

———. 1988. *Philippines Financial Sector Study.* Washington, D.C.: WB.

Yap, Josef T., Mario B. Lamberte, Teodoro S. Untalan, and Maria Socorro V. Zingapan. 1990. *Central Bank Policies and the Behavior of the Money Market.* Manila: Philippine Institute for Development Studies.

PART II

LATIN AMERICA

CHAPTER SIX

CHILE

Felipe Lagos and Carlos Díaz

Chile has a long history of financial repression which goes back to the 1940s. The intellectual origin of this repression lies in the idea that a small economy should develop the manufacturing sector to reduce its foreign dependence. To foster the development of indigenous manufacturing firms, the government restricted imports by imposing tariffs, quotas, and a battery of nontariff barriers and providing subsidies through preferential credit allocation. Only in 1975 did the process of financial liberalization begin in Chile. But lacking proper and practical regulation, the country's financial system became insolvent in the recession of 1982–1983, and the government was forced to nationalize major commercial banks. But, with the implementation of prudential regulation, these banks were later privatized again. In this chapter we look into the effects of financial repression and the subsequent liberalization of the Chilean economy.

Government intervention in the credit market consisted of interest rate controls, selective credit allocation, and quantity controls on the level and rate of expansion of credit. Credit allocation was initially directed to the manufacturing sector and later to the agricultural sector under a vast agrarian reform drive. Quantity controls on credit were introduced to free resources for the public sector and keep inflation under control. But the large public sector deficits financed by the central bank gradually raised the rate of inflation during the period of financial repression.

We conclude that financial repression has had a negative effect on economic growth of the Chilean economy. But we found partial evidence that there was a positive influence of selective credit on manufacturing investment. Due to economic and political instability, however, investment in this sector declined in both absolute and relative terms during the period of financial repression.

I. Structure of the Financial System

In Chile, the period of financial repression began in 1940 and continued until 1974–1975 when financial liberalization was finally undertaken. Because of data and other informational constraints, we focus our analysis on the characteristics of the financial system during the 1953–1990 period. During the period of financial repression (1953–1975), the Chilean government employed a complex system of control over credit allocation. Because different governments undertook subtle—and sometimes major—changes in the system throughout the period, it is best to think in terms of five subperiods that correspond to successive administrations: 1953–1958, the Ibañez administration; 1959–1964, the Alessandri administration; 1965–1970, the Frei administration; 1971–1973, the Allende administration, which was cut short by a military coup that ushered in the period of military rule under Pinochet; and 1974–1975, the first two years of the Pinochet administration, during which the government began to move away from financial repression and toward liberalization.

This periodization is intended to provide a frame of reference for the changing nature of financial policies which reflected the objectives of the different administrations. Despite several differences, the Ibañez, Alessandri, and Frei administrations all designed and implemented monetary stabilization programs; however, they all failed to achieve their macroeconomic objectives owing to their inability to control budgetary deficits. During the Allende period, the emphasis shifted to structural changes such as the nationalization of enterprises and income redistribution and away from price stability and external balance. The final two years of the repression period saw a transition toward liberalization.

Throughout all these periods, the Chilean financial system was composed mainly of the central bank, a state bank, private commercial banks, mortgage banks, mutual and pension funds, insurance companies, savings and loan associations, a few development institutions, the stock market, and the informal credit market. The Banking Superintendency and the central bank were in charge of regulating and supervising commercial banks. The Chilean Development Corporation (CORFO)—the principal government agency created in 1939 to promote sectoral development—acted as a financier and entrepreneur and was the most important institution specializing in financing long-term investment.[1] Other development institutions that played an especially important role during the agrarian reform (1964–1973) are the Institute for Agriculture Development (INDAP) and the Agrarian Reform Corporation (CORA).[2]

The role that the various financial institutions played as providers of credit changed significantly during the years under examination. As shown in Table 6.1, during the repression period of 1953–1975, financial savings at private institutions declined steadily. From 1950 until the mid-1970s, the stock market played a minor role as a source of new funds for the corporate sector as a whole, a fact indicated by the precipitous decline in the volume index of the stock market when transactions plummeted from 100.0 in 1940 to 8.4 in 1971.[3] Additionally, from 1940 to 1968, the real value index of equities dropped 80 percent. In contrast, the role played by public institutions, such as the state and central banks and development institutions, increased during the same period. As expected, the informal credit market was also an important, albeit declining, source of credit, and was more important than were other financial institutions, especially between 1940 and 1950. But this market did not play a significant role in the agricultural sector in terms of loans outstanding, in spite of high interest rates charged on those loans.

Both the market and the ownership structure of the Chilean banking industry have traditionally been highly concentrated. In 1938, Banco de Chile and Banco Español, the two largest banks in terms of credit outstanding, together provided more than one-half of the total private bank credit in the economy (Jeftanovic 1961). The share of equity held by the top thirty stockholders was 17.5 percent for Banco de Chile and 32.5 percent for Banco Español. Banco Edwards, the third-largest bank

1. CORFO extended credit for both working and investment capital, guaranteed foreign loans to domestic enterprises, participated in the equity of both public and private enterprises, and established artificially low interest rates and favorable amortizations.
2. INDAP was created in 1962 to help the agricultural sector with credits and technical assistance and to encourage small farmers to organize into cooperatives. Since 1965, INDAP has taken an active role in these endeavors. CORA was also created in 1962 to promote land reforms and help small farmers and cooperatives with credit. Its role was insignificant until the agrarian reform process was intensified. A generous share of investment outlays was concentrated in hydroelectric power, steel, and petroleum projects.
3. This situation is explained by the absence of a stable dividend policy, a discriminatory tax treatment against equities, and the political and economic instability during this period.

Table 6.1. Financial indicators, 1940–1990 (by percentage)

Year	M_1/GDP[a]	M_3/GDP[b]	Time deposits/GDP	Time deposits/M_1
1940	12.0	na	1.9	15.8
1950	10.5	na	0.4	3.8
1960	9.0	12.7	1.9	21.1
1970	10.2	14.1	0.8	7.8
1973	22.2[c]	28.5	0.1	0.5
1980	7.3	24.0	2.5	28.7
1985	5.0	27.9	36.1	302.1
1990	5.7	34.0	20.6	361.1

	Commercial banks' average annual real interest rate for credits[d]	Private bank credit/GDP	State and central bank credits/GDP	Development institutions' credits/GDP
1940	−0.7	11.0	11.3	na
1950	−1.0	9.5	5.9	1.5
1960	13.6	6.3	9.4	1.7
1970	−8.1	3.9	14.6	4.1
1973	−75.7	3.4	74.3	5.2
1980	15.2	27.5	18.6	2.4
1985	9.4	41.9	27.1	3.5
1990	13.3	34.1	12.9	na

	Mutual funds' financial assets/GDP	Insurance companies' financial assets/GDP	Informal estimated credits/GDP	Stock market volume of transactions index
1940	0.0	2.6	15.9	100.0
1950	0.1	2.6	12.9	61.3
1960	0.1	1.0	5.4	32.4
1971	0.0	0.5	2.3	8.4
1980	2.6	na	na	568.2
1985	0.8	3.5	na	98.5
1990	1.7	7.4	na	1,107.4

Sources: Central Bank of Chile 1989; Superintendencia de Bancos e Instituciones Financieras, various years; CORFO, various years a; Cahmi and Fielbaum 1978; and Superintendencia de Valores y Seguros, various years a, b.

Note: na = not available.

[a]M_1 = private money.

[b]$M_3 = M_1$ + time deposits + private quasi money.

[c]In 1973, money supply increased dramatically, which led to an acceleration of the inflation rate.

[d]Until 1973, the real interest rates were calculated based on the maximum legal rate of interest, deflated by the consumer price index. From 1980 to 1990, the real interest rates correspond to the annualized real rates for operations within 90–365 days.

with a 4.9 percent share of total private bank credit, was closely controlled by a very highly concentrated ownership.

In 1956, the two largest banks—Banco de Chile and Banco Español—together still accounted for a significant 43.1 percent of total private bank credit, with ownership concentration slightly higher for the former. Even after eighteen years, the market structure remained basically the same: the top three banks accounted for almost 50 percent of total private bank credit. The higher ownership concentration in smaller banks also remained basically unchanged between 1938 and 1956. There is no available information on credit allocated to ownership-related nonfinancial institutions.

By 1982 the structure of the banking industry had become less concentrated, with the two largest banks accounting for 38 percent of total private bank credit. Nevertheless, many banks were controlled by large conglomerates or economic groups, becoming an important source of credit for other companies belonging to the groups. For example, Banco de Santiago, the second-largest bank in size, had 43 percent of its total outstanding credit allocated to ownership-related firms. A similar pattern of credit allocation was also observed in the case of Banco de Chile and Banco Nacional (Valdés and de la Cuadra 1990).

II. Financial Repression

As noted earlier, the government interfered with the credit market by controlling the interest rates, as well as the amount, rate of expansion, and allocation of credit. In this section we analyze the motivations that led to market intervention and the instruments that were used to achieve the desired objectives during the 1953–1973 period. We then examine the effect of government intervention.

Interest Rate Controls

The policy of the central bank and the superintendency was to keep interest rates low by fixing nominal interest rates on credit and deposits at a low rate.[4] The results of this policy are reflected in Tables 6.2 and 6.3, which provide data on the legal maximum interest rates for credit and the interest rates charged by the central bank and commercial

---

4. For credits, the maximum nominal rate of interest was defined as the maximum rate that could have been legally charged by a commercial bank.

Table 6.2. Average real and nominal interest rates charged on credits by the central bank

Period	Bank's rediscounts		Public sector credits[a]		Private sector credits	
	Nominal rate	Real rate	Nominal rate	Real rate	Nominal rate	Real rate
1944–1952	4.5	−11.5	1.9	−13.7	6.4	−9.8
1953–1958	5.0	−28.2	1.8	−30.4	11.3	−23.6
1959–1964	12.3	−6.5	1.0	−19.1	13.2	−9.4
1965–1970	na	na	na	na	16.7	−7.3
1971–1973	na	na	na	na	26.7	−44.4
1974–1975	na	na	na	na	na	na

Sources: Central Bank of Chile, various years.
Note: na = not available.
[a] The public sector includes the fiscal sector, public agencies, autonomous institutions, and municipalities.

Table 6.3. Average real and nominal interest rates charged by commercial banks

Period	Average nominal rate			Average real rate		
	Rate charged by banks	Legal maximum rate	Effective rate	Rate charged by banks	Legal maximum rate	Effective rate
1953–1958	13.5	16.5	19.7	−22.3	−20.3	−18.1
1959–1964	15.4	18.5	22.6	−7.5	−5.0	−1.8
1965–1970	17.1	20.6	26.0	−7.0	−4.3	−0.1
1971–1973	24.2	29.0	na	−46.1	−44.4	na
1974–1975	34.4	● 37.5	na	−32.3	−31.6	na

Sources: Tapia and Olivares 1970; Fleischman 1972; Central Bank of Chile 1989.
Note: na = not available.

banks. Interest rates on deposits were freed in October 1957, but this change did not attract savings because restrictions remained on nominal interest rates on credit.[5]

Although there was excess demand for credit, commercial banks did not always charge the maximum legal rate because of the central bank's policy of low interest rates. If a commercial bank made a loan at a rate lower than the maximum established rate, it was allowed to rediscount a certain proportion of the loan with the central bank at a rate lower than the lending rate. This policy became particularly effective in controlling credit allocation in 1953–1958 because during this period, refinancing

5. Interest rate control for credit operations remained during the entire period of repression, thus constituting a ceiling.

constituted the most important source of subsidized funds for commercial banks. For example, in 1957 and 1958 the amount of rediscounts was on average equivalent to 70 percent of a typical commercial bank's capital and retained earnings. This instrument was also used, albeit with less strength, during the 1964–1970 period.

In practice, however, the commercial banks' announced interest rates differed significantly from those effectively paid by their clients. This discrepancy came about because the banks made an advance collection of interest payments and because of specific taxes and other fiscal surcharges on bank loans.[6] These fiscal charges amounted to an average of 20 percent of nominal effective rates from 1953–1958, 22 percent from 1959–1964, and 30 percent from 1965–1970.

From Table 6.3, which presents the real and nominal rates of interest charged by commercial banks and the effective rates paid on credit, it is clear that although the nominal effective rates were higher than the legal maximum, the real effective rates were negative during the period of repression. This situation was particularly dramatic during the 1953–1958 period.

Given these negative effective real interest rates, one wonders how the banks survived all those years. Also puzzling is the fact that during this period, there was a strong interest on the part of the private sector to create new banks. One possible explanation is that the cost of external funds to banks was very low as interest rates on deposits and the central bank's rediscount rate were both low; consequently, the banks could make profits from the positive spread between their lending and borrowing rates. The cost of internal funds such as the banks' capital and retained earnings could not, however, have been low given that they had more profitable alternative uses. In fact, according to Jeftanovic (1961), the banks suffered persistent losses from 1936 to 1957 and a diminution in their capital.

The most plausible explanation for this phenomenon is that the banks allocated part of their capital and retained earnings to ownership-related firms, as in the case of Banco de Santiago, which had 43 percent of its total outstanding credit allocated to ownership-related firms. That is, the banks were basically used as a source of cheap credit for the bank owners' personal and other businesses. While the banks were losing money, other ownership-related firms were reaping the benefits of cheap credit, because what mattered was the total profits for the entire group and not those of the group's bank.

6. In short, the effective rate was the sum of the interest rate formally charged by the bank, the bank's informally charged extra points, and the government surcharges.

Quantitative Credit Control

During the period of financial repression the government, through the central bank, controlled both the amount and expansion rate of commercial banks' outstanding credit. As shown in Table 6.4, the central bank constituted the financial system's most important source of funds and was, at the same time, the entity in charge of regulating the system. The motivation for intervening in the financial system in such a way came from the necessity of financing the fiscal deficit through

Table 6.4. Credit of the central bank, state bank, and private commercial banks

Central bank

		Relative to total	Distribution			
Period	Index (Avg. 1953–1958 = 100)	bank's credit (%)	Local currency[a]	Foreign currency	Public sector	Priv sect
1953–1958	100	24.5	92.8	7.2	73.9	26
1959–1964	385	43.0	14.5	85.5	86.0	14.
1965–1970	806	55.0	11.6	88.4	93.3	6.
1971–1973	2,708	76.1	55.3	44.7	96.1	3
1974–1975	3,780	84.8	20.8	79.2	99.3	0.

Private commercial banks

		Relative to total	Distribution			
Period	Index (Avg. 1953–1958 = 100)	bank's credit (%)	Local currency	Foreign currency	Public sector	Priv sect
1953–1958	100	42.0	96.7	3.3	2.4	97.
1959–1964	174	36.3	76.0	24.0	1.1	98.
1965–1970	201	24.3	88.8	11.2	0.6	99.
1971–1973	161	8.4	89.0	11.0	11.4	88.
1974–1975	171	6.7	44.9	55.1	8.2	91.

State bank

		Relative to total	Distribution			
Period	Index (Avg. 1953–1958 = 100)	bank's credit (%)	Local currency	Foreign currency	Public sector	Priv sect
1953–1958	100	33.5	99.9	0.1	10.2	89.
1959–1964	124	20.7	92.9	7.1	7.5	92.
1965–1970	219	20.7	89.1	10.9	14.8	85.
1971–1973	382	15.6	81.4	18.6	8.8	81.
1974–1975	271	8.5	57.0	43.0	43.6	56.

Sources: Banking Superintendency, various years; Central Bank of Chile, various years.
[a] Credit in local and foreign currency.

monetary expansion. Quantitative controls allowed the government a higher degree of freedom in financing the fiscal deficit than otherwise as the quantitative controls could be used to control credit expansion. Even then, however, the rate of inflation increased during the repression period because the fiscal deficit was financed with new money created by the central bank. As can be seen in Table 6.5, there is a close correspondence between the size of the fiscal deficit and the rate of inflation during the 1944–1975 period.

To control credit expansion, the central bank issued periodic instructions, established quotas on credit expansion, and supervised their fulfillment. These quotas were expressed either as a maximum rate of credit increase or as a fixed total amount of credit. The central bank also threatened the commercial banks in a credible way by not allowing access to the rediscount window if their credit surpassed these limits. The overall experience with this type of control was negative, however. Quotas became a central point of concern for the banks, and lobbying to obtain preferential treatment became intense.

In 1959, the central bank started using reserve requirements, dropping quantitative control on credit expansion, as an instrument for controlling inflation. In addition to the basic reserve requirement rate, the central bank, in conjunction with the Banking Superintendency, established a marginal rate that was applicable to deposits beyond a certain amount. This rate was higher on average on demand deposits than on time deposits and was changed periodically. It was raised in 1959 to a level in excess of 60 percent on both types of deposits and kept at higher rates on demand deposits until the end of the repression period (Table 6.6).

The use of quantitative controls had the effect of channeling a major part of the funds of the financial system into the public sector at the

Table 6.5. Fiscal deficit and inflation rate

Period	Fiscal deficit as a percentage of fiscal income	Fiscal accounts as a percentage of GDP			Average yearly inflation rate (Dec.–Dec.)
		Income	Expenses	Deficit	
1944–1952	4.4	15.4	16.1	0.6	18.5
1953–1958	17.6	14.4	17.0	2.5	48.0
1959–1964	26.2	16.5	20.9	4.3	26.0
1965–1970	9.9	21.7	23.8	2.1	26.6
1971–1973	82.0	19.6	35.7	16.1	169.0
1974–1975	29.2	23.4	29.9	6.6	358.0

Sources: Cortés and de la Cuadra 1984; Central Bank of Chile 1989.

Table 6.6. Reserve requirement rate (as a percentage of deposits)

Period	Local currency			
	Demand deposits		Time deposits	
	Basic	Marginal	Basic	Marginal
1953–1958	20.0	20.0	8.0	8.0
1959–1964	20.0	67.9	8.0	66.4
1965–1970	37.5	68.8	24.8	21.5
1971–1973	68.7	75.0	18.0	8.0
1974–1975	90.0	80.0	8.6	8.6

Sources: Central Bank of Chile, various years.
Note: On average, effective reserve requirement rates, defined as total reserves/total deposits, were 20 percent in 1953–1958, 26 percent in 1959–1964, and 32 percent in 1965–1970.

expense of the private sector. In 1944–1952, credits to the public and private sectors made up 42 and 58 percent, respectively, of total central bank credits and investments, but by 1965–1970, the distribution had shifted dramatically to 86 percent to the public sector and 14 percent to the private sector. The distribution became even more skewed under Allende, and by 1974–1975, the private sector was receiving less than 6 percent of total central bank credits (Cortés and de la Cuadra 1984).

Credit Allocation Controls

Beginning in the 1930s, the manufacturing sector began to receive special government attention and preferential treatment. Although political and emotional factors were powerful in establishing the drive for industrialization, the Great Depression and the emergence of a new theory of economic growth contributed to the adoption of an interventionist policy. As observed by Mamalakis and Reynolds (1965), "The wave of liberalism and balanced growth attitudes that had almost uninterruptedly swept Chile until the Great Depression, was replaced by protectionism favoring a 'big push' leading to self-sufficiency" (pp. 14–15). Indigenous manufacturing industries were seen as key for putting the economy on the path of independent growth. Industrial policies were gradually implemented and came in two distinct stages. First, during 1931–1938, the government undertook restrictive measures, including tariffs, quotas, import licenses, exchange controls, and multiple exchange rates, to protect indigenous manufacturing industries. Second, from 1938 until the end of the financial repression, the government granted direct subsidies, tax exemptions, and low-cost credit to the manufacturing industries. CORFO was created in 1939 as the principal institution for carrying out these policies for industrialization.

As was to be expected, other sectors, such as mining, agriculture, and services, were neglected during this period. Relative prices turned against them, and funds were seldom available for their development. In fact, there were periods during which the government took away resources from these sectors and diverted them to manufacturing. Such a situation was especially true in the case of mining, where the government imposed strong discriminatory measures, such as high direct taxes and unfavorable exchange rates. The large, foreign-owned copper and nitrate concerns were particular targets of these measures.

Even though the policy of protecting the manufacturing sector against imports continued, in the 1950s the government began to shift its emphasis from promoting manufacturing to promoting "productive activities" in general. Many existing institutions were restructured, and new policies to develop productive activities were implemented. In the mid-1960s, agriculture became a sector receiving preferential treatment through CORA and INDAP, especially with the adoption of agrarian reform.

To control credit allocation, the central bank frequently sent notices encouraging commercial banks to allocate credit to productive activities. Rediscounting was also selectively allowed to banks extending credit to productive activities, especially to those extending credit to agriculture, under specific terms and interest rates. This practice was stopped in 1959 mainly because of its ineffectiveness. The government did not have the ability to process the information related to the allocation of credit and was consequently unable to control its ultimate use.[7] This problem of credit diversion was particularly important in the case of funds advanced through the rediscount operation.

Quotas on credit expansion were also used to intervene in credit allocation. For instance, larger quotas were granted to regional banks and the agricultural and industrial departments of state banks. On average, limits established for these banks were from 15 to 40 percent higher than those for other institutions.

As another means of controlling credit allocation, the authorities exempted new credit from the marginal reserve requirement if it satisfied certain conditions in terms of the interest rate and other terms of the loan. Given the persistently high levels of reserve requirements,

7. To supervise the credit allocation process, the central bank demanded from commercial banks all relevant information related to new credit when its total amount exceeded a predetermined quantity.

exempting new credit from the reserve requirement became the most important and most frequently used instrument. Given the use of marginal reserve requirements to achieve several policy objectives, however, calculation of the right percentage for the requirement became excessively complicated, and thus in 1965, the reserve requirement was abandoned as an instrument of credit allocation.

During the 1959–1964 period, central bank funds were made available under favorable terms to commercial banks to meet the needs of specific sectors at low lending rates. Direct credit was also continually granted to private sector industries but at a decreasing rate until 1965. This practice was later suspended as it became too difficult for the central bank to maintain a close and direct relationship with a large number of clients.

Several specific lines of credit were created after 1965 to exercise further effective control over credit allocation and to provide cheap credit to a broad class of firms. The support for productive, nonservices activities continued with subsidized credit. In August 1970, funds allocated to such activities through these specific lines of credit represented 43 percent of total commercial bank credit.

Commercial banks were required to allocate their new credit through more than ten different lines until certain predetermined goals in terms of amount and/or percentage of the outstanding credit were reached. The most important line was the cash flow budget credit line, which operated on the basis of an agreement between a client and a bank or a consortium of banks. This credit line gave the client access to all funds necessary for operation according to the client's cash flow budget; but in exchange for the access, the client was required to make all payments in cash and hand over to the bank or the consortium the collection of all bills. In 1966, the central bank ordered commercial banks to allocate funds through this line until they reached an amount equal to at least 13 percent of their total credit outstanding, an amount later raised to 19 percent in 1967 and 25 percent in 1968. Although the cash flow budget credit line was created to help all productive activities, a major part of the funds went to the manufacturing sector. Thus, at the end of 1968 the manufacturing sector accounted for more than 70 percent of the total amount of funds allocated through this line. The remainder went to the agricultural sector.

In 1970–1973, the government tightened its control over credit allocation. It also began to nationalize commercial banks, bringing more than 90 percent of all commercial banks under state ownership by 1971. During this period, the authorities tried to allocate credit to productive activities that were deemed most important according to criteria established by the Ministry of Development.

III. Evaluation of Credit Allocation

Although the central bank's direct credit was allocated to the private sector, there is little information on how it was distributed across sectors and activities. Some authors such as Ffrench-Davis (1973) argue that the major part of the credit went to large companies, but this argument is based largely on the fact that until the end of the 1970s, many members of the central bank's board of directors had some financial interest in these corporations. Also, no information exists on CORFO's allocation of credit by sectors, but it is known that a major part of its funds was allocated to designated sectors.[8] With respect to CORA and INDAP, evidence indicates that all their funds were allocated within the agricultural sector (CORFO, various years a, b; Cahmi and Fielbaum 1978).

Evidence on the allocation of bank credit shows that with the exception of 1971–1973, when the total amount of commercial bank credit contracted dramatically as a result of economic chaos and hyperinflation, much of private commercial bank credit ended up in the manufacturing sector, although "productive activities" in general were supposed to be promoted (Banking Superintendency, various years; Central Bank of Chile 1989). The manufacturing sector was heavily protected against foreign competition, and consequently, its rate of return would have been high and its risk low. Because they were free to allocate credit across several productive activities, the banks simply allocated credit to the activities with the highest rate of return. Such allocation would have been especially easy when some of these activities were carried out by ownership-related firms. The econometric results presented later in this paper support this thesis.

The mining sector received very little credit from private banks, probably because bank owners and the government did not have any economic interest in this sector since the large mining companies were owned by foreigners. The share of private bank credit going to the

8. By law, CORFO's objectives were to improve the standard of living of the population and the balance of international payments. These vague criteria were finally materialized as an import substitution criterion and as investments in activities of high capital intensity. Within these categories, emphasis was put on power, raw materials, and intermediate goods.

agricultural sector declined over the 1965–1975 period, and the ratio of credit allocated to the value added of the agricultural sector also fell. In contrast, the ratio of credit to value added for the manufacturing sector remained relatively constant (Banking Superintendency, various years; Central Bank of Chile 1989).

With respect to the distribution of credit across sectors by the state bank, the state bank granted a higher proportion of its credit to agriculture than to manufacturing. This difference is even greater if one compares the distribution of credit relative to GDP or capital stock (Banking Superintendency, various years; Central Bank of Chile 1989). In our opinion, this bias in credit toward agriculture reflects the government's attempt to offset the unfavorable side effects resulting from tariffs on manufacturing imports (Krueger, Schiff, and Valdés 1990).

Fuenzalida and Undurraga (1968) examined more than thirteen thousand bank debtors at the end of 1965 to determine if credit allocation was concentrated in large companies. Bank debtors were first sorted by sectors and then classified into nine categories according to the size of their capital stock. Debt was measured as only direct bank credit (in local and foreign currency). As shown in Table 6.7, whereas debtors in categories one through four owned 26 percent of the total stock of capital, they received 42 percent of the total credit outstanding. It is thus small and medium-sized firms that received a large share of credit. To

Table 6.7. Credit and capital distribution by capital categories, 1965

Capital category[a]	Stock of capital (millions of 1977 US$)[b]	Percentage	Percentage excluding capital category 9	Credit (millions of 1977 US$)	Percentage	Percent excludi capita categor
1	1,304	2.1	3.2	810	7.8	8.2
2	4,957	8.0	12.0	1,447	14.0	14.7
3	3,919	6.3	9.5	905	8.7	9.2
4	6,258	10.1	15.2	1,363	13.1	13.8
5	8,358	13.5	20.3	1,783	17.2	18.1
6	3,428	5.5	8.3	712	6.8	7.2
7	3,619	6.9	10.3	849	8.2	8.6
8	8,733	14.1	21.2	1,993	19.2	20.2
9	20,749	33.5		494	4.8	
Total	61,326	100.0	100.0	10,356	100.0	100.0

Source: Fuenzalida and Undurraga 1968.
[a] For each capital category, a firm's capital stock range is as follows: 1, 0–0.5; 2, 0.5–1.6; 3, 1.6–2.6; 4, 2 5.3; 5, 5.3–16.0; 6, 16.0–26; 7, 26–53; 8, 53–264; and 9, 264 or more.
[b] Sum of all the firms' capital stocks that were under each category.

avoid any distortion owing to the presence of excessively large companies, the same calculation was carried out with the debtors in the ninth category excluded. Even so, small and medium-sized firms received a larger share of credit. Thus the argument that a large amount of credit went to a small number of large enterprises that belonged to the owners of the banks must be rejected.

The manufacturing industry was heavily protected from imports and also received most of its credit from commercial banks. Within manufacturing, the most-protected industries received a relatively large amount of credit. For example, the food, textiles and clothing, and footwear industries—industries in which the effective protection was especially high throughout the 1960s and through the first half of the 1970s (Corbo and Meller 1981; Aedo and Lagos 1984)—were also the industries that received a relatively large amount of credit from commercial banks (Banking Superintendency, various years).

Given that credit allocated at fixed nominal interest rates provides a subsidy to borrowers, we would expect that this pattern of lending would influence resource allocation. To find the sectoral distribution of this subsidy, we have estimated the subsidy implicit in such loans using the following formula:

$$S_{tj} = C_{tj}\{(1 + i_t^*)(1 + \pi_t) - (1 + i_t)\}$$

where

S_{tj} = the amount of subsidy in sector j in year t,
C_{tj} = the amount of credit granted to sector j in year t,
i_t = effective interest rate charged on loans,
i_t^* = interest rate in the absence of the subsidy, and
π_t = the rate of inflation.

The London Interbank Offer Rate plus a 6 percent country risk rate is used as a proxy for i_t^*.[9] In a liberalized capital market, banks would charge i_t^* adjusted by the rate of inflation on their loans,[10] thus the difference between this rate and the effective rate corresponds to a subsidy. The subsidies for the agricultural, mining, manufacturing, and services sectors are shown in Table 6.8 as a percentage of sectoral output. As a proportion of output, the subsidies increased in the 1970s

9. Six percent is a reasonable estimate of the country risk for Chile (see Valdés, Muchnik, and Hurtado 1990).
10. Indexation in the capital market is actually a common practice in Chile and in economies with high inflation.

Table 6.8. Credit subsidy (as a percentage of sectoral output)

Year	Agriculture	Mining	Manufacturing	Services
1965	2.4	0.1	1.0	0.6
1966	0.9	0.0	0.5	0.3
1967	1.6	0.1	0.8	0.4
1968	2.7	0.1	1.3	0.6
1969	3.5	0.1	1.3	0.6
1970	4.1	0.2	1.4	0.7
1971	4.6	0.3	1.4	0.8
1972	25.5	2.9	12.4	4.7
1973	56.7	0.4	8.6	4.7
1974	39.8	2.8	17.2	2.3

Sources: Central Bank of Chile 1989; Banking Superintendency, various years.

because of the high rate of inflation, with those in the agricultural sector being especially significant.[11]

The principal question is whether this pattern of subsidized credit had any effect on the sectoral distribution of investment. To test this hypothesis, we used a model of sectoral investment developed by Coeymans (1989) and added a credit variable. The modified model explains the allocation of a given amount of investment (savings) among the different sectors (agriculture, mining, manufacturing, and services). In Figures 6.1, 6.2, and 6.3, sectoral investment relative to total investment and credit in each sector relative to total credit is plotted. In mining, credit is minimal; in agriculture, a weak negative relationship exists between the two variables; and in the manufacturing sector, there is a negative contemporaneous relationship (that is, the correlation coefficient is -0.25), but a positive correlation with credit lagged one period (the correlation coefficient is 0.27).

Coeymans's model follows the portfolio approach, and the sectoral share of investment thus depends on the expected marginal rate of return in each sector. The specification adopted implies that the rates of return rather than the desired stock of capital determine the share of investment. An increase in the expected rate of return in sector i, given the rate of return in other sectors, will increase the share of investment in sector i. The positive effect includes a change in the desired stock of capital in sector i and an increase in the speed of adjustment in the actual stock toward its equilibrium level.

11. It should be recognized, however, that this subsidy partially compensated for the low effective protection granted to this sector. Thus, its net effect on resource allocation is ambiguous.

The expected marginal rate of return of each sector corresponds to the expected marginal profits arising from a unit of additional capital valued at the replacement cost. For econometric analysis, however, it is possible to use only the average rate of return, defined as after-tax profits divided by the value of fixed capital.[12] The expected rates of return are constructed as the fitted values of AR(3) regressions—autoregressive with three lagged periods—with a variable representing foreign exchange restriction (FEC). This variable, constructed by Coeymans (1989), corresponds to the maximum real imports that are possible and is equal to the value of exports less financial services plus autonomous capital movements and international reserves at the end of the preceding year. It thus captures the terms of trade and foreign interest rate shocks and summarizes the news on external foreign crisis.[13]

Sectoral investment behavior is affected not only by the expected rates of return but also by the transitory or unexpected rates of return. This variable captures new information not contained in the expected rates. The transitory effect is obtained as the difference between the actual and the estimated expected rate.

In a manner analogous to the wealth effect of the portfolio model, the investment model includes total investment normalized by the capital stock of the previous year. Overall investment conveys information about expectations on the future growth of the economy, where an increase in total investment implies that the expected growth of the economy will be higher. Lagged shares of investment are also included in the model. This variable captures the fact that actual investment depends on decisions made in preceding years. The difficulty of predicting the future in the Chilean economy also justifies the presence of inertia in the investment process.

Finally, to capture the effect of credit on sectoral investment, we include in the model the stock of credit of each sector relative to total bank credit. To differentiate between the period of financial repression (1965–1975) from the period of financial liberalization (1976–1982) in the sample,[14] we used two dummy variables: a free dummy that takes a value of zero for 1965–1975 and a value of one for 1976–1982, and an interactive dummy with the credit coefficient.

12. Profits are computed from national accounts data, and the value of capital corresponds to the price of capital as constructed by Coeymans (1989).
13. In the Chilean economy, most recessions are associated with external shocks. The variable FEC includes the price of copper, total exports, net financial services, and capital movements.
14. To gain degrees of freedom, we ran the regression for the period 1965–1982, for which complete data are available.

For each sector, with the exception of services,[15] the following equation is estimated using the full-information maximum likelihood technique:[16]

$$S_i = a + b_1 R_1 + b_2 R_2 + b_3 R_3 + b_4 R_{iT} + b_5 I/K_{t-1} + b_6 S_{i,t-1} + b_7 C_i/C_T$$
$$+ b_8 (C_i/C_T)*D + b_9 D + b_{10} D_{73} + b_{11} D_{74}$$

where

S_i = I_i/I, the share of sector i in total investment (i = agriculture, mining, and manufacturing),

R_1 = expected rate of return in agriculture,

R_2 = expected rate of return in mining,

R_3 = expected rate of return in manufacturing,

R_{iT} = transitory component in the rate of return,

I = overall investment,

K_{t-1} = lagged stock of capital,

C_i = bank credit in sector i,

C_T = total bank credit,

D = dummy variable, with a value of zero for 1965–1975 and of one for 1976–1982,

D_{73} = dummy variable for the year 1973, and

D_7 = dummy variable for the year 1974.

The evidence presented in Table 6.9 shows that the own expected rate of return is positive and significant in all sectors, with the strongest effect in the manufacturing sector. The cross effect between mining and manufacturing is negative and significant, reflecting a substitution relationship. The transitory component in the rate of return is significant only for the manufacturing sector. The effect of total investment is negative in agriculture, mining, and manufacturing, indicating that when total investment increases, only the share of the services sector increases, which may be because public investment is oriented toward the latter (roads, ports, public hospitals, public schools, and so forth).

The result in which we are especially interested is the effect of the share of credit on the investment share. The evidence indicates that an increase in the share of credit does not have a statistically significant effect on the investment share in agriculture and mining and is only

15. The system allocates a given amount of investment, so the adding up restriction should hold. The sector that is excluded is services.
16. The problem of simultaneous equations arises because of the expected returns. To avoid a loss of degrees of freedom, homogeneity and symmetry restrictions are incorporated.

Table 6.9. Determinants of investment shares

	Agriculture		Mining		Manufacturing	
	Coefficient	T-statistic	Coefficient	T-statistic	Coefficient	T-statistic
Constant	0.17	4.1	0.30	5.60	0.05	6.90
R_1	0.60	4.0	—	—		
R_2	—		0.50	3.10	-0.30^a	
R_3	—		−0.30	−2.40	1.70	5.90
R_{iT}	—	—			1.40	6.90
I/K_{t-1}	−1.60	−3.8	−2.50	−3.90	−4.60	−4.20
$S_{i,t-1}$	0.50	3.9	—		—	
C_i/C_T	0.03	0.4	0.02	0.01	0.20	1.80
C_i/C_T*D	−0.40	−2.2	−2.70	−1.10	−1.10	−4.90
D	0.70	2.1	0.06	1.20	0.30	4.50
D73	—		0.08	1.50	—	
D74	—			2.60	−0.30	−7.00
$(C_i/C_T)_{t-1}$					0.30	2.30

Note: A dash indicates that the coefficient was not significant.
[a] Coefficient obtained from the restrictions.

marginally significant in the manufacturing sector. The lagged credit variable is significant for manufacturing, however; that is, there is a time lag between borrowers' receiving credit and their making the actual investment.

During the period of financial repression, the manufacturing sector was one of the dynamic sectors, albeit not the most dynamic, and it held the largest share in terms of total credit (Table 6.10).[17] In contrast, the more dynamic sectors such as transport and other services had only a modest share of credit and even a negative credit flow in the case of services. The agricultural sector received the second-largest share of credit, an amount that includes credit from the government institutions of CORA and INDAP, which was important especially during the 1964–1973 period, when the agrarian reform was being carried out.

In spite of the large share of credit going to the manufacturing sector, the investment share of this sector declined from 1967 through 1974 with the exception of 1973 (Figure 6.3). Even worse, the absolute amount of investment began to decline in 1968. But manufacturing is

17. Credit flow corresponds to C_t-C_{t-1}. The share of credit is influenced by the share of output in total output of the specific sector as well as its growth rate of output. A sector with a large share of output may need credits to maintain the existing level of output, even though it is not growing at all.

In 1975, a year of recession hit the manufacturing and construction sectors very badly. To avoid a bias against these sectors, 1975 was excluded from the analysis.

Felipe Lagos and Carlos Díaz

Table 6.10. Sectoral growth and credit share and flow, 1965–1974 (by percentage)

Sector	Average output growth	Share of total credit	Average flow of credit relative to output
Agriculture	2.90	32.9	−0.4524
Mining	2.38	1.4	0.0071
Manufacturing	3.33	37.4	0.0429
Trade	1.64	13.1	−0.2895
Construction	1.08	4.5	−0.1064
Transport	3.60	1.4	0.0066
Services[a]	4.57	9.4	−0.0774

Sources: Central Bank of Chile 1989; Banking Superintendency, various years.
[a] Includes financial, municipal, personal, consumption, and other services.

also the sector with the highest private rate of return. During 1965–1974, the average real rate of return for manufacturing was 30 percent (with a very small variance), compared with 12 percent for agriculture, 19 percent for mining, and 15 percent for services. How do we reconcile the decline in investment in manufacturing with its high rate of return and its large credit share? One possible explanation is that economic and political instability in those years deterred investment, although some microeconomic policies such as the imposition of tariffs maintained a high profit rate for the sector.

Finally, we note that the dummy variable that discriminates between the period of financial repression and financial liberalization has a positive and significant effect in the manufacturing and agricultural sectors. This finding implies that financial liberalization had a positive effect on investment shares in these sectors. It is to the liberalization process that we now turn.

IV. Liberalization of the Financial Sector

Beginning in 1975, the Chilean government undertook the process of financial liberalization with the following principal measures:

(1) All banks controlled by the government, except the state bank, were transferred to the private sector through an auction process.
(2) Credit ceilings were gradually lifted and were eliminated once the fiscal deficit was under control. Ceilings on foreign borrowing by banks were gradually lifted and eliminated in 1979.
(3) All credit controls, special credit lines, selective rediscount policies, and other forms of credit allocations by administrative means were gradually eliminated.

Table 6.11. Real interest rate and spread (by annualized percentages)

Year	Interest[a]	Spread[b]
1974	−48.0	na
1975	0.0	na
1976	49.4	8.1
1977	56.5	17.4
1978	45.9	10.7
1979	19.6	7.3
1980	11.4	5.2
1981	34.5	6.3
1982	31.4	9.6
1983	8.7	11.0

Source: Adapted from Valdés and de la Cuadra 1990.
Note: na = not available.
[a] Interest rate for short-term loans (thirty to eighty-nine days).
[b] Spread between lending and borrowing rates in thirty-day operations.

(4) Lending and deposit interest rates were freed.
(5) The reserve requirement on demand deposits was lowered from 85 percent in 1976 to 10 percent in 1980. For time deposits, the requirement went down from 55 percent to 4 percent. The reserve requirement on foreign borrowing, which was established in 1978 as a way of taxing short-term capital inflows, was also reduced. For loans with a maturity of less than thirty-six months, the reserve requirement was reduced from 25 percent to zero.
(6) Late in 1979 all credit operations of the central bank with the public sector were prohibited. The central bank could lend money only to financial institutions.

The Real Interest Rate and Financial Liberalization

Immediately following financial liberalization, real rates of interest increased greatly (Table 6.11). According to Valdés and de la Cuadra (1990), this occurrence was an overshooting in the interest rate resulting from the supply of credit rising slowly relative to demand. That is, savings were slowly channeled to the financial market, whereas the demand for credit expanded rapidly as the firms that were previously excluded from the capital market quickly increased their demand for credit. The rise in the real interest rate was also a consequence of the stabilization program launched by the government in early 1975. Inflation, which reached 340 percent in 1975, declined to 175 percent in 1976, and this unanticipated decline in inflation increased the ex post real interest rate.

As shown in Table 6.11, the spread between the lending rate, that is, the real rate of interest that banks charge to their clients, and the borrowing rate, or the real rate of interest that banks pay to the public for deposits, increased soon after liberalization. This may reflect an increase in credit risk because of the banks' inexperience in evaluating such risk. Valdés and de la Cuadra (1990) argue that it takes some time for banks to learn the business and reduce the intermediation cost.

Prudential Regulation and the 1982–1983 Crisis of the Banking Sector

In a liberalized capital market, the government should exercise prudential regulation, especially if it guarantees bank deposits. Prudential regulation is necessary because in the banking industry, there is an externality and a public-good problem; that is, the social value of information about the risk of bank insolvency is greater than its private value. But prudential regulation also gives rise to problems of structural contingent subsidies, moral hazard, and rollover of unrealized loan losses (Valdés and de la Cuadra 1990). If the government gives a free guarantee to deposits, this constitutes a subsidy, from which the banks will try to obtain the most. Moral hazard is the typical problem of asymmetric information because regulators cannot see the risk taken by the banks. Rollover of unrealized loan losses is also a problem of asymmetric information, for a bank may continue to operate when it is, in fact, insolvent. To deal with these problems, regulators may set debt-capital ratio limits, restrict the kind of assets that banks can hold, control entry to and exit from the banking industry, and assume the power to decide when a bank is insolvent.

In Chile, prudential regulation was established only in 1980 after the government had given support to depositors at five large financial institutions. The government, however, was not effective in limiting banking risk. The problem was that the regulators did not control the key parameters, namely, the exchange rate and interest rate risks, which depended on macroeconomic policies.[18] The exchange rate was fixed from the middle of 1979 to the middle of 1982, and even on the eve of the recession in early 1982, the government announced that there was to be no devaluation and that the interest rate would fall shortly.[19] Under these circumstances, the regulators could not force the banks to make provisions for risk without confronting their superior authorities (that is, the finance minister).

18. For an exhaustive analysis of this point, see Valdés and de la Cuadra 1990.
19. Recall that international interest rates rose from 1.5 percent in 1980 to 10.7 percent in 1981.

Nevertheless, we believe that at least some agents expected a devaluation toward the end of 1981 and in early 1982. Consider, for example, the ratio of the current account deficit to GDP, which was 14 percent in 1981. This magnitude of the deficit would have led many to expect a devaluation. Even with such an expectation, some business groups that were in a very poor financial situation continued to use their banks to obtain foreign credit. One reason for this behavior is moral hazard, the expectation that the government would come to their rescue. But there was no escaping from a banking crisis when a severe recession occurred in 1982 and 1983, with GDP declining by 14.1 percent and 0.7 percent, respectively.

The Effect of Financial Liberalization on Savings, Investment, and Financial Intermediation

The effect of financial liberalization on total savings is not clear. An increase in the real interest rate will produce a substitution effect that increases savings, but its income effect will have a negative impact on savings. Thus, the net effect of a higher interest rate is ambiguous. A study by Foxley (1986) for the 1963–1983 period found no significant relationship between the interest rate and savings in Chile. In a study by Hachette (1987), domestic savings were correlated with variations in income; the finding was that savings increased in 1965–1969 because of the positive income effect of a higher copper price. Recessions in 1975 and 1982–1983 reduced savings. And from 1987 there is a sustained increase in savings owing to an increase in public savings, which reached the highest level in 1990. Thus, it appears that financial liberalization had a positive effect on external savings, but the increase substituted for internal savings with little positive effect on total savings. This finding is also reported by Foxley (1986) as a negative effect of the current account deficit on total savings. The decline in national savings during the 1980s is evidently due to the debt crisis.

Even though higher real interest rates have an uncertain effect on total savings, they have a clear effect on portfolio composition. Financial liberalization causes substitution away from real assets such as consumer durables and foreign currency via capital flight into financial assets. Thus, the ability of the capital market to channel savings toward investment can be illustrated with data on financial savings and total credit of the banking sector.

Financial savings—which include money, demand deposits, time deposits, savings deposits, central bank documents, treasury documents, and deposits in foreign money at the banking system—represented 27.6

Table 6.12. Incremental capital-output ratio

	1961–1971	1978–1981	1985–1990
ICOR on net investment	2.94	0.99	1.73
ICOR on gross investment	7.15	2.52	4.30

Source: Central Bank of Chile 1989.

percent of GDP in 1980 and 54.5 percent in 1988. Total real credit by the banking sector, on the other hand, increased by 2,373 percent between 1975, the year when liberalization began, and 1987. Thus to the extent that the capital market channels savings to more profitable projects, we should expect financial liberalization to increase the productivity of investment and hence the rate of growth of output. To examine this, we looked at investment productivity as measured by the incremental capital-output ratio (ICOR) for a period of financial repression (1961–1971) and for two periods of liberalization, 1978–1981 and 1985–1990. Those years in which GDP declined and the three years following a recession were omitted from the analysis.[20] The ICOR data in Table 6.12 suggest that investment did, in fact, become more efficient after the liberalization of the capital market.

Although there is no evidence of a positive link between the real interest rate and savings, financial liberalization may have a positive effect on economic growth through its effect on the efficiency of investment. The argument is that a higher real interest rate increases financial savings by inducing a switch of some savings from real to financial assets and from foreign to domestic assets; this financial deepening, in turn, increases the productivity of investment. Our regression results support the view that the effect of financial deepening, as measured by the ratio M_3/GDP, is to reduce the ICOR.[21]

Repression, Liberalization, and Economic Growth

To gain some insight on the relation between financial liberalization and economic growth, we tested a relationship between economic growth, on the one hand, and the ratio of investment to GDP and a variable that measures the foreign exchange constraint, on the other.

20. After a recession, the ICOR usually declines because of more intensive use of existing capacity.

21. More specifically, the results of the regression are as follows:

$$\text{ICOR} = 4.85 - 0.14 \ M_3/\text{GDP}$$
$$(3.02)$$
$$R^2 \quad = 0.26; \ \text{DW statistic} = 1.86$$

This relationship is predicated on the new theory of economic growth which postulates increasing returns to scale at the economy level and thus allows investment to have a positive influence on the rate of growth.

Most recessions in the Chilean economy have been triggered by foreign factors (Cortés and de la Cuadra 1984). To capture this effect, we include a variable constructed by Coeymans (1989) that measures the foreign exchange constraint of the economy (FEC). This variable corresponds to the maximum real imports that are possible and is equal to the value of exports less financial services plus autonomous capital movements and international reserves at the end of the previous year. The FEC variable captures the terms of trade and foreign interest rate shocks, which are the most important foreign shocks that have hit the economy. We expect this variable to have a positive effect on economic growth.

The FEC variable also captures the outward orientation of the economy through exports. Openness to trade has a positive effect on growth by reducing distortions in the economy, which is, however, a static effect. Dynamic effects come from technology transfer and scale economies made possible with an outward-oriented trade policy. Furthermore, the diversity of inputs made available through openness to trade increases factor productivity. To capture the effect of financial liberalization, we include in the regression a dummy variable for financial distortion. The dummy has a value of one for the periods of real rate of interest less than -5 percent.

In the regression, the ratio of investment (lagged one period to avoid simultaneity) has an insignificant effect on the rate of per capita GDP. The FEC variable has a positive and significant effect, and financial distortions have a strong negative effect. In fact, financial repression lowers growth by 3.5 percent. Such a result appears only for very negative real interest rates of -5 percent or less. But when we ran the regression with a dummy variable for the periods of negative real interest rates, the basic conclusion did not change.[22]

22. The results of the regression were as follows:

Per capita GDP growth $= -1.21 + 0.27$ (I/GDP)$_{t-1} - 3.5$D$_2$ $- 12.9$ DGDP $+ 0.07$ FEC
$\phantom{\text{Per capita GDP growth} = -1.21 + 0.27 \ \text{(I/GDP)}}$ (1.05) (2.29) (4.39) (2.2)

where

(I/GDP)$_{t-1}$ = investment to GDP ratio lagged one period,
D$_2$ = dummy variable for periods when the real interest rate was less than -5 percent,
DGDP = dummy variable for recession years 1975 and 1982, and
FEC = foreign exchange constraint.

T-statistics are reported in parentheses, and $R^2 = 0.73$ and Durbin-Watson statistic $= 1.83$. Data are from 1960–1990.

During the period of financial repression, when the government fixed interest rates, established quantity controls on credit, and managed credit allocation, the Chilean capital market virtually stagnated. Although quantity credit controls were introduced to free resources for the public sector and keep inflation under control, the large public sector deficits financed by the central bank gradually raised the rate of inflation, and toward the end of the period, the economy was in a state of incipient hyperinflation. Not only did the economy suffer accelerated inflation, but it also experienced reduced per capita GDP growth.

Government intervention in the process of credit allocation was initially directed to achieving industrial development and later to improving the agricultural sector under a vast agrarian reform. Our study found partial evidence of a positive influence of credit on investment in the manufacturing sector but none in the agricultural and mining sectors. But because of economic and political instability, investment in the manufacuring sector declined in both absolute and relative terms during the period of financial repression. Agriculture and manufacturing grew at a similar rate and, in some cases, at a lower rate than did the mining and services sectors, which received only a negligible amount of credit. Overall, financial repression had a severely negative effect on per capita GDP growth.

The recent experience of the Chilean economy holds mixed lessons. On the one hand, the success of the structural reforms of the 1980s appears to vindicate the case for well-defined property rights, minimal distortions, minimum constraints on factor mobility, macroeconomic stability, fiscal balance, and openness to foreign competition. But the Chilean experience also suggests that the market for financial services is inherently different from a market in, say, peanuts, and free-market arguments for the latter on efficiency grounds do not necessarily apply to the former. Financial liberalization with market-determined interest rates and high competition among financial institutions must be accompanied by prudential regulation to overcome the problems of information asymmetry and moral hazard, thus minimizing the possibility of financial crises.

References

Aedo, Cristian, and Lagos, L. F. 1984. Protección Efectiva en Chile. Working Paper no. 94. Santiago: Pontificia Universidad Católica de Chile.

Banking Superintendency. Various years. *Boletines*, various issues. Santiago: Banking Superintendency.

Cahmi, Rosa, and Germán Fielbaum. 1978. Análisis del Crédito Agrícola en Chile, 1960–1976: Un Intento de Cuantificación del Subsidio vía Crédito Entregado al Sector. Universidad de Chile. Unpublished manuscript.

Central Bank of Chile. 1989. *Indicadores Económicos y Sociales, 1960–1988*. Santiago: Central Bank of Chile.

———.Various years. *Boletin Mensual,* various issues.

Coeymans, Juan. 1989. Allocation of Resources and Sectoral Growth in Chile: An Econometric Approach. Ph.D. diss., Magdalen College, Oxford, England.

Corbo, Vittorio, and Patricio Meller. 1981. Alternative Trade Strategies and Employment Implications: Chile. In *Trade and Employment in Developing Countries*, ed. Anne O. Krueger, Hal B. Lary, Terry Monson, and Narongchai Akrasanee. Chicago: University of Chicago Press.

CORFO. Various years a. *Balances Anual,* various issues. Santiago: CORFO.

———.Various years b. *Memoria Anual,* various issues. Santiago: CORFO.

Cortés, Hernán, and Sergio de la Cuadra. 1984. Recesiones Económicas, Crisis Cambiarias, y Ciclos Inflacionarios: Chile, 1926–1982. Santiago: Pontificia Universidad Católica de Chile. Unpublished manuscript.

Ffrench-Davis, Ricardo. 1973. *Políticas Económicas en Chile, 1952–1970*. Centro de Estudios de Planificación Nacional, Ediciones Nueva Universidad. Santiago: Ediciones Nueva Universidad.

Fleischman, Diego. 1972. Costo Nominal del Crédito Bancario. Washington, D.C.: Comisión Económica Para América Latina. Unpublished manuscript.

Foxley, Juan. 1986. Determinantes Económicos del Ahorro Nacional: Chile, 1963–1983. *Cuadernos de Economía* 68(April): 119–27.

Fuenzalida, Javier, and Sergia Undurraga. 1968. *El Crédito y su Distribución en Chile.* Editorial Lambda.

Hachette, Dominique. 1987. El Ahorro y la Inversión en Chile: Un Gran Desafío. In *Desarrollo Económico en Democracia*, ed. Felipe Larraín. Santiago: Ediciones Universidad Católica.

Jeftanovic, Pedro. 1961. Investigación sobre el Impacto de la Inflación en las Utilidades Bancarias en Chile. Working Paper no. 15. Santiago: Pontificia Universidad Católica de Chile.

Krueger, Anne O., Maurice Schiff, and Alberto Valdés. 1990. *Economía Política de las Interacciones en América Latina*. Santiago: Centro Internacional para el Desarrollo Económico (CINDE).

Mamalakis, Markus, and Clark Reynolds. 1965. *Essays on the Chilean Economy.* Homewood, Ill.: Richard D. Irwin.

Superintendencia de Bancos e Instituciones Financieras. Various years. *Información Financiera,* various issues.

Superintendencia de Valores y Seguros. Various years a. *Boletin Mensual Valores y Seguros,* various issues.

———.Various years b. *Revista Seguros,* various issues.

Tapia, Daniel, and Eduardo Olivares. 1970. Tasas de Interés, 1958–69. In *Estudios Monetarios 2*. Santiago: Central Bank of Chile.

Valdés, Alberto, Eugenia Muchnik, and Hernan Hurtado. 1990. *Trade, Exchange Rate, and Agricultural Pricing Policies in Chile.* Washington, D.C.: World Bank.

Valdés, S., and Sergio de la Cuadra. 1990. Myths and Facts about Financial Liberalization in Chile, 1974–1982. Paper no. 128 (October). Santiago: Pontificia Universidad Católica de Chile.

CHAPTER SEVEN

BRAZIL

Daniel L. Gleizer

The development of financial markets can be regarded as a dialectical
process in which the government promotes changes by regulating the
financial system to achieve certain objectives, and these changes in turn
engender reactions by private agents. In this process, the financial
system often unfolds in ways that frustrate the original expectations
and goals of policymakers, inducing additional waves of change and
adaptation. The evolution of a financial system, therefore, can be studied as the dynamic outcome of a process in which conscious intervention
is combined, and often constrained, by the reaction of the system and
by the need to adapt initial policies to unexpected sectoral and
macroeconomic problems.[1]

In the introduction, Lee and Haggard emphasize that the structure of
financial intermediation which results from government intervention
will depend heavily on the state's capacity to intervene effectively to
achieve its objectives. Their emphasis, however, was primarily on the

The author is an economist at the European 1 Department of the International Monetary
Fund. The views expressed in this article are those of the author and do not necessarily
reflect those of the IMF.

I thank Leslie Armijo, Benedict Clements, Jeffry Frieden, Stephan Haggard, Chung Lee,
Nathaniel Leff, the Brazil Desk at the IMF, the participants in the East-West Center's
conference Government, Financial Systems, and Economic Development, and an anonymous reviewer for their insightful and useful help.

1. This description of financial policy assumes that the government actively intervenes in
the financial system. In some countries, however, the government is much less interventionist and relies on market forces to carry out the desired objectives. In the latter case, the
above definition is less appropriate. Nevertheless, given the widespread market failures
that permeate financial systems, government regulation, even if limited, is an almost
universal phenomenon. The description is certainly appropriate for Brazil.

microeconomics of financial markets. Though this played an important role in Brazil, the central problems of financial market policy and development were related to the country's extreme macroeconomic instability. High and unstable inflation played a major role in undermining the government's stated objectives, both with regard to its liberalization efforts and with respect to those areas in which the government sought to intervene. In this chapter I analyze the evolution of the Brazilian financial system since the mid-1960s, stressing the interaction of market forces and government regulation in the context of recurrent efforts at stabilization and structural adjustment.[2]

I. Nature of Financial Policy

The economic strategy adopted by the government that emerged from the 1964 military coup in Brazil consisted of a series of stabilization measures designed to restore internal and external balance and of a variety of institutional and structural reforms. Of foremost importance were the reforms of the financial sector which were aimed at redefining the financing methods of both the public and the private sectors. In the public sector, priority was placed in the development of mechanisms that would make the financing of government expenditures less dependent on inflationary finance, a major characteristic of the previous period. With regard to the private sector, emphasis was on strengthening the debt-asset system, creating new institutions, improving overall credit conditions, and, particularly, developing medium- and long-term savings instruments that yield positive real rates of return in order to raise new savings and divert savings from curb markets, real estate, and capital flight.

The sudden change in worldwide and domestic conditions in 1973 deeply affected the development of the Brazilian financial system. In contrast with the experience of the mid-1960s, when a preconceived design was introduced, post-1974 institutional reforms and changes in the regulatory framework of the financial system were, by and large, determined by attempts to stabilize the economy. Most of these developments can be regarded as the (often unexpected) results of a fundamental conflict between short-run stabilization policies and long-run

2. Structural adjustment policies refer to policies that consciously attempt to redefine the economy's patterns of production and allocation, whereas stabilization policies are those that are specifically implemented in response to the recurrent macroeconomic disequilibria that afflict the economy.

structural adjustment policies. This conflict was manifested in the
frequent "crises" for specific subsectors of the system and in the
government's attempts to rescue them. This new pattern of financial
development would characterize the economy until the end of the
1980s.

The Nature and Objectives of the Financial Reforms of the 1960s

The analysis carried out by the military government of Castello Branco
emphasized the perverse effects of inflation on the development of
financial markets. The high rate of inflation was seen as the result of
conflicting claims over the distribution of national product. Federal
government spending in excess of revenues was perceived as the main
cause of the continuous increases in the money supply, which, in turn,
induced higher levels of private spending and prices. The resulting high
rates of inflation were responsible for large distortions in the economy.
The coexistence of a legal limit on nominal interest rates (12 percent
according to the Usury Law of 1933) and high and uncertain rates of
inflation generated negative real rates of return on financial assets,
driving all long-term instruments out of the market. As a result of this
financial repression, the economy was forced to rely on an obsolete
banking system to finance its activities. A similar affliction prevailed in
the housing market, where long-term credit for construction and mortgages was extremely scarce. Government revenues were also seriously
affected by high inflation. Given the reduction in the real value of tax
payments because of the high rate of change in the price level, it became
profitable for firms and households to delay tax payments, even when
penalties were imposed. Finally, high rates of inflation gave rise to
overvalued exchange rates and disequilibria in the balance of payments.

The government diagnosis indicated, therefore, the urgency of implementing stabilization policies and carrying out profound reforms in
order to redefine the financial arrangements of both the private and the
public sectors. In the public sector, priority was given to the development of a technology that would make the financing of government
expenditures less dependent on increases in the money supply. With
regard to the private sector, the analysis indicated the necessity of
strengthening the debt-asset system, creating new institutions, improving
consumer credit, and, in particular, developing medium- and long-term
financial instruments that yield positive returns so as to increase financial savings.

To reach these goals, the government introduced a set of laws, de-
crees, and resolutions between 1964 and 19\66. Three sets of reforms

were fundamental in shaping the new financial system: the Law of Banking Reform (Law 4594 of December 31, 1964), the Capital Market Law (Law 4728 of July 14, 1965), and laws on idexation (monetary correction) and the National Housing Bank (Law 4357 of July 16, 1964, and 4380 of August 21, 1964).

The Law of Banking Reform restructured the monetary authorities—and created the National Monetary Council and the Central Bank of Brazil—with the purpose of redefining responsibilities and imposing discipline in money and credit policies. Underlying the redesign of the structure of the monetary authorities was the perception that the previous structure of the monetary authorities in Brazil—where the Superintendency of Money and Credit (SUMOC) shared its central bank responsibilities with Banco do Brasil, the country's largest commercial bank, which also conducted other typical central bank operations—resulted in uncoordinated and often conflicting policies. Indeed, an account called "Conta de Movimento" linked Banco do Brasil to the central bank in such a way that currency issued by the central bank could find its way to the voluntary reserves of commercial banks, which remained under the responsibility of Banco do Brasil. Although this account was intended to work in both directions, subject to weekly clearing, with the debtor institution paying interest to the creditor, Banco do Brasil had been the systematic debtor. Thus, Banco do Brasil was able to expand its loans above the ceilings determined by the newly created monetary budget.[3]

Most analyses of the reforms show that although its role as a monetary authority was somewhat reduced, Banco do Brasil retained its role as a currency issuer. In the years to come, on the other hand, the central bank would also assume, in addition to its monetary authority operations, important fiscal and development functions, including raising resources and supplementing them with transfers from the government which were then allocated to a variety of special programs.

The Capital Market Law, which dealt with the development of the capital market and the introduction of new savings instruments, was aimed at redefining the financial schemes of both the private and the public sectors. The new regulations deliberately created a specialized system where different institutions were the sole suppliers of credit to specified segments of the economy. In this spirit, short-term credit for working capital was the responsibility of commercial banks, which were, in turn, funded by demand deposits. The newly introduced investment

---

3. For more details, see Zini 1982, p. 77.

banks were the suppliers of long-term credit and carried out direct financial activities such as lending and purchasing shares, acting as a provider of financial services such as the underwriting of stocks and bonds.

In addition to long-term credit extended by investment banks, another solution for the lack of supply of long-term funds was the strengthening of the stock market and the recovery of the debentures market. To strengthen the stock market, the government altered the functioning of the market, redefined the role of brokers, introduced fiscal incentives favoring stockholders of open capital enterprises, regulated investment funds, and increased the allocation of institutional resources to the market, mainly through the creation of mutual funds, through Decree Law 157. This law authorized financial institutions to create "157 Funds," permitting them to deduct from their taxes the sums that were applied for purchasing shares from these mutual funds; this created a pool of potential savings to be channeled to corporations in need of financial aid.

Finally, external capital inflows were stimulated through a series of regulations. Direct loans became possible through Law 4131, and indirect loans channeled to firms by commercial and investment banks were legalized by the central bank's Resolution 63.

The laws on indexation and the BNH were instrumental in the creation of new savings instruments yielding positive returns. Indeed, as part of the strategy to revitalize the financial system, indexing was applied to a wide range of assets to compensate nominal returns for the changes in the price level. Indexing was particularly used as a means of recovering the real value of tax revenues, as a measure to free real interest rates, and, finally, as a way to stabilize the rate of inflation itself. To achieve these goals, the government established a standard of constant real value, the Unidade Padrao de Capital (UPC), making it equal to the value of a readjustable government bond (ORTN). Therefore, two units of account were used in the economy: the cruzeiro and the ORTN. Indexing meant that the two units had a fluctuating exchange rate, with the ORTN constantly appreciating in cruzeiro terms. This became known as the two-units-of-account system.

Indexing cannot be neutral or generalized if the indexation scheme is to be used as a policy tool to alter relative prices or to fight inflation. Indeed, indexing must be partial in the sense that only a subset of the economy's prices are indexed, or in the case of generalized indexation, it must be differentiated among the different agents or prices in the economy.

In the Brazilian case, monetary correction was first introduced as a device to help finance the government deficit. As pointed out earlier, the high rate of inflation encouraged firms and individuals not to pay their taxes on schedule. In response the government introduced monetary correction on agents' fiscal debts and issued ORTNs[4] as a means to recover the real value of its revenues and make noninflationary financing viable. The principal of the debt was reevaluated on a systematic basis, employing recent inflation rates as the index.

Later in 1964, indexing was introduced in the newly created Housing Financial System. The housing sector was seriously disrupted by the coexistence of inflation and limits on interest rates. The result was a decline in housing investment, a negative effect on a sector that is a high-employment generator, and creation of a serious housing shortage. In the new system, financial contracts were adjusted to real values and based on previous inflation rates, and rents were set free. The introduction of monetary correction on the newly introduced passbook savings and mortgages were the cornerstones of new finance for housing activities. Wage and salary indexation schemes, however, were subject to a different criterion, lagging behind other prices.[5]

For our purposes, however, the more relevant issue is the introduction of monetary correction on financial assets and its consequences for their real rates of return. The previously mentioned Usury Law was an obstacle for the increase in real rates of return. Although this legal ceiling was often circumvented by devices such as discounting, excessive commissions, and linked accounts, the uncertainty about future inflation made this kind of apparatus insufficient. Because market-determined discounts depended on expected rates of inflation, a mistaken forecast could have disastrous effects for one of the agents involved in the transaction.

Therefore, the principle of ex post monetary correction was introduced into the financial system. Long-term debt, a large portion of time

4. Two kinds of indexed government bonds were created. ORTNs could be indexed to the rate of inflation, on the basis of a monetary correction index set by the authorities, or they might carry the option of exchange rate or monetary correction, whichever is higher.
5. The way indexation is introduced in different economies reveals the distinct goals and political forces involved. In Brazil, indexation was first introduced in capital markets and for the adjustment of tax revenues. It is only later that wages were indexed and even then to a reduced extent when compared with capital. In Israel, on the other hand, wages were indexed much earlier than financial instruments. From the point of view of the objectives involved, it is clear that the Brazilian emphasis was on allocation and inflation control, whereas in Israel, the main concern seemed to be with equity considerations. The different timing, however, also reveals the political power of capital and labor in both countries.

deposits, and medium-term instruments were adjusted for previous inflation rates, with financial institutions being allowed to introduce monetary correction in their assets and liabilities. It has proven difficult, however, to introduce this scheme in short-term private securities, given the risk involved in borrowing in readjustable terms and paying the debt from unindexed receipts. Thus, a series of regulations introduced a pre-fixed indexing mechanism. Yields or interest rates on short-term instruments, exchange bills, and certificates of deposit were determined in advance and subject to a different treatment with regard to taxation. Postindexed gains were to be treated as capital gains, and preindexed gains were considered to be interest payments and were not included in taxable income.

In addition, to cope with the prevailing housing sector crisis, the government reorganized the corresponding financial subsystem. The Housing Financial System was created, and a National Housing Bank (BNH) was established to act as a central bank for housing financial institutions. This bank was allowed to issue indexed bonds and to index its loans to attract private savings to the real estate bills (*Letras Imobiliarias*) market. The sector was also the beneficiary of the proceeds of a newly introduced compulsory social security fund (Fundo de Garantia de Tempo de Servico, or FGTS), which was funded by an 8 percent payroll tax. Additionally, funds deposited at savings and loan associations, which were captured by the issuing of indexed passbook deposits, complemented the sector's resources.

Finally, the fixed exchange rate system that prevailed in Brazil could not be maintained in the face of high inflation rates. The frequent devaluations had a strong inflationary effect by pushing up domestic costs, and the expectation of large and sudden devaluations led to speculative attacks against the cruzeiro. Thus in 1968 the government adopted a crawling peg system, a system of frequent mini-devaluations.

II. The Structure of the Financial System

The System as It Emerged from the Reforms

As a result of the reforms, there was a rapid process of financial deepening in the Brazilian economy. Several nonbank financial institutions were created, and a variety of financial instruments became available to the public. A well-known indicator of the degree of financial deepening is the Goldsmith Financial Interrelation Ratio (GFIR), which is defined as the ratio of nonmonetary financial assets to GDP. As shown in Table 7.1, the Brazilian GFIR jumped from 1.5 percent in 1960 to 13.5 percent in 1970 and to 59.1 percent in 1985. In addition, the ratio of total financial assets to GDP, which oscillated around 23 percent during the first decade, jumped to about 42 percent in the late 1970s and 67.1 percent in 1985.

These figures indicate that the rapid increase in GFIR during the 1960s was the counterpart of a steady decline in the share of monetary assets to total financial assets. This seems to imply that the reforms managed to attract to the financial system the savings which were kept in monetary form but which were outside the system. The reasons for the large increase in the ratio of financial assets to GDP observed since the mid-1970s reflect the clear preference for financial instruments which characterizes the economy after 1974.

Table 7.1. Financial assets of the Brazilian financial system (as a percentage of GDP)

Year	Monetary assets	Nonmonetary assets	Total financial assets
1960	22.1	1.5	23.6
1961	22.4	1.3	23.7
1962	22.2	1.4	23.6
1963	20.0	1.2	21.2
1964	18.5	1.6	20.1
1965	20.6	3.2	23.8
1966	16.4	4.3	20.7
1967	17.9	6.6	24.5
1968	17.3	9.2	26.5
1969	17.3	10.7	28.0
1970	17.0	13.5	30.5
1971	16.7	17.5	34.2
1972	17.3	21.3	38.7
1973	18.4	24.2	42.6
1974	16.9	22.5	39.4
1975	17.1	27.3	44.4
1976	15.2	26.7	41.9
1977	13.8	27.0	40.8
1978	13.4	29.3	42.7
1979	14.1	29.2	43.2
1980	11.5	23.5	35.0
1981	10.1	32.7	42.8
1982	8.6	37.7	46.3
1983	7.3	49.7	57.0
1984	7.0	53.5	60.5
1985	7.9	59.1	67.1
1986	12.3	49.5	61.8
1987	8.7	77.1	85.8
1988	8.4	104.9	113.3

Sources: Central Bank of Brazil, various years.

It is also interesting to analyze the changes in the assets held by the
public. The share of nonmonetary assets to total assets increased from
7.2 percent in 1964 to 55.7 percent in 1973. Among nonmonetary
assets, savings deposits grew at a high rate, rising from 0.3 percent of the
total in 1967 to about 6.7 percent in 1973. These funds, deposited in
savings and loan associations, benefited from unconditional guarantees
from the government and became an important source of funds to the
Housing Financial System. Time deposits and government bonds also
grew substantially. Finally, growth in the amount of bills of exchange
(*letras de cambio*) held by the public was very rapid between 1968 and
1973, a period that saw the demand for consumer durables increase
substantially.

Another important indicator of the transformation of the financial
system is the change in both the volume and structure of loans extended
by the financial system. If the ratio of loans to the private sector as a
percentage of GDP is used as an indicator of the financial system's
importance in the financing of economic activity, a significant change is
clear; the ratio increased from 16.4 percent in 1965 to around 47
percent by the end of the so-called Economic Miracle in 1973. These
trends are accentuated when we look at the ratio of loans extended by
the nonmonetary system to the private sector, because this sector grew
much faster than did the monetary sector.

As a result of the reforms, a drastic change in the sources of loans to
the private sector also occurred. The share of loans from the monetary
system—which was made up of Banco do Brasil, other state-owned commercial banks, and private commercial banks—declined from 86 percent of total loans in 1964 to around 50 percent in the mid-1970s. Some
changes in the relative shares of the different components of the monetary system are also noteworthy. In 1965, Banco do Brasil accounted for
33.6 percent of the loans extended by the monetary system to the private
sector. In 1973, this share rose to 38.1 percent, although the share of
Banco do Brasil loans in total loans fell to 19.1 percent. The evolution of
loans from private commercial banks was unstable throughout the period, however.

The nonmonetary sector experienced a rapid increase in net lending from the Housing Financial System (SFH). Lending by credit and
finance companies increased during the Economic Miracle period,
peaked at 15 percent in 1973, and contracted in the second half of
the 1970s. A similar pattern is observed in the behavior of investment
banks. The share of loans extended by the National Economic and Social
Development Bank (BNDES) increased from 3.4 percent in 1965 to an

average of 6.4 percent in the second half of the 1970s during the implementation of the Second National Development Plan.

These developments in the financial system thus indicate that the reforms removed some of the obstacles that had constrained economic growth in Brazil. The financial conditions were now present for expansion of the construction sector and fuller utilization of the capacity installed in the late 1950s in the consumer durables sector. In addition, the state had recovered its fiscal capacity to operate as a leader in the investment process. The financial system that developed, however, had some limitations and was subject to systemic instability. The coexistence of various units of account could only work properly as long their rates of exchange were not subject to sudden and violent changes. Thus the system prospered as long as the rate of inflation was stable, the exchange rate followed a smooth path, and the economy's financing requirements were mainly of a short- and medium-term nature. These conditions, however, would drastically change in the decades to come.

Unattained Objectives

Extensive financial deepening occurred in the Brazilian economy from the early 1960s. One should be very cautious, however, in drawing conclusions about the evolution of the economy's overall savings rate as well as that of its components. National accounting data show that domestic savings as a percentage of GDP increased after the introduction of the reforms. Private savings as a percentage of GDP, however, was relatively insensitive to the innovations instituted. The main changes involved government savings, primarily in response to the fiscal reforms, and foreign savings (Table 7.2).

Despite the various aspects that distinguish the Brazilian reforms from the reforms advocated by the proponents of financial liberalization, some of the notions underlying the Brazilian experience are very similar. The formulators of the reforms were convinced that restoring market forces, "getting prices right," and raising real interest rates were preconditions for increased savings and investment and sustained growth in the future. The government's analysis of the situation, as quoted in Zini 1982, is illustrative of this point:

> In an economy suffering from high rates of inflation, where a rigorous anti-inflationary policy is being undertaken[,] an argument in favor of high interest rates can be made. By high interest rates we mean high in relative terms, including monetary correction. The economy will derive two main benefits, besides the probable increase in savings in the first round. Since

Table 7.2. Savings trends

	1960–1964	1965–1970	1970–1974	1974–1982	1982–1985
Inflation (WPI) (%)	82.9	31.3	20.7	60.9	178.7
Ex post deposit rate (%)	−15.0	10.0	4.0	−1.0	6.0
National savings (% of GDP)	16.0	18.7	18.9	18.5	15.1
Domestic savings (% of GDP)	16.6	19.6	19.8	21.0	20.5
Government savings (% of GDP)	1.6	4.2	5.5	2.5	−3.1
Private savings (% of GDP)	14.3	14.4	13.4	16.0	18.2
Foreign savings (% of GDP)	0.9	0.4	3.0	4.6	2.3
Gross investment (% of GDP)	16.9	19.1	21.8	23.2	17.4
Net factor payments abroad (% of GDP)	0.6	0.9	0.9	2.5	5.4

Sources: Central Bank of Brazil, various years.

the individuals receiving the interest payments belong to the classes with higher propensities to save, there will be an "income-effect" that might lead to higher savings. Additionally, higher interest rates will prevent relatively unproductive uses of capital (except those administratively selected). As monetary stabilization progresses, we can expect long rates to return to a normal level. (p. 74)

The rate of interest has always been considered a possible variable explaining the saving behavior of individuals. After a Keynesian interlude during which the level of income was regarded as the main determinant of savings, interest rates came back to the center of the discussion, mainly through theories of saving/consumption behavior based on utility maximization given the present value of lifetime resources. Despite agreement on the ambiguous theoretical effect of interest rates on savings, there is, however, considerable disagreement about the empirical evidence (a point to which I will return later). Nevertheless, in the development literature, the presumed positive effects of interest rates on savings became the intellectual cornerstone of the advice to liberalize financial markets and raise real interest rates.

Given the crucial role played by the elasticity of savings with respect to the real interest rate, a large number of empirical papers on the subject have appeared. A review of such work shows no consensus among economists regarding the significance of this variable. In a substantial study of twenty-five Asian and Latin American countries, Gupta (1984) concludes that generalizations about the appropriateness of raising interest rates as a means of increasing savings are not applicable. Financial conditions seem to affect savings in Asia but not in Latin America.

Despite the introduction of indexation, controls on both deposit and lending interest rates remained in Brazil throughout the period to varying degrees. The coexistence of instruments subject to different indexation schemes, subsidized credit lines, controlled rates, and market-determined rates gave rise to a wide dispersion of interest rates. But it does not seem reasonable to characterize the Brazilian financial system as a repressed one. Legal interest rates on certain segments of the market interact with free rates to generate a variety of financial instruments yielding high positive real interest rates. In fact, a major policy issue in the 1980s was the difficulty of resuming growth in the presence of such high real rates. Ex post rates frequently understate ex ante rates owing to unforeseen accelerations of inflation or thanks to government tampering with the relevant index. Therefore, if high real interest rates do promote higher savings rates, the postreform Brazilian economy should constitute a good test case.

It is informative to make a preliminary evaluation of the data by taking averages over the period in question. As shown in Table 7.2, there was an increase in the average real deposit rate from −15 percent during the period 1960–1964 to 10 percent in 1965–1970. If we look at only the changes in the domestic savings rate, we see a large increase from 16.6 percent to 19.6 percent of GDP over the same period. A look at the disaggregated numbers, however, reveals that most of this change is explained by a large increase in the government savings rate (from 1.6 percent to 4.2 percent), whereas the change in the private savings rate is very modest (from 14.3 percent to 14.4 percent). The increase in the government savings rate seems to be more a result of the fiscal reform than an implication of higher interest rates.

The increase in domestic savings in the 1970s is also associated with higher government savings, as well as with the considerable rise in the role played by foreign savings (from 0.4 percent in 1965–1970 to 3.0 percent in the first half of the 1970s). Only in the first half of the 1980s do private savings increase along with real interest rates. But, as will be discussed later, this result is largely explained by the big jump in the rate of inflation observed in the period. The table also shows the problems involved in measuring the country's savings effort by looking at domestic as opposed to national savings rates given the economy sent 5.4

percent of its GDP abroad during 1982–1985 in the form of factor payments.

Results obtained in econometric tests performed for the Brazilian economy from 1965 to 1985, using both the savings functions and the Euler equation approaches, confirm the insights derived from the correlation exercises (Gleizer 1990, chap. 3). Domestic savings in general, and private savings in particular, respond negligibly to real interest rates in Brazil. One is therefore led to conclude that neither theory nor empirical evidence offers support for a policy of high interest rates as a mechanism to increase the savings rate.

The observation that private savings were insensitive to changes in the interest rate and that increases in domestic savings were basically determined by increases in public sector savings leads to another interesting observation. A long-run strategy designed to strengthen the private sector gave rise to an increasing role of the state in the savings-investment intermediation process. It might be argued that such an outcome is not inconsistent with the original goal, because the state channeled savings into infrastructure and mobilized cheap capital for private investment. There can be no doubt, however, that the attempts to increase private domestic savings were unsuccessful and that the rising contribution of government and foreign savings was crucial in the period. This phenomenon also reveals itself when we look at the sources of long-term finance in the economy.

When evaluated from the point of view of the main goals of the authorities, the major limitation of the financial system that emerged from the reforms was the inability to create a market for long-term financing. The causes and consequences of the lack of private domestic sources of long-term finance and the ways through which such problems were addressed are fundamental to an understanding of the evolution of the financial system in the last two decades. In the financial system envisaged by the formulators of the reforms, investment banks were the institutions designed to provide long-term industrial loans and support corporations in the issuing of new underwriting. The sources of funds were to be long-term savings deposits from the public in exchange for certificates of deposit (CDs), rechanneled government and foreign funds, and the issue of new underwriting. In this respect, the establishment of investment banks was a clear effort to revitalize and strengthen the stock market.

Although it is true that investment banks were able to increase the share of CDs in the total amount of assets held by the public from 0.4 percent in 1967 to 8.9 percent in 1980, it is important to emphasize that the loans offered by these institutions never achieved the terms envisaged by the formulators of the reforms. Most loans are medium-term loans aimed at providing firms with working capital, a segment previously reserved to commercial banks, rather than long-term loans for investment. Some analysts argue that part of the failure of investment banks to provide long-term loans is due to the inappropriateness of their liability structure in supporting long-term operations.

A more fundamental reason for the lack of long-term credit is the degree of uncertainty that characterizes economies with chronic inflation. Two related considerations are important here. The first involves the reluctance of nonfinancial agents to borrow under indexed clauses and to use their resources for productive investment. The second is related to the financial institutions' unwillingness to lend for a long term unless under floating rates or indexed clauses. Inflation affects the demand for funds in a variety of ways. Most important, it increases the uncertainty surrounding profit forecasts, reducing the attractiveness of investment projects. This reduction in the attractiveness of investment projects may result from the expectation that in its effort to control inflation, the government might interfere with pricing policies of firms or may try to reduce aggregate demand by increasing taxes or interest rates or by reducing its own demand. If any of these possibilities occurs, a firm's expected profitability may be reduced, and the marginal efficiency of capital will therefore go down, reducing investment and the demand for long-term funds.

Still, from an economic point of view, it is important to consider the impact of inflation on financial costs and, in particular, on their variations in real terms. These variations constitute an element of uncertainty which tends to reduce the contracted terms of financial operations. Inflation leads to "front-loading" of debt repayments, generating the need for debt-financed investment projects to start producing cash very soon. Otherwise, the firm will have to borrow continuously until the project matures to service its debt. This may work as a deterrent to long-term investment.

From the lender's point of view, a basic effect of inflation is to reduce the capacity to evaluate the default risk associated with each borrower. All the standard methods used to ensure that the probability of default is low (that is, estimation of a project's profitability, consideration of a borrower's income, security over assets, risk spreading, and so on) become more uncertain. These effects lead risk-averse agents to seek a shortening of terms in financial transactions in order to allow for more-frequent recontracting opportunities.

Given the very nature of financial intermediation, institutions involved in maturity transformation assume a certain degree of liquidity risk. When operating in chronically inflationary environments with rapidly changing nominal interest rates, however, these institutions face an additional kind of risk. By committing its funds to long-term applications at given interest rates, a financial intermediary may run into serious trouble as it tries to roll over its liabilities. Indeed, it might be faced with the need to increase the rates of interest offered to depositors as a means to attract funds continuously, while on the asset side it is locked into precommitted fixed interest rates. Therefore, both borrowers and lenders prefer short-term contracts.

Indexation, although it alleviates some of these difficulties, does not eliminate the fundamental problem of inflation risk, at best transferring the risk from lenders to borrowers. When servicing an indexed debt, a borrower will have to pay interest and a principal adjusted for inflation, which would pose no additional risks if the borrower's income increased by the same rate as that used to index its liabilities. Given the average nature of an index, however, no guarantee exists that the real income of a borrower will keep pace with its real obligations if indexation is used. In this sense, indexation reallocates the inflation risk from lenders to borrowers (Baer 1983, p. 236).

This reallocation of the inflation risk also explains the refusal of private financial institutions to issue liabilities with postfixed monetary correction and their preference for pre-fixation (liabilities with a discount reflecting expected inflation). Under these circumstances, the issue of long-term finance remains a problem. Financial institutions have to borrow to relend and in fact prefer to do so without monetary correction, thus attracting mainly short-term resources. On the asset side, financial institutions prefer to lend with postfixed monetary correction, but borrowers resist. In sum, agents are happy to hold indexed assets but consistently refuse to issue indexed liabilities. The risk premium is so high that the market operates only in the provision of short-term credit.

Given the failure to revitalize the stock market and the unavailability of long-term credit, the only alternatives available to medium-sized and large private firms, besides retained profits, were (1) debt financing contracted with government institutions such as the National Economic and Social Development Bank (BNDES) and the state development banks, and (2) foreign resources. Both developments would have important macroeconomic effects: the first because of the increasing difficulty to raise noninflationary resources to finance the public sector, and the second because the rapid accumulation of foreign debt would leave the country's economy extremely vulnerable to further external shocks.

The Financial System in the 1970s

The sharp rise in oil prices in October 1973 caught the Brazilian economy operating close to full capacity, overheated by an expansionary monetary policy, and running growing current account deficits. In addition, the incoming administration was committed to a process of political decompression that was perceived as incompatible with the implementation of austerity measures.[6] After an initial attempt to cool down the economy through the application of orthodox monetary and fiscal policies, the administration adopted an aggressive development strategy aimed at preserving high growth rates while adjusting to the oil shock. Given the risks involved in this strategy, it can be explained only by the importance of continuous growth for the process of political opening and by the assumption of policymakers that the shock was temporary.[7]

Embodied in the Second National Development Plan (PND II), this expansionary policy was aimed at achieving a rate of output growth of about 10 percent a year, with emphasis on the need to implement structural reforms in the economy in order to eliminate the constraint imposed by the new external environment. These reforms were to be centered on a substantial import-substitution process and directed toward the capital goods and basic inputs sectors, along with heavy investments in infrastructure, especially energy. This effort was coupled with a series of export-promoting measures, such as fiscal and credit subsidies to manufactured exports, and an increase in tariff and non-tariff protection.

Parallel to the investment program, the PND II introduced modifications in the financial system as a means to channel funds to the newly established priorities. Because the system that emerged from the reforms lacked private domestic sources of long-term finance, the resources needed by the new projects were provided by foreign sources and the

6. See Fishlow 1986 and Baer 1983 for discussions of political determinants of economic policies and performance.
7. Standard macro theory suggests that governments should finance temporary shocks and adjust to permanent ones, a distinction that is extremely hard to make as events are taking place. As Taylor (1988) puts it, "One initially tries to ride out a shock by supporting domestic demand, and learns only as the 'dark forces of time and ignorance' play their hand that it is permanent" (p. 10).

Brazilian public sector, mainly through BNDES. The latter was altered through the creation of new subsidiaries such as Mecanica Brasileira S/A and Insumos Basicos S/A, which were to offer favorable financing terms, supported by fiscal resources and funds from two compulsory saving schemes. In addition to these policy changes, endogenous transformations resulted from the interaction of stabilization attempts and the intrinsic characteristics of the system. Indeed, the abrupt acceleration in the rate of inflation and the sharp deterioration in the balance-of-payments position deeply affected the evolution of the financial system.

Because the authorities regarded lax monetary policy as one of the main causes for the recrudescence of the inflationary process, the financial system faced a period of restricted liquidity and uncertainty. Indeed, the acceleration and increased variance in the rate of inflation led to mounting uncertainty as to the future behavior of prices and financial asset returns, including those assets subject to indexation (since until then the rate of monetary correction was decided on a month-to-month basis without a clear rule). In addition, the government's decision to intervene in the Halles Group (the fourth-largest commercial bank and an important financial conglomerate) in April 1974 led to widespread panic. Until that time, there prevailed a consensus in the financial system that any solvency problem would be subject to a negotiated solution between the monetary authorities and another financial group.[8] Simonsen (1983), however, clearly identified such solutions as a source of moral hazard and decided to reintroduce the concept of risk into the system. The lack of confidence in the solvency of the system led to an enormous resource flow from private to official institutions and from the "nominal" to the "real" (indexed) fraction of the financial system. To reduce such uncertainties and speculation that the government would tamper with the index, the authorities decided to make the monetary correction rule explicit by equating it to a weighted average of the wholesale price index (IPA) in the previous three months and of the monthly rate equivalent to 15 percent yearly inflation.

A reduction in the rate of growth of the real money supply in 1974 managed to cool down the economy but was unable to reduce inflation significantly. The combination of high inflation, lower industrial activity, and the poor performance of the government in the elections of 1974 led the government to reverse the anti-inflationary policy in 1975 and

---

8. See Tavares and Assis 1985, p. 52, for a discussion of the intervention.

attempt to expand the economy.[9] But economic agents also showed an increased preference for liquid assets at the expense of investment projects. Moreover, the difficulties involved in forecasting future inflation and real yields on nonindexed assets led to a flight away from such securities with a compensating increase in the holdings of savings deposits and indexed government bonds.

The result of such portfolio changes, in conjunction with the announcement of the explicit rule for monetary correction and the uncertain path of inflation, was a massive speculative wave in the financial system. Brokerage firms sold indexed bonds of long-term maturities but agreed to repurchase them at a later date, at a preestablished price, by issuing a repurchase agreement (RP) of, sometimes, one business day (overnight). In this way, financial institutions could overcome the legal impediment of issuing securities of very short maturities and shorten the maturity of indexed bonds. The RPs became the true financial instrument, with the indexed securities serving merely as a collateral. Thus, from the point of view of the agent buying the securities, these operations were a secure means of lending short-term funds at fixed prices with virtually no risk. The financial institutions, on the other hand, could make huge profits based on the difference between the preestablished price promised on the RPs and the rate of monetary correction, as long as the rate of inflation (and monetary correction) accelerated faster than expected inflation. While such conditions prevailed, brokerage firms had an incentive to increase their leverage continuously, which in some cases reached up to a hundred times a firm's capital. The fragility of the system was evident. Brokerage firms were the actual holders of indexed bonds and had to refinance their positions with the public in what became known as the overnight market. Therefore, they were exposed to runs that could occur in response to changes in the overnight rate (a function of expected inflation) or in the monetary correction rule. The potential difficulties were exacerbated by the fact that the RPs were not subject to rediscount mechanisms.

This speculative scheme reduced the authorities' degrees of freedom to operate monetary policy. On the one hand, an abrupt contraction in the money supply could disrupt the system and lead to several bankruptcies. On the other hand, the system was clearly rendering ineffective the government's attempts to fuel production by increasing the money supply, for funds were being channeled to financial assets rather than

9. Carneiro (1989, p. 303) analyzes the policies of the period, stressing their stop-and-go character. He questions the strength of the monetary squeeze in place before such measures were implemented.

investment. The coup de grace came with the announcement that supply shocks would be purged from the index that was used to calculate monetary correction. By raising the suspicion that the basic condition for the perpetuation of the speculative bubble was being violated, this announcement triggered a run on financial institutions and led to widespread liquidity problems.

The hands-off policy exemplified by the Halles affair was reversed when the authorities perceived that a domino effect could occur. The decision to rescue the system had important implications. First, it validated the financial institutions' bets and thereby increased moral hazard. Second, it resulted in large increases in the money supply, underscoring the restrictions imposed by the financial system on the conduct of monetary policy. Third, as larger institutions were called on to absorb smaller, insolvent firms, conglomerates headed by commercial banks began to form, and the system became much less segmented than planned by the original reforms. Within these conglomerates, the investment banks—which many had hoped would be a source of long-term credit—became merely an extension of commercial banks providing medium-term credit for working capital.

The combination of a heavy industrialization program with a financial structure reluctant to engage in the financing of long-term projects set the tone for a pattern of resource supply characterized by an increased role of foreign debt and a growing importance of government funds. The increase in the use of foreign resources resulted from a combination of supply and demand for foreign capital. Favorable supply conditions stemmed from the situation in the international credit market. A decrease in the demand for loans from the usual sources, reflecting the economic conditions within the industrialized world, turned the Eurocurrency market toward some Latin American countries. With generous terms, long maturities, and declining spreads, lending increased rapidly in the early 1970s. Under these circumstances, access to foreign financial markets appeared as a very positive opportunity to replace the inadequacy of internal intermediation. The mechanisms designed to stimulate external inflows were Law 4131, which regulated direct loans, and the central bank's Resolution 63, which regulated indirect loans channeled to firms by commercial and investment banks.

Through Law 4131, direct external credit became extremely important. Initially, the private sector contracted most resources borrowed through Law 4131; in 1972, for example, private debt accounted for 75.1 percent of the resources borrowed through Law 4131. Over time, however, a transformation occurred in the relative shares of the private and the public sectors. By 1981 the public sector was already responsible for 69.6 percent of the resources.[10] It is interesting to note that the bulk of the private sector loans is contracted by foreign firms, followed by joint ventures and domestic firms.

Despite their smaller share in the total volume of resources, funds channeled via Resolution 63 had a more direct impact on the structure of the financial system. This impact is a result of a tighter link between the domestic and foreign financial systems, a link that resulted from the introduction of relending operations. These operations allowed domestic financial institutions to borrow long-term funds abroad and relend them in the domestic market for shorter periods of time. Given the peculiarities of the system that developed, such loans were virtually free of exchange risk for the borrowing institution, because this risk was first transferred to the final borrowers and later to the public sector. As a result, these operations greatly enhanced the activities of commercial and investment banks, which were no longer restricted to deposits as their sources of funds, and contributed to the rapid growth of these institutions during the period.

An interesting outcome of this process was the increased importance of foreign banks in the intermediation of funds. Participation of foreign banks rose from 8 percent of the total in 1972 to 22.3 percent in 1981. This observation gains importance when one recalls that the financial system in Brazil is highly protected from foreign competition. The reforms of the 1960s maintained a series of existing restrictions for the entry of new foreign banks into the country and limited the scope for the creation of new agencies for the banks already installed in the market. Although such regulations constrained the growth of deposits captured by foreign banks, they were less successful in limiting the growth of their active operations as is evidenced by the increase in the ratio of foreign bank loans to domestic bank loans from 13.8 percent in 1970 to 40.2 percent in 1981 (Davidoff Cruz 1984, p. 130).

The other source of long-term credit was government funds. These funds were transferred to the private sector, frequently through private financial institutions, in the form of subsidized credits and to targeted

---

10. The process of "statization" of the foreign debt was common to most highly indebted countries. It has led to the suggestion that the government operates under a political-economic constraint, referred to by Arida and Taylor (1989) as a "bankruptcy constraint." The conjecture is that the government will not allow widespread bankruptcies to develop because they have high economic and political costs. In the context of the debt crisis, the need to constantly devalue the exchange rate imposed large bankruptcy risks for private firms indebted in dollars. As a result, the government was forced to offer hedges and guarantees, basically absorbing the exchange risk. See also Diaz-Alejandro 1985.

sectors such as agriculture and exports of manufactured goods, which were perceived as priority sectors in the new economic policy.

The growing importance of the nonmonetary system, a trend observed in the late 1960s and early 1970s, is maintained during the period under consideration. The ratio of nonmonetary financial assets to GDP oscillated around an average of 26.4 percent from 1974 to 1979, up from 16 percent during the Economic Miracle; thus, there is an increasing trend. The choice between monetary and nonmonetary assets in the portfolios held by the public shows the same pattern as before. The share of nonmonetary financial assets in total holdings increased from 55.7 percent in 1973 to 65.2 percent in 1979. Savings deposits continued to grow rapidly, whereas holdings of government debt jumped from 15.8 percent of the total in 1973 to an average of 19.0 percent over the period. One important aspect is the flight from non-indexed to indexed assets in response to higher and more uncertain rates of inflation. If we take the ratio of savings deposits and holdings of indexed government bonds to holdings of time deposits and bills of exchange as an indicator of the relative preference of indexed to nonindexed assets in agents' portfolios, we observe that from a value of 0.58 in 1973, this ratio jumped to 0.81 in 1974 and 1.35 in 1977. Also noteworthy is that bills of exchange, which showed high growth during the Economic Miracle, lost participation rapidly, reflecting the lower demand for consumer durables.

In 1976, interest rates were set completely free. This initiative was part of a more comprehensive package that was aimed at raising the cost of funds in the domestic market with the purpose of inducing a foreign capital inflow to help finance the balance of payments. The high interest rate, however, also contributed to increased segmentation of the financial system. Demands for subsidized credit multiplied quickly. Given the state's deteriorating capacity to extract and transfer fiscal resources, such subsidies were basically financed by credit from the central bank.[11]

The evolution of loans to the private sector during the first half of the 1970s is similar to the pattern that prevailed in the previous period. Total loans to the private sector as a percentage of GDP continued to grow, rising from 46.9 percent in 1973 to 51.1 percent in 1974 and stabilizing at around 55 percent for the rest of the period. The participation of the nonmonetary system in the total volume of loans extended to

---

11. The World Bank estimates that by 1978 the annualized flow of credit subsidy had amounted to almost 5.5 percent of GDP (WB 1984, p. 27).

the private sector, which had been growing rapidly since the reforms, stabilized at about 49 percent. From 1974 to 1978, Banco do Brasil loans to the private sector as a share of total loans extended by the monetary sector was 44.4 percent, up from 36.2 percent during the period following the reforms to the end of the miracle; that is, the share of Banco do Brasil loans exhibited a reduced rate of growth. Loans from Financeiras to the private sector also suffered a large reduction in the second half of the 1970s, falling from 15.1 percent of total loans in 1973 to only 6.9 percent in 1979, reflecting decelerating demand for consumer durables.

It is also interesting to note that the importance of credit from official sources, such as BNDES, fell in the first half of the 1970s when compared with the years that followed the reforms. This reinforces the idea that credit was very important in propelling the recovery. In the second half of the decade, with the implementation of an ambitious investment program, the importance of BNDES loans grew again.

Thus, the developments of the 1970s would bring to the fore the main limitations of the financial system. The first limitation was the difficulty in mobilizing additional savings when the economy was at or near full employment, as it was in the beginning of the decade, and in transforming them into long-term investable funds. The second limitation, which is intrinsically related to the first, is that because of the multiple units of account that coexisted in the economy, stability of inflation and the exchange rule were fundamental elements to the overall stability of the financial system. The acceleration of inflation in the mid-1970s and the break with the exchange rule by the end of the decade disrupted this stable scheme.

The Financial System in the 1980s

The second oil shock, the sharp increase in world interest rates, and the world recession in the late 1970s brought the process of debt-led growth to a sudden end. The openly expansionist policies implemented when the external shocks hit in the early 1980s epitomized the attempt to deny the need for adjustment and had an adverse impact on macroeconomic performance.

At first, the Figueiredo administration hinted at a strategy change as Mario Henrique Simonsen, the finance minister, insisted on lower growth rates as an unavoidable cost for adjusting the economy. But he was quickly dismissed in favor of a promise of another miracle made by Delfim Netto, who replaced Simonsen as finance minister. Strict nominal interest ceilings were established, many administered prices were liberalized, and a new "inflation plus" indexation scheme for minimum wages was put in place. A maxi-devaluation of the currency of 30 percent was implemented, which broke with more than a decade of a crawling peg. In addition, the rates of monetary correction and exchange devaluation were preannounced in an attempt to dampen inflationary expectations.

Delfim's attempt to contain inflation by manipulating expectations rather than by contractionary demand policies proved disastrous and was quickly abandoned. Inflation soared, eroding the relative price effects of the maxi-devaluation undertaken in late 1979.[12] The impact on the financial system was strong. The combination of nominal interest controls and rising inflation turned real returns on financial assets negative, inducing a flight to foreign exchange and physical assets.

Orthodox policies returned only in the last quarter of 1980, as central bank holdings of foreign reserves were rapidly depleted and Brazil was faced with a major liquidity crisis. To deal with the balance-of-payments crisis, bring inflation down, and, more important, retain international creditworthiness, contractionary monetary and fiscal policies were maintained during 1981. This generated the first downturn in Brazilian production since the Great Depression. The rate of credit expansion was limited to 50 percent, as was the target for money supply. GDP fell by about 1.6 percent, industrial output decreased by 5.5 percent, and unemployment soared.

The policy of interest rate controls was also reversed, and all controls were abolished. This, combined with the sharp monetary squeeze, was once again aimed at shifting the relative cost of borrowing in favor of foreign markets with the explicit goal of inducing domestic firms to borrow abroad for balance-of-payments purposes. High interest rates led to cuts in investment spending and an increase in the government's interest bill, as domestic debt was increasingly being used to finance the public deficit. Another impact of the restrictive policies on the financial system was an additional inducement to the process of mergers of institutions and growth in the share of financial intermediation in total output.

12. The relative price effects of the maxi-devaluation on the rate of inflation, however, remained. The jump in the rate of inflation, from around 40 percent until 1978 to 80 percent in 1979 and to 120 percent in 1980, seemed to many observers to be related to the perverse combination of supply shocks (such as the new wage law of 1979 and the maxi-devaluation of the currency) and widespread indexation schemes. The view was reinforced by the apparent inability of contractions to reduce inflation and led to the formulation of the "Inertial Hypothesis," which culminated in the Cruzado Plan and the following heterodox programs. For a more detailed discussion, see Arida and Lara-Resende 1985.

The exchange crisis and the jump in the inflation rate, in conjunction with the memory of the pre-fixation experiment and the tampering with the index of monetary correction, gave new impetus to the flight from nominal assets. Demand for dollar-denominated assets and gold increased. On the other hand, agents holding dollar-denominated liabilities were faced with increasingly risky obligations, for the expectations of additional large depreciations began to build.

Two main mechanisms were used to hedge against exchange risk. The first mechanism was to hold ORTNs with exchange correction. The second mechanism was the use of a facility created by the central bank through Resolution 432 and Circular 230, which allowed the private sector to deposit the domestic currency equivalent of its foreign obligations at the central bank, which absorbed the exchange risk, assuming debt service payments. These deposits, however, could be withdrawn at any time by the public, reducing the effectiveness of monetary policy. In the face of an expected maxi-devaluation or a decrease in the rate of interest, the private sector increased its demand for such deposits. On the other hand, if the authorities opted for a more contractionary policy, inducing a rise in the rate of interest, there was a tendency to withdraw these deposits, which would undermine the attempted monetary squeeze.[13]

The Mexican moratorium of August 1982 brought the process of voluntary debt rollover to an end. As a result, Brazilian external reserves were quickly depleted, and after some reluctance and a postponement caused by the November elections, the country had to apply for an IMF-supported program.[14] After several letters of intent were signed and domestic targets missed, it became increasingly clear that the good performance of the external sector was being achieved at the expense of internal equilibrium. The policies required to generate the large trade surpluses and service the external debt were adding to inflation, damaging public finances, and reducing resources available for investment.

From late 1984 onward, the level of economic activity gradually recovered, as domestic policies took an expansionary path. Industrial output increased, led by the production of exportables, with the economy generating large trade surpluses. The trend toward recovery strengthened when the first civilian government took office in early 1985 (following two decades of military dictatorship), and gradually, the

13. Dornbusch and Moura da Silva (1985) develop a model showing these effects. In December 1982, the value of such deposits at the central bank was around US $10 billion.
14. For details of the program and its implementation, see Oliveira 1989.

emphasis of economic policy turned from external adjustment to domestic growth and income distribution in response to previously repressed
social demands that were now coming to the fore. As a result, the upturn
continued in 1985 and 1986, with real GDP increasing by 8.3 percent
and 7.5 percent in these two years, respectively. In contrast to what
happened in 1984, however, growth was led by domestic demand fueled
by wage increases and rising government consumption expenditures.
Investment remained at modest levels because the recovery used up
existing productive capacity.

At the beginning of 1986, however, the economy was perceived to be
on the brink of hyperinflation, and the government responded by
launching a heterodox program, the Cruzado Plan, based on a price
freeze, an incomes policy, and monetary reform. The sudden stop in
inflation which followed the announcement of this plan led to a series
of changes in the financial system, ones that resulted mainly from a
reduction in the expected profitability of the sector. The lower rate of
inflation implied a loss in the banking system's capacity to collect its
share of the inflation tax. Also, the higher demand for real cash balances
which accompanied the fall in the rate of inflation resulted in a reduction in the demand for banking activities, in the number of jobs in the
financial system, and in the number of branches. Explicit fees and
charges replaced revenues previously collected through the inflation
tax.

With the implementation of the Cruzado Plan, interest rates were set
at low levels with the goal of affecting inflationary expectations and as a
means of spurring investment. This led to a large increase in real credit.
After a few months, however, it became clear that the program had
failed.[15] Widespread shortages and the associated premiums became a
common phenomenon. Trade balance figures deteriorated quickly as a
result of expanded spending and exchange rate speculation.

The process culminated with a debt moratorium in early 1987, inflation explosion, and an abrupt reduction in the levels of economic
activity. Many of the small and medium-sized firms that borrowed heavily
during the period of low nominal interest rates were now faced with
unbearable financial costs and went bankrupt. Special lines of credit
were extended by the monetary authorities to provide assistance to such
enterprises. Credit to the private sector declined by 10 percent in real
terms during 1987. These trends continued in 1988. The final years of

---

15. For a description of the Cruzado Plan, the causes of its failure, and the plans that
followed, see Modiano 1989.

the decade were characterized by stagnation, a permanent threat of hyperinflation, and several stabilization attempts that ranged between orthodox and heterodox experiments.

The main developments in the financial system were responses to the constant changes in the rules of the game, the rapid acceleration in the rate of inflation, and the ever growing financing needs of the public sector (which are discussed in more detail below). The major feature of the decade was the rapid process of demonetization in the economy, with a rapid reduction in the participation of monetary assets to total assets. Provisional data show that in 1990, this share was only 6.3 percent, down from an average of 37 percent in 1974–1979 and 21 percent during the first half of the 1980s.

One implication of the flight away from currency and demand deposits was the increasing sophistication, as well as cost, of the liabilities issued by financial institutions. Highly liquid, interest-paying current accounts and a variety of funds, mainly based on portfolios of government securities, were introduced, raising the average funding cost. Nevertheless, the profits that could be obtained on the reduced volumes of deposits led the financial institutions to engage in a frenetic drive to capture resources through an increase in the number of branches, the introduction of sophisticated computer systems, and the like.

On the asset side of financial intermediaries, a recent study shows that there was a marked reduction in the share of loans to total assets, compensated by a large increase in the institutions' portfolios of government securities (Almeida et al. 1988). This trend was observed not only in private financial firms but also in Banco do Brasil. This behavior reveals, once again, the financial institutions' preference for indexing their loans and the public's reluctance to take such loans. Under these circumstances, the option of lending to the government under indexation clauses, high liquidity, and low risk became extremely attractive. Among nonmonetary financial assets, we also observe the increasing importance of government securities as well as savings deposits in the total volume of assets held by the public, which reflects the attempt to hold indexed assets. Fixed deposits also increased as a consequence of the innovations described.

After the onset of the debt crisis, overall credit followed a contractionary trend. Total loans to the private sector as a percentage of GDP fell from around 40 percent in the late 1970s to 35.6 percent in 1982 and to a mere 18 percent in 1989. From 1982 to 1989, there was a reduction of around 40 percent in real credit extended to the private sector.

The policy of credit restriction had a strong impact on Banco do Brasil: its credit to the private sector fell from around 21 percent of total loans in 1979 to 10.5 percent in 1985 with some recovery by the end of the decade. (The decade average, however, is only 14.6 percent, which is lower than the 21.4 percent in the 1970s.) One of the main reasons for this reduction in credit was the transfer of rural credit to private commercial banks through an increase in the share of rural applications for compulsory loans. Commercial banks experienced an increase in the participation of loans, since they had the opportunity to engage in operations subject to fewer restrictions, such as the intermediation of foreign funds.

The recessionary character of the economy throughout the decade, with the exception of the two-year recovery of 1984–1986, explains the retraction in the amount of loans extended by Financeiras and investment banks. Credit from development banks suffered lower reductions. The participation of BNDES loans was on average 3.9 percent of the total, whereas that of state development banks was 3.3 percent, which is, in fact, an increase, one that was due to an increase in financial assistance provided by these banks to private firms with liquidity problems.

Another important feature of the decade is the notorious increase in the share of total credit that was directed to the public sector. The real rate of growth of loans to the public sector between 1980 and 1984 was, on average, 10.7 percent a year, whereas loans to the private sector grew on average −5.5 percent a year over the same period. In 1988, 31 percent of all loans extended by the financial system was directed to the public sector, whereas in 1980 this ratio was only 17.5 percent. The increasing importance of domestic sources in the financing of the public sector was one of the major features of the decade.

The fiscal and financial reforms of the 1960s had a strong positive impact on government finance. The combination of increased tax revenues and the introduction of monetary correction on government debt instruments (which created the possibility of domestic debt financing of government expenditures) allowed the state to save 4.8 percent of GDP on average, at least until the mid-1970s. These savings made it possible for the public sector to finance its investments with no pressures exerted on the financial sector. As shown in Table 7.3, the borrowing requirements of the public sector, as defined in the national accounts,[16]

16. The public sector borrowing requirement, as used in the table, is defined as the difference between government savings and investment. The figures in the column that correct for inflation deduct monetary correction from current expenditures. These figures

Table 7.3. Sectoral balances (as a percentage of GDP)

Year	National accounts			Inflation-adjusted	
	Government sector	Private sector	Foreign sector	Government sector	Private sector
1965	2.46	−4.08	1.62	2.46	−4.08
1966	−1.11	0.92	0.19	−1.45	1.26
1967	2.15	−1.39	−0.76	1.66	−0.90
1968	−1.03	2.52	−1.49	−1.64	3.13
1969	5.01	−4.26	−0.75	4.39	−3.64
1970	−1.04	2.36	−1.32	−1.66	2.98
1971	−1.61	4.27	−2.66	−2.30	4.96
1972	−1.90	4.43	−2.53	−2.52	5.05
1973	−2.29	4.30	−2.01	−2.86	4.87
1974	−0.44	6.89	−6.45	−0.97	7.42
1975	0.25	4.91	−5.16	−0.31	5.47
1976	−0.26	4.17	−3.91	−0.98	4.89
1977	−0.63	2.91	−2.28	−1.89	4.17
1978	0.77	2.70	−3.47	−0.68	4.15
1979	0.12	4.69	−4.81	−1.13	5.94
1980	1.25	4.18	−5.43	0.45	4.98
1981	1.48	2.94	−4.42	0.60	3.82
1982	2.70	3.04	−5.74	1.72	4.02
1983	2.85	0.47	−3.32	0.69	2.63
1984	4.64	−4.66	0.02	0.97	−0.99
1985	10.25	−10.14	−0.11	1.96	−1.85
1986	10.02	−8.08	−1.94	0.91	1.03
1987	9.21	−8.74	−0.47	−0.30	0.77
1988	15.72	−14.52	−1.20	2.89	−1.69

Sources: Central Bank of Brazil, various years.

were negative throughout the period, which shows that the sector was generating a surplus.

After the first oil shock and in view of the adjustment strategy chosen by the authorities, the government's current account began to deteriorate. Given that government investment spending oscillated around 4 percent of GDP until 1976 and started to fall steadily thereafter, whereas consumption spending remained at around 9.6 percent of GDP throughout the decade, the deterioration of the government current

should not be taken as a measure of the overall public sector deficit. It is widely known that, among other difficulties, a number of subsidies are paid directly by the monetary authorities and are therefore deducted from the measure of public savings. On the other hand, the savings effort of state-owned enterprises is included in the private sector savings measure. Although the figures should be looked at with suspicion, the trends are representative of the developments I want to stress in the context of this work.

account seems to be explained by the evolution of net revenues. That is, the fall in savings resulted from a reduction in gross revenues, mainly because of inflation, and an increase in transfers to the private sector and state-owned enterprises. Also, at the end of the decade, interest payments on the internal and external debts represented 1.12 percent of GDP, which is twice as much as in 1973, a problem that was extremely aggravated in the 1980s. As a result, the sectoral balances depicted in Table 7.3 show a substantial deterioration in the public sector accounts around 1974 and a turn from a net creditor to a net debtor in 1978.

Since the early 1980s, the government's current account position has deteriorated further. A variety of factors are responsible: growth of sectors subject to fiscal incentives (such as exports and agriculture), a large reduction in revenues because of higher inflation (the so-called Olivera-Tanzi effect) and tax evasion, increasing subsidies and transfers to the state enterprises and the private sector, rising domestic and foreign debt service, and mounting consumption expenditures.

The emergence of the debt crisis checked the strategy of financing the public deficit with foreign resources. The state was therefore forced to resort to domestic indebtedness as a major source of finance. The shift in the sources of finance is, once again, shown by the data in Table 7.3. After 1983, there is a virtual disappearance of foreign savings, but the private sector borrowing requirement turns negative, thus indicating that it had become a net creditor to the government. In other words, the government sector was using up private savings to finance itself.

The deterioration in the public sector deficit cannot be dissociated from events in the external front. The huge surpluses obtained in the goods and nonfactor services account of the balance of payments, which characterizes the external adjustment of the Brazilian economy, had perverse effects on the public accounts. The use of credit and fiscal subsidies to private exporting firms, the control of public prices as a means to control inflation,[17] and the real exchange rate devaluations undertaken to increase the competitiveness of the tradable sector all adversely affected the public accounts.

Moreover, because the government was responsible for about 80 percent of the foreign debt, it was faced with a further difficulty: even in the event that the economy was able to generate the net exports of goods and nonfactor services equivalent to 5 percent of GDP (which is necessary to service the external debt), the public sector found itself having to

17. For an analysis of the use of state-owned enterprises as an instrument of short-run macroeconomic policy, see Werneck 1987.

effect a transfer of resources from the private sector to itself. For it was the private sector that produced the bulk of the foreign exchange used for debt service, whereas the government was the main debtor. Theoretically, there exists several different ways in which the government could raise the extra revenue to pay for these transfers. It could increase taxes and/or reduce expenditures, or it could increase domestic indebtedness, either by printing money or by issuing securities.[18] Given the notorious difficulties involved in tax increases and expenditure cuts,[19] the alternative that was followed was a combination of increased money supply and domestic debt.

The need to resort to domestic debt financing brought to the fore a serious shortcoming of the financial system: the virtual absence of a secondary market for government securities. The market for government securities in Brazil consists of three segments: the primary market, where treasury paper is issued and placed by the central bank on its behalf; the secondary market, where government securities are traded among financial institutions and where the central bank intervenes to dampen unexpected fluctuations in reserves; and an overnight market where the central bank conducts its monetary policy operations. Operations in the primary and the secondary markets are final, whereas those conducted in the overnight market are accompanied by a twenty-four-hour repurchase (or resale) agreement. The central bank announces the interest rate in the overnight market every business day and supports it by acting as a residual purchaser or seller. Thus financial institutions finance their holdings of government bonds through the acceptance of overnight deposits from the private sector, which pay a percentage of the overnight rate, and through the use of repurchase agreements with the central bank. It is estimated that by the end of the 1980s, around 70 percent of the stock of public domestic debt was rolled over daily in the overnight market,[20] thus revealing the government's difficulty in finding final holders for its securities.

The perception by the private sector that the government's accounts were on an unsustainable path led to a flight from nominal assets in

18. If state-owned enterprises are taken into account, at least two other possibilities exist: increases in public sector prices and the sale of public assets.
19. Attempts at increasing taxes are generally frustrated by tax evasion and a growing "underground economy." Current expenditure cuts are usually blocked by political and private interests. Most expenditure reductions in the public sector were concentrated on public investment rather than on current spending. It is definitely much easier to postpone new projects than to cut current expenditures.
20. In June 1988, this meant the need to roll over a stock of around US $33.7 billion daily.

general and from money in particular.[21] Indexation, however, created a buffer between nominal and real assets; that is, the flight away from money was reflected immediately not as a capital outflow or as an increase in the demand for real assets but as a rise in the demand for indexed assets of ever shorter maturities. These assets are bought mainly in the overnight market and are highly liquid. The government has responded to this situation by attempting to create an effective secondary market and to place longer securities.[22] Nevertheless, given the existence of alternative assets, such as gold and foreign exchange in the parallel market, the private sector insisted on holding either "indexed money"—namely, indexed securities in the overnight market—or requested real rates of return which were not sustainable in view of the government's intertemporal budget constraint, that is, they led to explosive paths. Therefore, it became increasingly difficult and costly for the government to finance itself domestically. The result was an unstable equilibrium, subject to the constant fear that if the stock of indexed money found its way to real asset markets, hyperinflation would be inescapable.

III. Credit Allocation and Real Investment

Against this general background of macroeconomic instability, we can now finally turn to the questions of credit allocation and real investment. There are at least two dimensions to the problem. The first relates to the evolution of aggregate credit in the economy and its effects on key prices—interest rates, exchange rates, and wages—and expenditures. The second dimension is the use of credit policy as an allocation instrument. The first set of issues is usually studied in the context of stabilization policies, whereas the second is typically considered in connection with structural adjustment policies. Of course, this stark separation between the two sets of policies is artificial, for many variables connect the two groups. Here I concentrate on the second group because the evolution of credit has been treated above. I argue that the style of government intervention in the Brazilian economy, as well as the state's

21. The velocity of circulation of money achieved a value of around 37 in 1988, up from an average of 8.1 in the 1970s.
22. The difficulty of replacing Letras Financeiras do Tesouro (LFT)/Letras do Banco Central (LBCs) (securities that paid the average interest rate in the overnight market and therefore had their return indexed by the cost of financing) with Obrigacoes do Tesouro Nacional (OTNs) of lower liquidity in 1988 is representative. The auctions indicated that the government had to offer rapidly increasing yields in order to reduce the liquidity of its debt.

financial constraints, contributed to the linking of these two sets of policies in ways that undermined the effectiveness of both.

The evolution of the Brazilian financial system in general and the utilization of selective credit policies in particular must be understood as being part of an overall development strategy that emphasized import-substitution industrialization and was, therefore, consciously interventionist. In very broad lines, the Brazilian style of intervention can be described as follows: the state sets national goals, establishes sectoral investment priorities, and defines the role to be played by the government and the private sector, domestic and foreign, in the economy. To guarantee the attainment of its priorities, the government offers the private sector two main incentives: a reduction in the cost of investment through fiscal and credit subsidies, and a market reserved for domestically produced goods through the manipulation of trade policy. Here we will concentrate on the role of credit as an instrument of industrial policy.

Selective or sectoral credit policies (SCP) are designed to channel resources gathered by financial institutions to priority sectors, groups, or regions at subsidized rates of interest. The objectives are to stimulate investment in priority activities that the authorities believe will not be undertaken otherwise and to redistribute income and wealth. Such objectives are attained by directing investable funds to specified projects through the use of nonprice rationing mechanisms. The six major categories of SCP instruments are subsidized loans for priority sectors, differential discount rates or reserve requirements, direct budgetary subsidies, credit floors, credit ceilings, and the proliferation of specialized financial institutions. Brazil has used a variety of these instruments, with an emphasis on the establishment of special funds and controlled interest rates.

The attempt by the government to foster selected sectors by allocating credit according to its developmental plans is not new. Even the capital markets reform law of the 1960s, with its increased emphasis on the role of market forces, envisioned the establishment of financial funds to be managed by the monetary authorities and used for developmental purposes. Zini (1982) divides the official funds into three groups according to the agents that managed them:

(1) Sectoral funds, provided by the Treasury for the development of particular geographical regions, such as the Northeast and the Amazon.
(2) Financial funds under the responsibility of the central bank. Examples include the General Fund for Agriculture and Industry (Fundo Geral

para a Agricultura e Industria, FUNAGRI), the fund for manufactured
export financing (Fundo de Financiamento a Exportacao, FINEX), and
the Alcohol Program Fund. Zini lists eighteen funds that were under
the supervision of the central bank. Some of these—FUNAGRI, for
example—are made out of dozens of subfunds that are lent to the
private sector through other financial institutions, private or public,
that is, the so-called authorized agents.

(3) Funds managed by Banco do Brasil, the BNDES, and BNH. In addition
to the funds under the direct responsibility of these institutions, they
also operate as agents of the central bank.

With the exception of the rural credit facility for marketing and
working capital (*custeio*), all these funds are of a medium- or long-term
nature, responding to the absence of private domestic sources of long-
term credit in Brazil. The main source of long-term finance for industrial projects in the last few decades has been the National Economic and
Social Development Bank. Indeed, it is estimated that in 1978 the
BNDES system was responsible for 80 percent of all institutional
financing used for industrial programs in Brazil (World Bank 1984,
p. 67). In that same year, total outlays of the bank were equivalent to
approximately 40 percent of the gross fixed capital formation in the
country. In addition to its financing role, BNDES can be regarded as the
government's leading vehicle for the implementation of its industrial
policy, having as its main beneficiaries private firms, state-owned enterprises, and government entities in general.

The BNDES was created in 1952 and has undergone several transformations.[23] Initially, the bank operated predominantly to support and
promote the public sector, focusing on sectors such as transportation
and electrical power. After the reforms of the mid-1960s, the range of
the bank's activities increased, as it started increasingly to utilize a system
of transfers of resources through development banks and private
financial institutions. This provided private financial firms with a whole
new set of opportunities. With the implementation of the PND II, the
focus of BNDES shifted toward the support of private sector enterprises,
which were perceived as the weak leg of the so-called tripod of state-
owned enterprises, multinational corporations, and private domestic
firms. During the first years following the financial reforms, the bulk of
BNDES operations with the private sector were carried out with
postfixed monetary correction. When the rate of inflation began to
accelerate in the mid-1970s, the cost of borrowing rose rapidly, and the

23. See Willis 1986 and Zoninsein 1985 for analyses of BNDES evolution and impacts.

private sector resorted to these operations only when nothing else was available (though it has consistently complained about such contracts).

Following the execution of the PND II, the structure of the BNDES was altered through the creation of new subsidiaries, including Mecanica Brasileira S/A, which targets the capital goods sector, and Insumos Basicos S/A, which focuses on the promotion of basic input projects. These two subsidiaries provided subsidies in the form of credit with favorable financing terms supported by central bank loans, fiscal resources of newly transferred funds from the compulsory saving schemes, and an increasing use of foreign finance (on directions from the executive government, despite strong resistance on the part of bank staff). Consistent with the need to engage the private sector in its ambitious investment plan, the government ceded to pressures to limit indexation of the BNDES's operations. Thus, in the mid-1970s, monetary correction was limited to 20 percent a year for most lending projects, particularly for those in new priority sectors such as basic inputs and capital goods.

In spite of the replenishing of the BNDES's resources with forced savings from public trust funds, however, the extension of loans at preferential interest rates led to mounting financial difficulties because of the increasing cost of funds and the rise in the share of third-party resources. Indeed, the need to secure a rate of return on its loans which was compatible with the cost of its liabilities led the technical staff of the bank to suggest that its solvency could be maintained only by an increase in overall interest rates or by full indexation of its credits. Despite political resistance to this move, the BNDES's credit programs slowly moved toward increasing degrees of indexation after 1978, thus reducing the subsidy element involved in its operations. The bulk of subsidized credit in the last decade has thus been directed to agriculture through the Rural Credit System, to exports through the Export Financing Program, to small-enterprise development, and to sectoral and regional funds.

An evaluation of the effectiveness and efficiency of selective credit policies runs into severe difficulties. First, an endemic lack of data exists[24] and is particularly pronounced in the area of interest rates. Second, the large number of special funds[25] aggravates the problem because of the common practice of accounting transfers among the funds and the multiplicity of operational procedures. Moreover, the use

24. Note also that the value of the available information is questionable to the extent that, in many cases, the system provides strong incentives for misinformation.
25. Zini (1982) counts more than one hundred different funds.

of a system of "transfers" (repasses), by which most of the resources are transferred from official agencies to other development banks, private commercial banks, and nonbanking financial institutions, allows final lenders to charge fees and commissions, to require compensating balances, and to create a variety of other circumventing devices that result in a whole new set of complications for the analysis of selective credit policies. Therefore, the following discussion is limited to a brief analysis of two of the most important targeted sectors.

Manufactured Exports

Brazil has been singled out by many observers as a Latin American country that managed to combine import substitution with a successful export performance from the late 1960s onward. This performance is explained by the combination of a sizable, preexisting industrial base and a set of active policies aimed at promoting exports. The main elements of the export-promoting policies were the adoption of a crawling exchange rate system in 1968 (which generated a "realistic" exchange rate) and the use of credit and fiscal subsidies to foster exporting sectors.[26]

Credit incentives to manufactured exports took the following forms: subsidized credit for projects linked to the export sector, the financing of actual exports, and preferential credit for export-oriented services such as overseas marketing facilities. Both preexport and postexport financing were available. The bulk of preexport financing is granted through FINEX, the export-financing program. By the late 1980s, interest rates for export financing were equal to market rates charged by the commercial banks operating the system (around 20 to 25 percent per year in 1988 plus monetary correction), less a subsidy determined by FINEX, the amount of which depended on the kind of product involved, where the subsidy varied between five and fifteen percentage points. Another type of preshipment operation (*Adiantamento sobre Contrato de Cambio*) involves advances in domestic currency of up to 100 percent of foreign exchange receivables, to be repaid at the time the foreign exchange is surrendered.

A variety of programs make postexport financing lines available for domestic firms. FINEX resources, administered by CACEX (the Foreign Trade Department of the Bank of Brazil), can be used for direct financing of the foreign importer. In one program, FINEX funds make up for

26. Fiscal incentives were based mainly on tariff exemptions (drawback provisions allowing for tariff-free imports on inputs used in the production of exports), indirect tax exemptions, and tax credit premiums (*credito premio*).

the difference between a foreign loan contracted by a Brazilian commercial bank in the international market and the cost that a foreign importer of Brazilian goods has to pay on a similar loan. A separate Banco do Brasil program allows the exporter to provide credit to the importer and then rediscount the paper at subsidized interest rates.

The banking system has also been instrumental in the government's effort to promote exports. The central bank offers reduced reserve requirements in the case of loans to export firms or trading companies and lower rediscount rates for manufacturing production for exports and for exporting firms (trading companies). A major source of preexport credit subsidies was established through Resolution 71 (1967) of the central bank, which allowed commercial banks to obtain resources from the discount window at low rates (4 percent per year) for lending to the export sector. By obtaining a certificate indicating that it will export, a firm could borrow funds of up to 80 percent of the exporting value for 120 days at an interest rate of 8 percent per year. A similar line of subsidized credit is available on a postexport basis, that is, for exporting firms which had not borrowed before and which need financing for future projects.[27]

The system of export subsidies used by Brazil created frictions abroad. Conflicts with the United States increased during the 1970s and culminated at the end of the decade when, in response to pressures from the international community, an agreement to eliminate the *credito premio* (credit premiums) and reduce credit subsidies was adopted.[28]

Total Brazilian exports grew at an average of 17.3 percent per year from 1970 to 1985, whereas manufactured goods exports grew at around 30 percent per year over the same period. This extraordinary increase in nontraditional Brazilian exports over the last two decades suggests the success of the selective credit policy described above. As mentioned before, however, an evaluation of these policies runs into several obstacles. To have a clear idea of the impact of these policies, it is necessary to consider the volume of funds released for these particular purposes in relation to the aggregate capital available to the export sector. An estimate of funds is not available, and therefore, the effectiveness of this policy is hard to assess. In addition, it is important to stress that exports have been simultaneously subject to a multitude of incentives, and the relative efficiency of each instrument is difficult to estimate.

27. For more details on the various incentive schemes, see Musalem 1984.
28. In 1981, given the difficulties in the balance of payments, these subsidies were reintroduced.

In his attempt to quantify the volume of subsidies provided to manufactured exports, Musalem (1984) has shown that the package of incentives used to promote growth of manufactured exports clearly succeeded in inducing an increase in their share of total sectoral output. Although he concludes that the subsidies used had decisive effects on export performance, the author was not able to reach a conclusion as to the relative effectiveness of each of the incentive schemes, thus confirming that it is very difficult to disentangle the impact of credit policies on exports from that of other incentives.

Agriculture

For many years, Brazilian agriculture has benefited from a series of incentives aimed at its modernization and increased output. Indeed, since the creation of the National System of Rural Credit (SNCR) in the mid-1960s, subsidized credit for the rural sector has been the most important incentive mechanism for the transformation of the Brazilian agricultural sector.

From its outset, the goal of transforming Brazilian agriculture was viewed as a twofold process in which increased capital and the utilization of modern inputs should go hand in hand. According to this conception, the system was designed in such a way that the use of chemical fertilizers and pesticides was compulsory for those who obtained subsidized credit. Moreover, the acquisition of inputs itself was subsidized. In addition, farmers could acquire machinery at subsidized rates. Accordingly, financial incentives to agriculture mainly took the form of lower interest rates for agricultural production and the purchase of modern inputs and were used in conjunction with a set of regulations which attempted to ensure the volume of credit allocated to the sector by imposing that a minimum share of total bank loans be dedicated to agriculture.

Banco do Brasil, which was responsible for about 65 percent of total agricultural credit in the late 1980s, has always been the major provider of agricultural credit through its vast network of branches. In addition to the resources it captures through deposits, Banco do Brasil can resort to central bank funds through the Conta de Movimento, an account connecting the central bank of Brazil to Banco do Brasil. The potentially inflationary character of this source of funds has been the focus of heated debates on the effects of agricultural credit in Brazil.

In addition to credit extended directly by Banco do Brasil, the authorities have established a series of selective credit mechanisms to ensure the participation of private financial institutions. After early attempts to induce commercial banks to provide credit to agriculture (by allowing them to use up to 10 percent of their reserve requirements for rural loans) proved not to be very successful, the system was reformed, and by the mid-1980s, the main source of compulsory funds to the agricultural sector was the requirement that a certain share of a commercial bank's assets (with the exception of relending operations and rediscounts) be held in the form of agricultural loans. Given the flight from monetary assets in response to the ever increasing rates of inflation, the authorities responded by increasing the share of an institution's assets which was to be dedicated to such loans from 10 percent in 1972 to 35 percent in the mid-1980s.

Because agricultural loans are extended at subsidized interest rates that are in many instances even lower than the rate of inflation, the rate of interest charged by the financial intermediaries on their other assets is pushed upward to restore the overall return of their loan portfolio.[29] Thus, an important side effect of this policy is the increased segmentation of the credit market, an effect that is reflected in significantly higher interest rates on loans to the remaining sectors of the economy.

In spite of the constant claims that subsidized agricultural credit was being diverted from its intended uses and channeled to the financial system where high real rates of interest could be obtained at low risk, analysts of the agricultural sector maintain that, despite its various shortcomings, the existence of subsidized credit contributed decisively toward the modernization of the Brazilian agricultural sector since the mid-1960s. It is also claimed, however, that in most cases the use of subsidized credit was taken too far and used for too long. It is also argued that over time, the economic justifications for the use of the policy lost force, to the extent that the subsidy policy was no longer an active incentive but rather a compensation for other distortions present in Brazilian agriculture, such as the export quota system (Correa do Lago et al. 1984, p. 42). Moreover, as mentioned earlier, given the mounting volume of subsidized credit in place and the way such credit from Banco do Brasil was financed, complaints about its inflationary effects became common. Another often-mentioned shortcoming of the policy was its bias in favor of medium-sized and large firms at the expense of smaller units.[30]

29. For a discussion, see Correa do Lago et al. 1984, p. 43.
30. A critical view of the rural credit system in Brazil is offered by the World Bank (1984). According to its report, the system induces direct on-farm misallocation, is discriminatory, leads to considerable diversion, increases financial system segmentation, and has inflationary effects.

In the late 1970s, the amount of preferential credit began to be reduced. First, in mid-1983, the rate of interest charged on agricultural loans was fixed at 85 percent of the rate of monetary correction plus 3 percentage points. Later that year, the system was extended to other sectors receiving preferential treatment, such as exports and small enterprises, in conjunction with the move of all rates to positive values that were made equal to 100 percent of monetary correction plus 3 real percentage points. This move toward total indexation of credit caused widespread concern about its effects on the rate of growth of the agricultural sector. The outcome, however, did not validate these worries, for the sector continued to exhibit high rates of growth during the 1980s, performing extremely well by the end of the decade.[31]

Selective credit policies were used in areas other than agriculture and exports. Reserve requirements, for example, have been used to provide incentives for the purchase of government bonds and stocks for the purpose of stimulating growth in less-developed regions and for the development of small enterprises. That is, commercial banks acquire the right to reduce their compulsory reserves if they lend to these sectors or regions.

These examples suggest that despite some problems (such as the choice of wrong targets, the excess of bureaucracy, and the concession of unnecessary subsidies), these policies, which are regarded as part of a more comprehensive package of measures, were able to stimulate the sectors that were being targeted. The cost, however, was the increased fragility of the public sector accounts. The state was operating with a negative spread; on the one hand, it became the foremost debtor in indexed terms, while the other side of its balance sheet was made up of assets denominated in nominal terms with rates of return which, in most instances, were lower than the rate of inflation. The reemergence of inflation in the 1970s and the debt crisis transformed this unstable system into an open financial crisis for the public sector, one with widespread negative implications.

An alarming feature of this process is the behavior of the investment rate. In fact, after the international financial market was paralyzed in 1982, the private sector and the government reduced their investments, the latter both directly and through state enterprises, to levels of about one-half of those recorded in the mid-1970s. Gross capital formation fell to 16.9 percent of GDP (measured in 1980 prices). The falling trend in the investment rates continued in the first half of the decade. There was

---

31. See Rezende 1989 for an analysis at the aggregate and disaggregate levels.

some recovery in 1986, but the rates did not increase to the levels observed in the late 1970s and was followed by another two years of decline.

If we look at investment data in current prices, a large and increasing discrepancy in the two measures of the investment rate are observed. The difference is the result of the relative increase in the price of capital goods in terms of goods and services in general. The evolution of the relative price of capital goods—defined as the ratio between the implicit deflator of gross capital formation and the implicit deflator of GDP—shows a marked increase from 100 in 1980 to 106 in 1983, to 122 in 1987, and to 126 in 1988. This point is important because real investment spending depends, holding everything else constant, on the relative price of investment goods in terms of consumption goods.[32]

A source of additional, and probably related, concern stems from the changing composition of aggregate investment. Machinery and equipment shows a falling share in total investment, from an average of 41 percent in the first half of the 1970s to 36 percent in the second half of the 1970s and to 29 percent from 1980 to 1988. On the other hand, the share of construction has been increasing. Such investments contribute less toward sustained output growth. Finally, the rapidly declining share of imported capital goods to total investment is worrisome in a world economy subject to constant, and extremely rapid, technological change.

The considerations above indicate that not only has the "quantity" of investment spending been largely reduced but also its "quality" has deteriorated in the sense that it has become less supportive of output growth. This trend is also manifested by the behavior of the incremental capital-output ratio, which has been rising consistently since the last decade, averaging around 4.04 in the 1980s, as compared with 2.81 in the 1970s. The rising ratio exhibits the compounded growth difficulties facing the Brazilian economy: not only is the investment rate falling and showing a trend toward an adverse composition, but the investment requirements per unit of output growth are also increasing (Table 7.4).

Lack of resources and the increased instability generated by high and unstable inflation rates seem to be the reasons for the fall in investment. On the one hand, there has been a reduction in the availability of foreign savings and a transformation in their composition. From 1965 to

32. The possibility that the increase in the relative price of capital goods reflects the increasing sophistication of investment does not seem to find empirical support. The relative price of machinery and equipment is falling in fact, and with this item, increased technological sophistication should be captured. For a discussion, see Chami 1989.

Table 7.4. Investment in Brazil

| | Gross fixed investment | | | | |
Year	In 1980 prices	In current prices	Relative price of capital goods[a]	Equipment and machinery[b]	Capital-output ratio
1970	20.60	18.54	91.46	40.91	2.11
1971	21.30	19.91	93.45	42.36	2.17
1972	22.20	20.34	91.54	41.77	2.30
1973	23.60	20.37	86.35	39.62	2.51
1974	24.70	21.85	88.45	39.91	2.76
1975	25.80	23.32	90.50	41.18	2.97
1976	25.00	22.41	89.59	39.34	3.21
1977	23.60	21.35	90.60	36.90	3.38
1978	23.50	22.26	94.70	36.85	3.34
1979	22.90	23.36	102.12	34.48	3.38
1980	22.90	22.87	100.00	35.66	3.99
1981	21.00	22.82	108.92	33.46	4.66
1982	19.50	21.37	109.51	31.29	4.87
1983	16.90	17.94	106.06	30.19	4.30
1984	16.10	16.45	101.93	31.20	3.52
1985	16.70	16.98	101.53	29.03	3.22
1986	19.00	19.22	101.10	25.62	3.69
1987	18.10	22.05	121.58	25.08	4.04
1988	17.30	21.79	126.11	29.73	—

Sources: Castelar and Matesco 1989, p. 17, and statistics from Fundacao Instituto Brasileiro de Geografia e Estatistica.
[a] Calculated as fixed capital formation deflator/GDP deflator.
[b] Share of total fixed capital formation as measured in constant 1980 prices.

1975, the ratio of net factor payments abroad to GDP remained at around 1 percent, and the bulk of foreign savings was in the form of net imports of goods and nonfactor services. After 1975, the relation changed. By 1983, a new phenomenon in the Brazilian economy had appeared: a substantial surplus in goods and nonfactor services was being generated to service the foreign debt.[33]

From the investors' viewpoint, on the other hand, the uncertain environment is clearly not conducive to productive investment. Given the long delays involved and the irreversibility of investment decisions, private agents will avoid expanding productive capacity. The planning

33. The period after 1983 illustrates why it might be misleading to use the current account deficit as a measure of the economy's absorption of real foreign resources. Data show that net absorption of real resources from abroad turns negative, which indicates that the positive current account deficits ceased to be associated with an excess of domestic demand over GDP. In fact, domestic absorption has become lower than domestic production, with the reduction in spending falling heavily on investment, although consumption spending also dropped, most probably as a result of the fall in output.

horizon of firms shrinks in response to accelerating rates of inflation. Moreover, the need to effect large transfers of resources abroad introduces additional uncertainties because the private sector fears that the government may resort to higher taxation. As a result, firms increasingly hold financial assets at the expense of investment in real resources. As demand increased, the financial system continuously adapted itself to the situation by creating liquid, relatively safe, and remunerative investment opportunities at the expense of the government's accounts. Nevertheless, capital flight increased in later years, revealing an increased perception of the fragility of the state's fiscal position and of the possibilities of drastic changes in the rules governing financial accumulation.

During the last twenty-five years, the Brazilian financial system has undergone various transformations. No doubt exists that the reforms of the 1960s created a system that contributed enormously to the high-growth period of the late 1960s and early 1970s. In addition, the system was instrumental in creating alternatives to the high volume of capital flight observed elsewhere in Latin America. Nevertheless, several difficulties remained. Despite its increased sophistication, the system was never able to generate domestic sources of credit which could supply the economy with the long-term resources needed to expand productive capacity. High inflation has proven to be an obstacle even in Brazil's indexed economy. Moreover, indexation itself generated new problems in view of the rapidly changing inflation and exchange rates and the segmented financial system.

The alternative has been the continuous utilization of government credit. This support, however, was consistent with the style of government intervention in the economy—a style that has been capable of promoting the economic growth of the country from the 1930s to the late 1970s, when it attained its peak during the implementation of the PND II.

As industrialization proceeded in the 1970s, however, too many priorities existed, as did a whole new set of macroeconomic difficulties. The counterpart of the government's increasing intervention was the private sector's development of mechanisms designed to preserve the benefits it received. As a result, pressures were brought to bear from a variety of groups. Since the state lacked the political power to implement its programs fully, it was confronted with the need to develop indirect and disguised mechanisms to distribute resources as direct techniques were likely to be resisted by the affected groups.

The basic pattern was one where at each new stage of the growth process, a new set of policy tools and institutional arrangements were used by the government to redirect incentives in accordance with the newly established priorities. In an attempt to postpone conflict by creating the illusion that all sectors were equally protected, however, the government implemented the new arrangements without explicitly canceling those incentives extended in the previous stage. Given the private sector's increased sophistication and awareness, each new stage required the extension of more-effective and lasting advantages.

From an institutional and structural point of view, the outcome of this policy style is the establishment of a highly complex economy with allocation mechanisms characterized by a total lack of transparency, and a legislation distinguished by a plethora of incentives based on regulations and exceptions, taxes and subsidies, with the consequent canceling of real allocation effects. Moreover, as the discussion of credit policies clearly illustrates, because each incentive provided by the state is subject to different channels and mechanisms according to the specificities of the targeted sector, an evaluation of the public resources allocated to each sector is extremely difficult. For a comparison of incentives extended to different sectors, the difficulty is compounded. It is not farfetched to suggest that the authorities themselves had no clear idea of the net allocation incentives provided to a specific sector or of the costs involved.

From a macroeconomic point of view, the main lasting consequence was an ever increasing fiscal drain. Real relative incentive effects were obtained at mounting costs, worsening a situation that was already difficult in face of the deterioration in the external environment and questionable adjustment choices. Rising deficits and inflation led to persistent macroeconomic disequilibria. The high interest rates that characterized the stabilization policies undertaken since the early 1980s contributed to increased segmentation of the financial system. Sectoral imbalances in the financial system led to ever changing rules and growing inconsistencies. A piecemeal approach was substituted for a conscious financial policy. As inflation escalated and the indexation of loans became widespread, the demand for subsidized credit increased quickly. Given the deterioration of the government's capacity to extract fiscal resources from the economy, such subsidies were increasingly financed by credit from the central bank. Inflation and debt accumulation are consequences of this policy stance but are also instruments for conflict postponement. Stabilization and a profound financial reform, particularly in the public sector, are urgently needed to restore growth and development.

References

Almeida, J. S. Gomes, C. K. Ferreira, M. P. Freitas, and P. M. Figueiredo. 1988. Sistema Bancario Publico e Privado, Mudanca na Estrutura de Recursos e Tendencias de Custo e Lucro. Texto para Discussao 13. Sao Paulo: Instituto de Economia do Setor Publico/Fundacao do Desenvolvimento Administrativo.

Arida, P., and A. Lara-Resende. 1985. Inertial Inflation and Monetary Reform in Brazil. In *Inflation and Indexation: Argentina, Brazil, and Israel*, ed. John Williamson. Washington, D.C.: Institute for International Economics.

Arida, Persio, and Lance Taylor. 1989. Short-Run Macroeconomics. Chapter 17 in *Handbook of Development Economics*, vol. 2, ed. Hollis Chenery and T. N. Srinivasan. New York: North Holland.

Baer, Werner. 1983. *The Brazilian Economy, Growth, and Development*, 2nd ed. New York: Praeger.

Carneiro, D. D. 1989. Crise e Esperanca: 1974–1980. Chapter 11 in *A Ordem do Progresso, Cem Anos de Politica Economica Republicana, 1889–1989*, ed. Marcelo de Paiva Abreu. Rio de Janeiro: Ed. Campus.

Castelar, A., and B. Matesco. 1989. Relacao capital/produto incremental: Estimativas para o periodo, 1948/87. Texto para Discussao Interna no. 163, Instituto de Planejamento Economico e Social/Instituto de Pesquisa Economica Aplicada, Rio de Janeiro.

Central Bank of Brazil. Various years. *Annual Reports*, various issues. Rio de Janeiro: Central Bank of Brazil.

Chami, J. Batista. 1989. Uma Nota Sobre o Preco Relativo dos Bens de Investimento no Brasil. *Boletim de Conjunctura Industrial* 9(2).

Correa do Lago, L. A., M. Hanson Costa, P. N. Batista, Jr., and T. B. Ryff. 1984. *O Combate a Inflacao no Brasil*. Rio de Janeiro: Editora Paz e Terra.

Davidoff Cruz, Paulo. 1984. *Divida Externa e Politica Economica: A Experiencia Brasileira nos Anos Setenta*. Sao Paulo: Ed. Brasiliense.

Diaz-Alejandro, Carlos. 1985. Good-Bye Financial Repression, Hello Financial Crash. *Journal of Development Economics* 19(1/2): 1–24.

Dornbusch, Rudiger, and Adroaldo Moura da Silva. 1985. Taxa de Juros e Depositos em Moeda Extrangeira no Brasil. *Revista Brasileira de Economia* 38(1): 39–52.

Fishlow, Albert. 1986. A Tale of Two Presidents: The Political Economy of Brazilian Adjustment to the Oil Shocks. Working Paper no. 202, Department of Economics, University of California, Berkeley.

Gleizer, Daniel. 1990. Essays on Consumption, Saving, and Government Policy in Brazil. Ph.D. diss., University of California, Berkeley.

Gupta, Kar Dev. 1984. *Finance and Economic Growth in Developing Countries*. London: Croom Helm.

Modiano, Eduardo. 1989. A Opera dos Tres Cruzados: 1985–1989. In *A Ordem do Progresso, Cem Anos de Politica Economica Republicana, 1889–1989*, ed. Marcelo de Paiva Abreu. Rio de Janeiro: Ed. Campus.

Musalem, A. R. 1984. Subsidy Policies and the Exports of Manufactured Goods in Brazil. *Brazilian Economic Studies* 8.

Oliveira, Gesner. 1989. The Brazilian Experience with IMF Stabilization Plans. Ph.D. diss., Department of Economics, University of California, Berkeley.

Rezende, G. C. 1989. Agricultura e Ajuste Externo no Brasil: Novas Consideracoes. *Pesquisa e Planejamento Economico* 19(3): 553–78.

Simonsen, Mario. 1983. Indexation: Current Theory and Brazilian Experience. In *Inflation, Debt, and Indexation,* ed. Mario Simonsen and Rudiger Dornbusch. Cambridge: MIT Press.

Tavares, M. C., and J. C. Assis. 1985. O Grande Salto para o Caos. Rio de Janeiro.

Taylor, Lance. 1988. Fiscal Issues in Macroeconomic Stabilization. Background paper for the 1988 World Development Report. Washington, D.C.: World Bank.

Werneck, Rogerio. 1987. *Empresas Estatais e Politica Macroeconomica.* Rio de Janeiro: Ed. Campus.

Willis, E. J. 1986. The State as Banker: The Expansion of the Public Sector in Brazil. Ph.D. diss., University of Texas, Austin.

World Bank (WB). 1984. *Brazil: Financial System Review.* Washington, D.C.: WB.

Zini, Alvaro. 1982. Uma Avaliacao do Setor Financeiro no Brasil: Da Reforma de 1964/65 a Crise dos Anos 80. M.Sc. thesis, University of Campinas.

Zoninsein, Jonas. 1985. State Finance Capital and Industrialization: The Brazilian Economy. Instituto de Economia Industrial, Universidade Federal do Rio de Janeiro, Rio de Janeiro. Mimeographed.

INDEX

DATE DUE

GAYLORD			PRINTED IN U.S.A.